MW01628207

HURTUBISE

BY

BOB GATES

P.O. Box 34, Marshall, IN 47859

"Hurtubise"

by Bob Gates

© 1995 Bob Gates

Published by: **Witness Productions**
Box 34, Church Street
Marshall, IN 47859
317-597-2487

ISBN 0 9627653-5-X

Dust cover design by: Karen Hurtubise Sampson.
Cover photo by: Howard Woodring

Endsheet design by: Larry Wright

Printed in the USA

Most of the photos in this book are from the Hurtubise Family Collection and are indicated by [HFC]. Many have never been published. We have tried to credit the photographers whenever possible.

For

Karen, Pat, Andy and the Grandkids

Dedicated to

Mom and Pop— Ruth and Ernie

In Memory of

Mike Guglielmucci, Sr.

One of "Herk's" biggest fans.

Preface

Thirty-two years may seem like a very long time to most people, but my marriage to Jim for that period of time was way too short. Those thirty-two wonderful years seem like only yesterday and the love we shared lives on in our three children.

Jim actually had two distinct personalities, those of race driver as well as husband and father. People are amazed at how little I know or remember about different races and cars that Jim drove. Like many people who leave their work behind when they leave the workplace, Jim seldom discussed racing at home.

Through the good times, as well as the hard, the children and I never wanted for anything. I remember so vividly when Jim would buy something and let it slip to the children knowing that they would let it slip to me. I usually laughed about it, but there were a few times though: like the snowmobiles and the airplane.

He was so proud of his children and loved them, yet couldn't tell them. He would always tell someone else. The same with myself. Although he would always call and say "Love ya" after a race, and never failed to thank me for dinner or tell me how nice I looked, I always felt warm and good inside when at dinner he'd tell the children, "Eat all your food and something of everything. Your Mom didn't cook for her health."

Jim loved fishing but not hunting. He'd go on hunting trips with his friends, but always stayed behind at what he called "Mahogany Ridge," the local tavern. He simply liked talking to people from all walks of life whether they were farmers or millionaires. Like his dad, he never met a stranger. Perhaps that is why the fans loved him so much.

This book is not only a way for me to share Jim and my life with those who loved him, but is also a way for our children and grandchildren to know more about their father and granddad. To Karen, Pat and Andy; My love holds no bounds. My love and thanks to our dear friends, Al and Jeanette Krueger and Ken and Joni Jai for their love and support A special thanks to Pete and Sheila. My best wishes to all the race drivers, car owners and members of the auto racing fraternity who were a part of Jim's life.

Thank you Bob Gates for a superb job of writing and Ed Watson for believing in this story.

Jane Hurtubise

Aknowledgements

There are many people who were invaluable in making this book possible. They gladly shared their time, but more importantly their memories of a great man.

A special thanks to:

Jane Hurtubise, Karen Hurtubise Sampson, Andy Hurtubise, Pat Hurtubise Behrens, Pete and Sheila Hurtubise, Mrs. Ernest Hurtubise, John Sampson, Lee Bruss, LeRoy Neumayer, Danny Oaks, Don Shepherd, A.J. Shepherd, Hank Higuchi, Grayce Jones, Lisa Lingerich, John and Ginger Laux and Al and Jeanette Krueger.

Thanks as well, to my family and friends for putting up with me as I labored on this project, to Florrie Binford Kichler for her editing and Ed Watson for giving me the opportunity to record the deeds of my hero.

Bob Gates

It is not the critic who counts;
not the man who points out how the
strong man stumbled,
or where the doer
of deeds could have done better.
The credit belongs to the man who is
actually in the arena; whose face is
marred by dust and sweat and blood;
who strives valiantly;
who errs and comes short
again and again;
who knows the great enthusiasm,
the great devotions; and who spends
himself in a worthy cause;
who at best knows at the end, triumph;
who at worst, if he fails,
at least fails while doing greatly;
so that his place will never be
with those timid souls
who neither know victory nor defeat.

****Theodore Roosevelt****

HURTUBISE

HURTUBISE

1

Donald Barton photo -HFC

For the first time in a decade, rain had washed out the entire first weekend of qualifying for the world's most important automobile race, the Indianapolis 500. That left just two frantic days for the 92 cars entered to be pared down to the traditional starting field of 33. Though Saturday had fairly bustled with qualifying activity, Sunday May 21, 1978 dawned with thirteen starting spots still open.

With time rapidly running out, a bevy of talented drivers, A.J. Foyt among them, soon filled the field, and the rooting out process that attracted 75,000 fans and a nationwide TV audience began.

Called bumping, its explanation is simple, its execution formidable. If a driver can push his machine faster than the slowest car already in the field, that car is out, his is in. The next slowest car is then on the "bubble," and that driver has to endure the agony of helplessly standing by as driver after driver tries to best his speed and he is bumped, or the six PM gun sounds, mercifully ending the torturous routine.

As that Sunday in 1978 wound to a close, drivers, in their hungry search for speed, pushed closer and closer to the ragged edge of control. Two, Bob Harkey and Larry Cannon, crashed and a final practice session was cut short when Dick Simon crunched his car hard into the turn four concrete wall.

When the track again went green, just one precious hour remained. The tension hung dark and thick over the Speedway and permeated competitor and spectator alike. A long line of cars stretched from the head of the qualifying line, and in each was a driver praying for just one last banzai run against the clock.

Bob Harkey was the first away. He roared onto the track to the wild cheering of the fans grown restless with the long delays. They wanted action. But, unknown to them, a series of events had already been set in motion that would create an action filled spectacle unlike anything ever seen in the long, colorful history of the Indianapolis Motor Speedway.

As Harkey motored slowly down the backstretch, warming the tires and heating the motor, a gasp went up from the throng. A figure, clad in a white driver's uniform, broke away from a cluster of people gathered at the start/finish line, darted across the pit lane, cleared the low concrete barrier separating the pits from the track, and began a weaving run across the mainstretch.

Pursued by Speedway security people and race officials, the intrusive demonstrator was knocked to the track with a tackle from driver John Martin. Surrounded to prevent his escape, the protester was escorted back to the pit wall where the impromptu posse was met by a contingent of burly Indiana State Policemen.

The reaction of the crowd to the intense episode unfolding before them was at first peals of laughter, and cheers at the chase. That hilarity, however, soon shifted to anger. Choruses of boos rained down on the one who had disrupted qualifying, and so thoughtlessly taken precious time from those urgently trying to make the race.

But, as the uniformed patrol made its way down pit lane to the exit, the emotions of many of those watching changed to shock, then to sadness as they recognized the forlorn man being paraded before them. They looked away, knowing they were witnessing the uncalled-for humiliation of a hero.

Maybe it was the familiar, close-cropped hair. Maybe it was the twisted, gnarled hands, bloodied now from his tumble to the abrasive asphalt track. Or, maybe it was the bright blue eyes that usually danced with mischievous merriment, but now glinted with anger. But, there could be no doubt. This was Jim Hurtubise. Hercules to his legion of fans. Herk to his friends, who were legion as well.

The deplorable scene was tragically ironic, for it was just a few years previous that this same Jim Hurtubise had captured the imagination of yet another final qualifying day crowd. That day he won the hearts and accolades of the entire racing world when, as a still wet behind the ears rookie from the world of sprint cars and dirt tracks, he annihilated the track record at the world's most famous race track, and roared to within a few hundredths of a second of breaking the then seemingly insurmountable 150 MPH barrier.

That day in 1960 the crowd hadn't jeered, but rather had stood and screamed his name. That day Herk had not been surrounded by guards, but by photographers, journalists and well wishers. That day he had been lauded as the newest and brightest star in the constellation-filled firmament of Indianapolis.

Jim Hurtubise's prowess behind the wheel of a race car made him worthy of such acclamation. For as Indy car racing entered the decade of the sixties, the old guard was giving way to a group of talented, new, young chargers.

At the head of this company of young lions was a terrific triumvirate of drivers whose talents stood them head and shoulders above the rest; A.J. Foyt, Parnelli Jones, and Jim Hurtubise.

Jim was the first of that talented trio to assert his presence at the top echelon of open wheel racing. Taking over the seat of the car vacated by the injured driver, Johnny Thomson, Herk won the last Indy car race of the Fifties at Sacramento on October 25, 1959, and set the racing world on its collective ear during the first 500 of the Sixties with his extraordinary qualifying run.

There were those at the Speedway on that final qualifying day in 1960 who had already been privy to Jim's brash, thrilling exploits behind the wheel of dangerous, overpowered, fire breathing sprint cars. They nodded knowingly. It would be only a matter of time, they predicted, before this man nicknamed "Hercules" for his bravery, would win the Indianapolis 500.

That never happened for Jim Hurtubise. He never made it to racing's most important victory lane. That never diminished his esteem in the eyes of the fans, however, for they knew that save for a tragic fire that struck him down in his racing prime, his likeness very well would have joined that of his racing buddies, Parnelli Jones and A.J. Foyt, on the famed Borg Warner trophy.

In a near fatal accident, at Milwaukee in 1964, he was severely burned over almost half his body, but it was his hands that caught the brunt of the inferno. They were so ravaged that his doctors doubted he would ever regain normal use of them, much less be able to race again.

But race again he did.

Jim's miraculous return from those terrible burns rates as one of the most dramatic comeback stories in the history of any sport, and perhaps even more than his amazing feats on the racetrack, earned him the mantle of hero.

As a result, even after he curtailed his other racing activities in the late sixties and focused his efforts solely on the Indianapolis 500, his appearance there always brought an emotional, overwhelming response from the spectators. A roar would rise the moment he was spotted making his way from the garage area, and the cheering crescendo followed him like a cresting wave as he jauntily made his way down the pit lane to his waiting race car.

Invariably that car was a roadster. A car with its engine mounted up front and similar in appearance to the cars that had dominated the 500 until the rear engine revolution of the early sixties. Jim's roadster was a throwback to another era. It flew in the face of the technology of that day, for by then Indy cars were slim, low slung, track hugging rear engined speedsters.

Even this staunch refusal to change with the times brought him acclaim. The fans recognized that Herk's actions were not simply those of an old-timer stuck in the past. Rather, they saw him as a modern day David fighting racing's political Goliath. The underdog challenging the powers that be, as he protested changes he saw as being detrimental to the sport he loved so much.

Changes that, because of escalating costs, were taking racing at Indianapolis away from all but the very rich. Changes that were making it difficult for a young driver with dreams of winning the 500 to get there by talent alone. Changes that one day, Jim feared, would spell the doom of Indy car racing.

It can be argued that Jim went too far with that protest when his frustration finally boiled over into anger in 1978. Certainly many of the fans, and most of his competitors were dismayed by his actions.

But time has vindicated Jim Hurtubise. Those very changes that he then protested so vehemently have since come to pass. It is now virtually impossible for a driver with the sprint car and midget background of Jim, or Parnelli, or A.J., to get a ride for America's greatest race. The changes Jim once protested have now so fragmented Indy car racing that its leaders are scrambling to undo the damage as this once proud sport teeters on the edge of becoming a second rate racing league.

Jim has been lauded, and rightfully so, as heroic for his rare, remarkable talent behind the wheel of a race car, and for his soul-stirring return from near fatal injuries. He should also be applauded for his brave, quixotic stand. A lone voice, that the passage of time has proven to be prophetic.

Heroes are those rare individuals whose deeds enable those of us with ordinary, uneventful lives to share in and be inspired by the unlimited boundaries of the soaring human spirit.

Jim Hurtubise was such a man.

Hurtubise Family Photo

#98 Parnelli Jones leads #56 Jim Hurtubise and #1 A.J. Foyt at Indy in 1964.

HURTUBISE

2

Jack Fox photo -HFC

James Ernest Hurtubise was born on December 5, 1932 in North Tonawanda, New York, a small industrial town nestled snugly between the Erie Canal and the Niagara River, just ten miles south of Niagara Falls. Jim was of French-Canadian descent. His mother, Ruth, is English-Canadian, and his father, Ernest, or Ernie as he was known by everyone, was first generation French-Canadian, who didn't even speak English until he was eight years old.

Jim inherited more than just his middle name from his father. In personality they were virtually identical. Ernie was a robust, athletic, outdoors loving man who blustered his way through life without ever meeting a stranger. He played college football in the mid-twenties, first at St. Bonaventure, and then later with rival school, Canisius. His adventures on the football field earned Ernie a reputation that would serve him well when he opened a service station on the corner of Erie and Division streets in North Tonawanda.

Through hard work Ernie built his garage into a respected and successful business, although he really preferred to be hunting, fishing and tramping through what was then the wilderness-like country around North Tonawanda. This affinity with the outdoors led him to buy a small island, with a two story lodge, in Georgian Bay on Lake Huron near Parry Sound, Ontario. There Jim and his brother, Pete, born sixteen months after Jim on April 16, 1934, spent many memorable childhood days and developed a love for the outdoors that would remain with them all their lives.

Even in the heyday of their racing activities, Jim and Pete would often go to their father's island and let the peace and solitude they found there wash away the stress and trauma of racing. The island also became a favorite retreat for Jim's many racing friends, and they gathered there as often as their busy schedules allowed.

In contrast to his father, Jim's mother, though outgoing and friendly, is a reserved and proper lady, exuding an aura of class and inner strength. That gracious bearing can be attributed, in part, to her artistic nature. Ruth is an accomplished painter, whose work adorns the homes of a few selected friends as well as the walls of Pete's hundred year old farmhouse, where she now lives.

And Jim, no doubt surprising those who saw him only in the context of the roughneck setting of auto racing, inherited his mother's artistic bent. Ruth recalls that as a child Jim enjoyed drawing, especially, prophetically it seems now, the cars and airplanes that would later be so much a part of his life. As he grew older, Jim didn't express his talent with drawings and paintings, but rather revealed it in more practical ways. For instance, in the signs he enjoyed designing and making.

When Pete opened his landscaping business, "PeterPons," Jim designed and painted a sign that is still in use there today, and his artistic talent was also obvious in the color schemes he devised for his race cars. Even the number 56, that Jim used so often on his cars that it became synonymous with him, was chosen for artistic reasons.

"I like the style of the individual numbers," Jim once explained to Pete. "They have nice lines and curves, and I like they way they look when they are used together."

When Jim's mother speaks of her son's artistic ability, a hint of sadness is detected as she ponders what might have been, "Jim was such a creative, inventive person," Ruth says, "and he carried this over into his race cars. He would dream up all of these ideas and then he expected Peter to follow up and make them work. I often wonder what Jim would have been able to accomplish with his hands, had he not been burned."

In school Jim's grades were okay, but, much to his mother's chagrin, he didn't apply himself, because it was easy for him to get passing grades without expending a lot of effort. Although he didn't compete on the football or basketball teams because of his small stature, he did swim on the school team one year.

But other than that, the competitive spirit that would one day thrust Jim to the top of the racing world lay dormant until he became involved in his first motorized competition, power boats. Then those attributes of confidence, aggressiveness and natural talent erupted to the surface and a glimpse of what lay ahead was revealed.

Jim's first racing boat, according to Pete, who raced boats as well, was one that Jim built as teenager. It was a flat-hulled, plywood creation of his own design that used one of the many outboard engines his father had lying around the fishing lodge at Parry Sound.

When Jim became bored with the low speed that simple boat was capable of, he built a new one with a faster, V-shaped hull, and a larger, fifteen-horsepower engine. With this craft, Jim raced in the many regattas held in the waterways around his home. There was the Launch Club Regatta, the Swiftwater Regatta, held on the Niagara River, and the race run during the annual Parry Sound festival.

Pete recalls one Parry Sound event, "This was in the very early days of outboard motor boat racing, and by this time Jim had already built his V-hulled boat. He had a good motor on it, and led the race from the very beginning. In fact he had such a big lead that at one point he went way outside the marker buoys so he could get close to where the spectators were seated, and wave at the crowd."

Despite his crowd-pleasing performance and the lengthy lead he had at race end, Jim was sorely disappointed during the award ceremonies held afterwards. He expected a nice cash prize to go along with the first place trophy, but what he received instead was a nine by twelve foot piece of linoleum!

"We used the linoleum up at the island," recalls Ruth, "but, my, was Jim upset."

Jim often joked that the only auto racing he did before he went into the Coast Guard was from stoplight to stoplight, and, with one of the hottest cars in town, he did a lot of that. As a result the local constables were constantly on the lookout for the young Hurtubise and chased him home more than once.

As teenagers, both Jim and Pete were caught up in the great American love affair with the automobile that blossomed in those financially booming years immediately following World War II. Fostered by their father's interest in cars and things mechanical, the boys became enthusiastic hotrodders.

Working in a bay in the back of Ernie's service station, Jim and Pete created, from old Chevy and Ford coupes, exotic looking and sounding machines, resplendent in shiny paint, gobs of chrome, dual carburetors and Hollywood mufflers. But even then, Jim gave no indication that cars would be such an important part of his life. That, however, was soon to change.

In 1950 America still had a draft in effect, so serving in the military was never far from a young man's mind. Possibly in anticipation of being drafted anyway, or maybe because of his attraction to boating and water sports, Jim joined the Naval Reserve while a senior in high school. Upon graduation, he became less enthused about military life, and expended more effort trying to get out of the monthly training drills than he did attending them.

"Finally," laughs his mother, "they told him that he would either have to join the Navy for four years or the Coast Guard for two!" Jim opted for the shorter hitch in the Coast Guard and was assigned to the cutter, USS Nemisis, anchored in Boca Ciega Bay off St. Petersburg, Florida.

This proved to be a fortunate assignment for Jim, because it was while in St. Petersburg that his interest in auto racing was piqued. At first racing was little more for him than a distraction from the hum-drum, ordered drudgery of military life, but eventually it became a life changing passion. And, as is usually the case in life changing situations, the set of circumstances that put it all in motion came about by mere coincidence.

Wandering around St. Petersburg on a hot, Saturday afternoon in early 1953, Jim ventured into a small service station for a cold soda. Benny Moore, a respected racer in the Tampa/ St. Petersburg area, was working there and recalls his first encounter with the young Coast Guardsman.

"I was working at Sherry's gas station at that time," relates Moore, "when Jim came sauntering in. I was getting my stock car ready to run that night and he watched me work on it for some time. He asked a lot of questions about the car, then asked if he could go along with me to the track."

With his low budget operation, Benny was more than happy to have volunteer help, and readily agreed to let Jim join him. What Jim saw that night wasn't sophisticated racing machinery. Only Chevy and Ford coupes, with the fenders pulled off, and numbers painted on. Little else. But he was hooked on the noise, the smell, the fender rubbing excitement. He had to try it for himself, and in a matter of weeks Jim had his own car.

Calling on the mechanical experience he had acquired while working in his father's garage, and using parts donated by Moore, Bill Larimer and some other helpful, local drivers, Jim built his first race car. Based on a 1934 Ford coupe and numbered 56, the two hundred dollar racer wasn't much to look at, but it was a start. During the remainder of his two year stint in the Coast Guard, he raced all over Florida, testing his racing skills at tracks such as Speedway Park, Tri City Speedway, Gardenton, Plant Field and Sarasota. On occasion, he even ventured as far north as Maryland to race at tracks around Baltimore.

With his paltry service pay, Jim had little money to invest in his race car. Most of the time he just barely had enough to get back and forth to the track. Once he was so desperate for money just to keep racing that when he heard the promoter paid an extra ten dollars for a flip he deliberately rolled his car.

But, even then Jim's raw talent was evident to at least a few veteran observers. One who caught a glimmer of his natural ability was "Pop" Kramer, a savvy, old racer, affectionately known as the granddaddy of racing in St. Petersburg.

"Pop" was so impressed with the wild, young Hurtubise that he urged Benny Moore to put Jim in his car, just to see what he was capable of doing in better equipment. Benny complied, but was nervous about it the whole time. "Boy, I was worried," recalls Moore. "Jim was going really good, but, man, he just didn't want to let up on it!"

Besides the aggressive driving style that would serve as Jim's trademark his entire racing career, he also exhibited the tenacious desire to race at all costs that would later aid him in overcoming all obstacles in the pursuit of his racing dreams. One Saturday night at Plant Field in Tampa, Moore remembers that Jim cut his hand while working on his car. The cut was so deep that he had to be rushed to the emergency room for stitches. "Later that evening," says Moore, "I looked out and saw Jim's number 56 wheeling around the track. I asked, 'Who's driving Jim's car?' Someone said, 'That's Hurtubise, the nut's out there driving one-handed!"

What attracted Jim Hurtubise to racing is not known. It was something he never discussed, and he probably couldn't have explained the fascination anyway. Most drivers can't. It's simply something they love.

Whatever the allure, once racing snagged Jim's attention, it consumed him. From that point on it was all he wanted to do, and he pursued it with passion, dedication, and his own unique enthusiasm. His immediate goal was to overcome the one obstacle that then prevented him from racing more. The United States Coast Guard.

When Jim discovered that members of the Coast Guard boxing team were allowed extra shore leave, he took up boxing. Through the years many observers commented on how Jim carried himself like a boxer, walking with a confident, jaunty air, up on the balls of his feet.

The truth is he couldn't box his way out of a paper bag. But, that didn't matter. All Jim cared about was more free time to race. Jim's wife, Jane, recalls, "Jim had almost a perfect record while boxing in the Coast Guard. He lost every fight but one! The only fight he didn't lose was a forfeit when the other guy didn't show up."

Al Krueger, who became Jim's best friend, protector and confidant, recalls Jim telling him about one of those boxing matches. "Jim said he was fighting a guy," laughs Al, "who had a huge eagle tattooed on his chest. And, he thought that if he concentrated on hitting this guy on his tattoo, he might have a chance of beating him. So, that's what he did. Pretty soon the crowd caught on to his strategy, and every time Jim swung at the guy they would yell, 'Hit him in the eagle, Jim. Hit him in the eagle!' Jim lost that fight too!

When Jim couldn't get shore leave any other way, he would slip over the side of the ship and swim to shore. Writer Polly Roat, then a contributor to the *National Speed Sport News*, recalls seeing Jim show up at the track one night with his soaking wet uniform still on. He ran the feature, then rushed back to the ship before he even had time to collect his prize money. That he managed to avoid the shore patrol and a court martial for being AWOL is a miracle, but such was the strength of Jim's dedication to racing that he was willing to risk the consequences.

Back in North Tonawanda, Pete, too, had started racing in cars similar to those Jim was running in Florida; entry level, modified stock cars. Cutting his racing teeth at the quarter-mile paved oval in Buffalo's Civic Stadium, Pete used the same number, 56, that Jim was using on his car.

"I thought that since we were brothers, using the same numbers was the thing to do," says Pete. Later, when Jim and Pete raced together, Pete retained that number 56 theme by numbering his cars, 556.

While Jim was in the service, Pete towed his race car to Florida on two different occasions. On the first trip south, Pete stayed and raced for several months, keeping and working on his car at Bob Beam's Atlantic Service Station in St. Petersburg, the shop where Jim kept his car. In Florida Pete found work, first with a sand dredging company building beaches for luxury hotels, and then with a machine shop. With more disposable income to spend on his car, Pete often out-performed Jim in those days. It was during this trip that Pete won his first ever modified stock car feature at Saramana, Florida.

In early 1954 Pete returned to Florida, and he and Jim ran the Daytona Beach stock car race, the forerunner of today's Daytona 500. Neither finished the grinding event, then held on a combination highway and beach course, but, rubbing elbows with the big-time racers gathered there whetted their appetites to more zealously pursue their own racing efforts.

Despite his inferior equipment, Jim did manage one win before he was discharged from the Coast Guard and returned to North Tonawanda in late 1954. That was the consolation event during Tri City Speedway's annual Pearl Harbor Memorial race.

No sooner was Jim back home and resettled with a job at American District Steam in North Tonawanda, than he built another race car, a '37 Ford two-door sedan. Jim raced this little Ford in sportsman division races on an informal circuit that consisted of a half dozen tracks scattered from western New York state into Canada. There was Cuba Lake, Akron, Lancaster Speedway, and the Monroe County Fair Grounds in Rochester, all dirt ovals of various lengths. The track at Buffalo Civic Stadium was a paved quarter mile track. And, in Canada, a favorite track with all the drivers was the third mile dirt oval at Merrittville, Ontario.

Running as often as four nights a week, Jim raced and won against a group of drivers who would one day become legends in East Coast stock car racing circles. Frankie Schneider, "Dutch" Houge and Nolan Swift among them.

It was during these post-Coast Guard racing days that Jim befriended a young man, Lee Bruss, with whom he would share what was perhaps the most important two years of his racing life.

Lee didn't drive, but had been helping his cousin with his race car for some time when Jim appeared on the New York racing scene during the summer of '55. Lee was impressed, as was everyone else who watched him that summer, with Jim's prowess in a race car. But even more impressive to Lee was Jim's spectacular style, devil may care manner, and fun-loving attitude.

"Jim did real well with his Ford sedan," says Lee. "But what was so amazing wasn't the number of races he won, but the way he drove so damn hard! He might be leading a race, spin out, and drop all the way back to last place. Then, here he'd come, charging all the way back to the front and finish second, or third, or sometimes even win. He was always dramatic, spectacular, and the fans just ate that up. Even then he was a fan favorite."

"But," continues Lee, "whether he won the race, or flipped and finished last, Jim was always the same. Always laughing that funny little laugh of his. Always in a good mood. And, there always would be just as big a party afterwards. I never saw Jim happier than when he was in a race car. He raced for no other reason than the love and the fun of competition. In fact, I can honestly say, knowing Jim the way I did, that when he finally got the chance to run at Indianapolis, he would've gladly done it for nothing more than just the fun of doing it."

Being the consummate extrovert, Jim enjoyed the camaraderie and the off track hijinks he shared with his racing cronies as much as he did his on track escapades. While the race track was their main meeting place, the racing crowd hung out together even when there wasn't a race to go to. They gathered at dances and greasy spoon diners, or threw big backyard parties and cookouts in the country.

Then, when the cold, New York winter rolled in, curtailing the racing season, they rallied almost every evening at one of the many country western bars scattered in and around North Tonawanda and Niagara Falls. Smokey little joints with Hank Williams and Ernest Tubb blaring from the jukebox, and the beer flowing cold from the tap.

It was Jim who dubbed these raceless, winter evenings, "Honky Tonk Time," and whether he was leading the gang in boisterous pinball games, or loud contests on the bowling machines, he was in his social element.

"Jim was always the life of the party," laughs Lee as he recalls those many memorable nights. "But as much as he liked his beer, I can never remember seeing Jim drunk. He was the greatest guy for nursing a beer I've seen! He really liked the socializing that went with the drinking, more than the drinking itself."

"But," Lee goes on, "even if he'd been drunk, I don't think you could've told the difference anyway. He was always so happy-go-lucky, and crazy acting. Always having fun. Always wanting to do something."

"But what was so funny is that once he finally wore down, he'd go to sleep anywhere. We might all be sitting in a bar with five or six tables pulled together, and Jim would be laughing and carrying on. Then he'd get quiet for a few minutes and you'd look over and he'd be laying on somebody's shoulder sound asleep. Jim lived life at a hundred-miles-an-hour, and when he wore out he just needed a little bit of sleep and he was ready to go again."

It was on one such evening, with Jim and his racing buddies gathered in one of their favorite spots, Matt and Stan Janik's Villa Capri, that Jim made an unexpected announcement. Though he might not have realized it then, what he proposed would change the course of his life and propel him to the top level of his sport.

"You know," Jim proclaimed, "I'm just kinda' tired of staying up here. If you really wanna' be a race driver, you've got to go to California. In California they race all year round, and if you really want to make it big, that's where it is. That's where the action is! I'm going. Who wants to go along?"

In the passion of the moment, a half dozen voices shouted in agreement. They would all join Jim. They would all become famous race car drivers in California. That brave resolve, most likely fueled by a few too many beers, faded with the light of a new day. When it came time to make the trip only one of that initially enthusiastic crowd joined Jim—Lee Bruss.

"I had wanted to go to California from the time I could remember," explains Lee. "I had an aunt who lived in Los Angeles and she would occasionally send us the *Los Angeles Times*. I would grab it as soon as it came and read it from front to back a dozen times. Jim's invitation was just the opportunity I was looking for."

Although Jim owned a 1949 Ford coupe, and Lee a vehicle of some forgotten make and vintage, these were sold, along with a lot of other personal possessions, to raise funds for the trip. Their steeds of choice for the westward trek would be motorcycles; Jim on his new BSA Golden Flash, and Lee on his 1949 Harley Davidson. To forego the cost of motel rooms, they packed a pup tent and two sleeping bags. The clothes they took were limited to what they wore, and the few they could cram into their motorcycle saddlebags.

They planned to leave in mid-February, and to travel first to Daytona Beach, Florida for Speed Week, where Jim was sure he could get a ride in a car owned by an acquaintance from his Coast Guard days. Then, from Daytona they would take the southern route across the country in order to avoid the harsh Midwest winter weather.

On the eve of their departure, their friends threw the obligatory going away party, and the festivities blasted on through the night and into the early hours of the next morning. However, Jim and Lee were so excited about their impending trip, and the golden future they were sure lay at its end, that lack of sleep did not keep them from their pre-appointed rendezvous time of 7:00 AM.

That morning dawned cold and gray. Snow peppered them as they packed their motorcycles and said good-bye to their families. Their parent's reaction to the trip covered the full range of emotions. "They were worried that we had enough clothes, that we would eat right, that we would ride carefully, all the normal things," says Lee.

"Jim's mother was very sad, and my parents swore that we'd be back in six months. But Jim's dad was almost as excited as we were. 'You boys are doing the right thing. You'll do great out there, don't worry about a thing,' he said. I really believe that Ernie would have loved to have gone with us."

Jim's mother laughs as she recalls, "They wore ski masks because of the cold, and were bundled up in so many clothes that they looked like spacemen." But, comic recollections aside, it was a melancholy good-bye for Ruth. She cried.

On the back of a photograph she took of Jim and Lee with their motorcycles she wrote:

Remember this cold, February day?
This was the last time I saw
you - - and a sad one for me.

Even today Ruth says, "When Jim left North Tonawanda, we lost him. By this I mean he became part of another world."

That other world was exactly what Jim was seeking. Most of us dream, but too often those dreams are snatched away as we allow everchanging circumstances to pull us where they may through life. Jim was one of those rare few who dreamed, then set his own course. And, through the strength of his will, he stayed that route irregardless of the circumstances that surrounded him.

When Jim and Lee kicked their cold motorcycles to life and rumbled slowly through the still sleeping streets of North Tonawanda, Jim willingly bid his family, his home, and his friends good-bye, prepared to make whatever sacrifice necessary to see his racing dream through to fulfillment.

Hurtubise Family photo

The photo Mom Hurtubise wrote the note on.

V. H. Field photo -HFC

Jim at Merrittville Speedway June 18, 1955.

Hurtubise Family Photo

Stock Car racing in upper New York in the 1950s.

HURTUBISE

3

Hurtubise Family Photo

It had snowed for three days prior to the morning Jim and Lee left North Tonawanda. The roads they took south through New York and on into Pennsylvania were icy and treacherous. "It was so slick," remembers Lee, "that we never got over forty-miles-an-hour. The roads were so bad in places that we had to ride for long stretches with our feet dragging the road just to keep our balance. It was a hell of a tiring ride!"

Their destination that first day was Baltimore, Maryland, where they were to visit a friend of Jim's, Johnny Dodd. Johnny and his father owned a service station in Baltimore, and had both raced with Jim in Florida. Because of the unexpected slow pace, however, it wasn't until well after midnight that they were able to find the Dodds' shop. Of course, there was no one there at that hour.

With nowhere else to go and not wanting to dip into their travel fund so early in the journey, they hung around outside the shop until Jim finally was able to contact Johnny at six that morning.

"I'll get a case of beer and be right over," was Johnny's blithe response.

While Jim and Lee sipped beer and talked with the Dodds, time slipped quickly away. What was intended to be a short stay grew into an all day bench racing session. Finally, at four PM of the second day of the trip, and still without sleep, save for the three hours after the party back in North Tonawanda, Jim and Lee once again pointed their motorcycles south. Trying to make up for some of the time they had already lost, they rode late into that night before pulling into a small diner in Charleston, South Carolina.

The winter of 1956 was an extremely cold one, and although they had steadily made their way south, the temperature still hovered in the teens. On motorcycles, the sharp night air knifed through even the many layers of clothes they wore, chilling them to the bone.

While warming themselves with cups of steaming coffee in the cozy diner, Jim remembered hearing somewhere that newspaper was an excellent insulator. So, he bought several papers from the counterman, and he and Lee began stuffing them into their clothes.

Occupied with this task, they were startled and somewhat embarrassed when they noticed two truck drivers staring at them, mouths agape, eyes wide with amazement.

"What the hell are you boys doing?" the truckers gasped.

Jim, who never met a stranger, and certainly was never at a loss for words in any situation, not only explained in great detail all about the insulating qualities of newspaper, but went on to excitedly tell them how he and Lee were going to Daytona to run in the stock car races, then go on to California to become world famous racers.

Jim soon had the drivers doubled over with laughter, and so caught up in his infectious enthusiasm for his racing vision that they offered the boys what, on the surface, appeared to be the perfect solution to their travel problems.

The truckers were hauling straight through to Daytona Beach, and invited Jim and Lee to travel along with their motorcycles in the empty trailer. They would be warm and could catch some much-needed sleep as they motored peacefully to Daytona. It took only a few miles, however, for the fallacy of that plan to be revealed.

No sooner had they rounded the first sharp curve, than Jim's BSA tumbled over squirting gas onto the floor and pumping fumes into the air. Slipping and sliding in the spilled gas Jim and Lee desperately fought to right the overturned motorcycle in the pitch black dark of the jostling trailer. They finally got Jim's bike back on its wheels, and seeing no other way to secure the top-heavy motorcycles, leaned them in the trailer's corners and lay on their backs while holding them in place with their feet. Any chance of sleep, of course, was gone.

Adding to an already torturous experience, they soon discovered that an empty semitrailer was not designed for a smooth ride. Each bump in the road tossed them into the air, then slammed them back down. Boom, boom, boom! For three hours they rode like this, repeatedly dribbled against the hard, wood floor by the bouncing trailer.

Just when they thought they could stand it no longer, the truck eased to a stop. Jim and Lee yelled at the top of their lungs, and beat on the sides of the trailer. But, to no avail. They were trapped. The trailer, used for hauling refrigerated goods, was heavily insulated so the drivers couldn't hear them, and, assuming their passengers were asleep, didn't disturb them.

All too soon they were once more, literally, pounding down the highway. Desperate for some diversion from the agony of the black, fume filled hull, Jim said, "I know what we're going to do. We're going to sing! What song do you know, Lee?"

"Jim, right now I can't think of any songs I know," sighed Lee miserably.

"Well, I know *You Are My Sunshine*," said Jim, "Let's sing that."

So, for hours they sang "*You Are My Sunshine*" over and over again, enduring yet another stop before the doors of their darkened torture chamber were at last swung open in Jacksonville, Florida. As the morning light flooded into the darkened trailer, Jim and Lee, scrapped and bruised, looked at each other and smiled. Without speaking a word, they knew exactly what the other was thinking. They were free. Never had the sun looked better. Never had the air smelled sweeter.

Apologizing profusely for the misery they had put their new friends through, the truckers bought them breakfast, and, trying to make amends, again offered to take them on to Daytona Beach. Possibly they could make the remainder of the trip more bearable.

Jim and Lee's instant, unified response was, "Hell no! We're riding."

Jim and Lee were now into their third sleepless day, but with the powerful, growling motorcycles beneath them, a warm breeze in their faces, and a glowing Florida sun above, their spirits were rejuvenated. The excited anticipation of the adventure ahead quickly pushed sleep to the back of their minds.

They reached Daytona in a few hours, and located the friend Jim had hoped to drive for, but the ride did not materialize. Disappointed, but ever impulsive and always ready with a backup plan, Jim said to Lee, "Hell, let's ride on over to Tampa. I've got an uncle that lives there, and we can stay with him for awhile."

In Tampa Jim's uncle, his father's brother, Lawrence, listened with amusement and rapt amazement as Jim and Lee recounted their sleepless, three day ordeal. Then he fixed them, according to Lee, "The best steaks I've ever tasted in my life." Their stomachs full, the adventurers fell exhausted into bed and slept for twenty hours.

Restored by the rest and good food, they motored back to Daytona, where they took in all the activities of Speed Week through the day, and slept in their pup tent on the moonlit beach at night. With beautiful weather, races every day, and a town swarming with racing people, it was the closest thing to heaven a racer could find. But Jim was soon ready to head west.

"We stayed for three days," says Lee, "and then Jim was ready to take off. He always got restless quick. If Jim wasn't in a race car, or driving to a race, he was going nuts."

The motorcycle ride from Florida to California was leisurely. The country was different then. It was the last days of America's innocence. Ike was in the White House and people still kept their doors unlocked at night. Jim and Lee rode serenely all day, then slept, unafraid, wherever they chose to pitch their tent for the night.

Through tiny hamlets, along winding streams, returning the waves of passing motorists, they cruised across Alabama, Mississippi and Louisiana. Through Texas, New Mexico and Arizona, never failing to take time for a side trip should any place of interest prick their curiosity, Jim and Lee explored the Grand Canyon, Devils River Texas, and ventured into Juarez, Mexico.

"When we got to El Paso, Texas," recalls Lee, "Jim said, 'Hey, let's go to Mexico. We got plenty of time, and I bet we can have a lot of fun down there in Juarez!"

Having splurged for a motel that day, the boys had the luxury of being able to shower and spruce up for their trip across the border. But, by the time they got to Juarez, it had started to rain, and the fenderless front wheels of their motorcycles threw a streak of muddy water across their face and chests as they rode along.

In Juarez they cruised around until they found a likely looking beer joint, parked their bikes and strode in. Their reception was, to say the least, less than neighborly.

"Every eye was on us," laughs Lee. "I mean, here we were two Americans, dressed in blue jeans and leather jackets with a mud stripe up our fronts. The place was full of people. A bunch of guys drinking beer, and twenty five or thirty women sitting around talking, and they all just stopped."

"I whispered under my breath to Jim, 'Maybe we just better order a beer and get the hell out of this place.' But Jim thought everything would be okay. And when we got our beers, he went over to the women, and asked if anyone wanted to dance. One did. And when Jim started dancing with her, I noticed this one guy in particular. He looked mad. I don't know if it was her boyfriend, or her brother, or what, but he sure wasn't happy about the situation. I was starting to get worried."

Finally noticing the same unfriendly grimaces that had caught Lee's attention, Jim agreed that maybe they should depart for more friendly confines after all. They slipped out unscathed, and resumed cruising around town, trying to find a place with a friendlier atmosphere. Fruitless in their search, they spotted a group of men gathered on a street corner and stopped for directions.

Neither Lee nor Jim spoke Spanish, but one of the men in the group seemed to have a rudimentary grasp of English. After several minutes of trying to communicate in broken English, accompanied by a lot of arm-waving and hand gestures, they were getting nowhere. It would be easier, Jim decided, if the young Mexican would just hop on the back of his bike and direct them as they rode. With more distorted Spanish, embellished with more hand and arm signals, Jim finally made the man understand, and he happily agreed.

"We twisted and wound through the streets of Juarez for what seemed like a long time," says Lee, "before this guy finally signaled for us to stop. He pointed, grinned, and shook his head. I guess he was trying to tell us this was a great place. We looked, and, I'll be damned if he hadn't taken us right back to that same bar!"

Giving up their night of drinking and dancing in Mexico as a lost cause, they headed back across the border.

Continuing their journey to California, they hit the Golden State and rode into El Centro while the Imperial County Fair was in progress. The Imperial County Fair means just one thing to racers; sprint cars. Open wheeled, exotic, purpose-built machines. Jim got excited just seeing them sitting on trailers around town.

"Look at that! Look at that, Lee," he shouted over the roar of their motorcycles. "That's the kind of race car I want to run! That's it! That's what we're going to race!"

Spying a sprint car parked at a small diner, Jim insisted they stop. Inside they found the car's owner, Tony Gonzales, and the driver, Mike Schmader. After some brief introductory conversation, Jim launched into his pitch about how he and Lee had raced back in New York, and how they rode all the way to California to become great racers.

Perceiving that Jim and Lee did possess some mechanical aptitude, and glad to help a couple of young racers, Gonzales offered to buy them a pit pass for that afternoon's races if they agreed to help on his GMC powered sprinter. Jim and Lee jumped at the opportunity.

Sprint car racing had not yet gained the national popularity that it would enjoy in later years, so it is most likely that Jim Hurtubise had never seen a sprint car race before he arrived in California. Jim intended, according to Lee, to go to California to race midgets, those diminutive speedsters that had spawned a generation of Indianapolis stars such as the immortal Bill Vukovich, Johnnie Parsons, Walt Faulkner and Sam Hanks. It had been midget drivers who had taken the Speedway by storm in the early fifties, and Jim wanted nothing less than to emulate their accomplishments.

But when that first powerful sprint car engine roared to life, belching long plumes of blue flame, literally shaking the ground with its guttural growl, thoughts of midget racing were immediately cast aside. This was a defining moment in the life of Jim Hurtubise. These were the cars he was born to drive. These were the cars he was destined to make his name in.

"I'd never seen Jim so excited," insists Lee. "He was absolutely beside himself when they started running. 'Lee, look at that! Look at that one! This is great!' He was so excited I could hardly keep him on the ground."

From that moment, Jim resolved that he would drive sprint cars. When he and Lee finished helping Mike and Tony prepare their car, he dispatched Lee in one direction, while he went another. Jim's instructions: "Check out the best looking cars, and find out all you can about them." If he couldn't talk his way into someone's car, he reasoned, he would build his own.

Making his way through the pits, Jim introduced himself to anyone that dared make eye contact, and delivered his, by now, well-practiced spiel about coming to California to be a race car driver. He gleaned every bit of information he could from anyone willing to give him a minute of time, and went over every inch of their car with the tape measure he always carried. He checked wheel bases, ride heights, track widths, engine placement and any other dimension he thought pertinent.

Jim had a photographic memory so didn't bother to write anything down, but at day's end he assured Lee, "We know enough to build one of these things right now."

With but sixty dollars left between them, however, the plan to build a race car was temporarily put on the back burner. They first had to find jobs to restore their dwindling financial resources, and an incident following that first day of racing at El Centro dramatically demonstrated the need to find a more permanent dwelling than a pup tent.

As they had almost every night since leaving New York, they found a secluded spot to pitch their tent, and settled in for the night. After a few minutes of talking over the events of that afternoon, they drifted off to a peaceful sleep, their minds full of the promise the busy day had brought. Suddenly they were jolted awake by a loud voice, as a blinding light flooded the tent.

Shielding their eyes from the beam of a spotlight, they were terrified to see that they were staring down the muzzle of a double-barreled shotgun! "What in the hell are you punks doing here?" boomed a hostile voice.

"Wait a minute! Wait a minute," Jim pleaded.

"Wait hell," the faceless voice growled. "I ought to kill you SOB's right here. This is my property and I want you off it right now. Hell, I oughta just blow you off it!"

Jim, calling on all his considerable persuasive abilities, words tumbling out one on top of another, somehow placated the irate farmer, and convinced him they intended no harm. Jim again launched into his "came from New York to be great racers" story, albeit related this time with more panic than conviction.

When the farmer left, allowing then to stay where they were for the night, Jim said to Lee, as though he had actually been cool and poised through a potentially deadly situation, "You know, he wasn't really such a bad guy after all!"

"But," says Lee, "That was the most scared I'd ever seen Jim. He was probably one of the bravest people I ever knew. I never saw him when he was afraid in a race car. But, I'll guarantee you he was scared that time, and so was I. We were awake the rest of the night!"

Jim journeyed to California convinced that he would be able to find work in the then thriving and well paying aircraft industry. A couple of school friends had moved to Inglewood while he was in the Coast Guard and got jobs at Douglas Aviation. Jim believed they could help get Lee and him on there, so after the racing at El Centro ended, they rode to Douglas. Unfortunately, Jim's friends had no clout, and they were turned away without jobs.

With that door closed and their money dwindling fast, they rented a room at a cheap motel and early the next morning began pounding the pavement of Inglewood looking for work. By the second day Jim and Lee both had jobs. Lee, driving a truck for the National Lead Company, and Jim, as if his every move were an act of destiny, found work at a company that would figure prominently in his California racing future.

Brothers Charlie and Dave Chase owned two separate businesses that shared the same building. NeoGlo signs, which Charlie owned, made neon signs and was Jim's primary employer. Dave owned Az-Tech Manufacturing, and made fixtures and prototype parts for the aerospace industry. At this time Jim was already an accomplished welder and fabricator, so he often worked for Az-Tech whenever his special skills were needed.

With his solid work ethic and charismatic charm, Jim quickly gained the Chase brothers' confidence. They, like anyone Jim came in contact with, were caught up in his yearning to race. Within his first week on the job, they gave Jim a key to the building and permission to build a race car there after hours. This was a God send for Jim since the Az-Tech side of the business had many sophisticated machine tools and aircraft related materials that were perfect for a race car. Jim was given an open account for anything he used, and the cost was later deducted from his paycheck.

It was during this same period of time that Jim met Hank Higuchi, who would serve as Jim's chief mechanic at Indianapolis for many years, but, in 1956 he was the proprietor of a service station in Glendale and owned one of the finest sprint cars in California. Jim often tried to talk his way into the car, but Hank used only top notch talent, not raw rookies, and never gave Jim a ride. Then one afternoon Jim showed up at Hank's garage with a different request.

"When Jim first came out to California from New York," recalls Hank, "he came into my station in Gardena, and said to me, 'Henry, I don't have any money. If you loan me some, you can hold my motorcycle until I pay you back.' I didn't really know him from Adam, but I did know he wanted to race really bad. So I told him, 'No, I won't do that. I won't keep your motorcycle. But I'll loan you a couple hundred dollars, and you just pay me back when you can."

With the money Jim borrowed from Hank, and the pay that was starting to come in from their jobs, Jim and Lee bought an old twenty five foot house trailer, and rented a lot for it in an Inglewood trailer park for twenty eight dollars a month. The trailer was so small that they had to build bunkbeds to have room to sleep. The cramped quarters didn't matter, however, for in the busy days ahead they would spend little time there.

After a full day on their jobs and a quick bite to eat, they would rush to the NeoGlo shop and work most of the night building their race car. Getting little more than three hours sleep a night, they were sustained only by a racing dream and gallons of coffee. Unbelievably, in thirty two days they had a sprint car on wheels and running.

The car wasn't much to look at. By today's standards it was crude. But it was well thought out, and incorporated several of Jim's original ideas, the most innovative being the parallel, torsion bar rear suspension. Today torsion bars are the norm on sprint cars, but in 1956 they were rare, especially on home-built equipment. Jim's was especially unique in that it was made from flat steel stock, rather than the more common round tube. He even devised a mounting bracket for it that enabled him to quickly and easily make suspension adjustments at the track.

For power, the car used the hotrodder's mainstay, a Ford flat head engine. Jim bored and stroked the engine to a larger displacement, added a mild racing cam and three Stromberg carburetors. But with their short finances they could do little more. The car used a Ford rearend, Buick brake drums, a '37 Ford front axle, and the rear wheels were the old, wire spoke type. Jim built the body himself, forming the tail from two Cadillac fenders he welded together. He then painted the car white, and proudly emblazoned it with a huge maroon number 56.

Amateurish though the car might have been, Jim endured two years of intense, treacherous, wheel banging competition with it on the tough California Racing Association [CRA] circuit, and forged a reputation that would ultimately carry him to the top of the sport.

Incredibly, Jim almost won with his thirty-two-day-wonder the very first time out.

Hurtubise Family photo

Lee and Jim admire Jim's first flat head Ford powered sprint car.

HURTUBISE

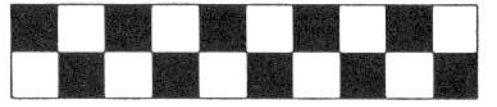

4

Hurtubise Family photo

Jim and Lee stared with awe as they rolled through the pit gate at Western Speedway in Gardena, California. Towing their pride and joy on a trailer they built themselves, with a truck they borrowed from Jim's boss, they were surrounded by the best sprint cars and drivers the CRA had to offer. This was Jim's first race with the new car, his first sprint car race ever. A beginning. A first tentative step towards his dream of racing success.

Jim didn't have the slightest notion about what the car should feel like, or what he needed to do to it to make it go fast, so he fiddled with the suspension some, and adjusted on the engine, but, mainly, he just ran a lot of practice laps. Those multiple laps paid off, and he qualified easily, surprising those observers who were skeptical of this green-as-grass sprint car driver in the homemade car.

When his eight lap heat race was flagged off, Jim jammed his throttle foot to the floor, the only way he knew to drive back then, and darted to the front from his outside, second row starting position.

By lap 2 he was leading and pulling away. Then, just as it appeared that Jim had his first win in the bag, the engine started to spit and sputter. Jim tried to nurse the car through the final two laps, but a radiator cap had worked loose and sprayed the magneto with water, causing it to short out. The engine misfired worse, and Jim was passed by two other cars right at the checkered flag.

Far from being angry Jim was ecstatic when he climbed from his car. Lee insists that Jim was as happy after that race as he ever was following any of the many races he would win later. "We had always heard," explains Lee, "that the best race car drivers were in California. And here we are, Jim's first time ever in a sprint car, and with a car we built ourselves from measurements Jim had in his head, and he almost won the darn race!"

"When he got out of the car, he was laughing and happy, a big grin on his face." continues Lee. "He said, 'Lee, this thing just quit running or we'd had those SOB's! I mean I was flying out there. We could have whipped their butts easy."

Jim's confidence, never in short supply, soared. He had proved to himself that he could race and win against the best, and that realization drove him to work even harder, to sacrifice even more. From that night on, Jim and Lee devoted every spare minute, every ounce of energy, and every extra dime to making the race car better. Recalls Lee, "Every payday we would cash our checks and dump our money out in a pile on the kitchen table. Then we would count out what we needed for our bills. So much for the rent. So much for utilities. So much for food. A little beer money. To make our money go even further, we ate a lot of what Jim called disappearing steak, cheap hamburger that disappeared when we fried it! All the rest of our money we put into the race car."

Even that was never enough. Racing, no matter the level, is expensive. So, to stretch their racing dollars even further, they scrounged parts that others discarded. Fellow California racer, A.J. Shepherd, recalls the time that Jim replaced the bad connecting rods in his engine with a set he dug out of the trash, and then won a race with the rebuilt engine that same night.

Tires were their biggest expense. While the top teams would go through three or four sets in one night, Jim and Lee made theirs last six or eight races by constantly re-grooving them. "I wish I had a nickel for every groove I've put in a tire," laughs Lee. "To get the most out of them, we'd groove them all the way down to the canvas."

With tires such a precious commodity, discarded ones became a prime target for scrounging. One night they spotted a particularly good set. "We were at Western Speedway, and pitted next to Art Bisch," says Lee. "Art drove for C&T Automotive, and they had top-notch equipment. The best of everything. They always had fresh tires, and changed them after hot laps, qualifying, and the heat races."

"While we were standing there watching them, they threw the set of tires they had just pulled off the car into this fenced-in, disposal area. Jim poked me and said, 'Hey, Lee, did you see that? Those tires look great. Keep an eye on them, and if they're still there after the race, we'll get 'em."

"Sure enough, when Bisch and his guys loaded up, they left the tires behind. But there were still a lot of people around, so we drank a few beers and waited for everyone to leave. We waited so long that they turned the track lights off, and the only people left were the CRA president, Walt James, and the person he was talking to out in the parking lot."

With the way finally clear, Jim and Lee sauntered over to the disposal pen, but while they were waiting, someone had padlocked the gate, and now a ten-foot-high fence separated them from those splendid, almost new tires.

"Damn! We'll have to climb over," Jim told Lee. "I'll stay up on the fence, and you get down inside, and hand the tires up to me. Then I'll throw them on over the fence from there."

Clinging to the side of the chain link fence with one hand, and trying to manhandle the heavy tires with the other, Jim got so tickled, cackling that distinctive, "Heh, heh, heh," laugh of his, that it was all he could do to get the tires clear of the barrier.

With that feat at last accomplished, "we flew back over that fence, grabbed the tires and hid them in the middle of our tire rack so fast no one had a chance to see us," laughs Lee. "I bet we used those damn tires for eight weeks!"

The constant need for financing led Jim and Lee to the convertible races at Balboa Stadium in San Diego. Stock car racing was then drawing tremendous crowds on the West Coast, and those large crowds generated huge purses.

"At the time," remembers Lee "if Jim cleaned house, at a sprint car race, that is set fast time, won the heat, and the feature, we would win from one hundred ninety, to two hundred bucks. But, the convertible races down in San Diego were paying five hundred, sometimes six hundred dollars just for winning the feature. That sounded great to us!"

A racing friend told them about a 1949, three-window, Plymouth coupe, that had been built and raced by the patriarch of the legendary Petty racing clan, Lee Petty. After Petty sold the car, it passed through a succession of owners before turning up in Southern California. Jim and Lee located that owner, but when they inquired about buying the car he told them, "Hell, I haven't got any use for it. My wife's been after me to get rid of it anyway. If you'll get the damn thing out of my way you can just have it."

They gladly took it off his hands.

To disguise the coupe as a convertible, they first chopped off the top, and then made what looked like a convertible top cover, complete with hold down snaps, from an old piece of canvas, and attached it to the back of the car. To complete the conversion, they installed a roll bar, and Jim painted his favorite number, 56, on the door. By the time they got the car race ready and to San Diego, they had just enough money left to buy one pit pass, a not so uncommon occurrence in those days. They would often go to a race without enough gas money to get home on, depending on Jim's winnings to finance the return trip.

For this particular inconvenience, Jim had already devised a plan. "You get in the trunk with our spare tires," he told Lee. "and, when we get into the pits, just pop out with a couple of tires like you were pulling them out of the trunk."

They pulled that bit of melodrama off without a hitch, but they still had to avoid getting caught by the pit stewards with their single pass. For that, Jim also had a plan. "Here's what we'll do," he explained to Lee. "We'll keep an eye out for the steward, and when we see him coming I'll jump under the car like I'm working on it, and you climb inside and bend down like you're doing something under the dash. I'll reach out and show him the pass, and then I'll hand it up through the floorboard to you."

Whether it was because their acting ability warranted Academy Award nominations, or the officials displayed compassion for a couple of obviously struggling young racers and simply looked the other way, they managed that charade, despite being checked numerous times throughout the course of the evening.

Calling on his three years of stock car racing experience, Jim won the feature that first night at Balboa, and returned to win there on several other occasions with the made over Plymouth.

It was with this prize money that Jim bought and installed his first Chevy V-8 engine in a sprint car. It would be several years before Jim and Parnelli Jones shook the world of USAC sprint car racing to its foundation by beating the expensive, purebred racing Offies with hot rod Chevy engines. But, even as early as 1957, Jim was one of the first to see the vast, untapped potential of the Chevrolet as a racing engine.

"I can't absolutcly vcrify it," says Lee today. "But, if Jim didn't have the first Chevy in a sprint car on the West Coast, or in the nation as far as that goes, he certainly had one of the very first."

Jim's first Chevy was a 1955 265-cubic-inch engine introduced by Chevrolet in their Corvette. In those days there was not the proliferation of over the counter speed parts available for the Chevy like there is today. All Jim was able to do, especially in his financially strapped condition, to gain more horsepower was to add three Stromberg "97" carburetors and a Dempsey Wilson racing cam. Dempsey, a driver/businessman who would later compete at Indianapolis, gave Jim the cam at a discount in return for carrying the Wilson Cam logo on the hood of his car.

Although the Chevy was much better than the old, flathead Ford, Jim's car was still underpowered when compared to the top competition.

"Before the races," recalled Lee, "they used to introduce each driver over the PA, and make some interesting comment about him or his car. Nick Valenta had a car with a big Dodge engine in it, and the announcer would introduce him by saying, 'And, here's Nick Valenta in his 400 horsepower Dodge powered car.' Once, while the announcer was doing that, Jim nudged me and said, 'I wonder if they're going to introduce me and our 140 horsepower Chevy!"

But doing without the best of equipment only spurred Jim to work harder. "Jim had unbelievable determination and dedication," says Lee admiringly. "He would never quit. Whatever it took to keep going, that's what he did. I remember one night he crashed during a heat race at LA Speedway, and it bent up the front axle and the steering arm. We had the welding equipment with us, so when the wrecker towed the car back in Jim went to work on it with the torch."

"He got the steering arm red hot, then pounded it against a wooden post to straighten it. He'd eyeball it, then heat it, and beat it against the post some more. And, he kept this up until he got it to where it looked reasonably straight."

"While he was working on the car, Walt James came over," continues Lee, "Walt said, 'Jim you can't run the car like that. You bent that arm when you crashed, and now you've heated it and bent it again trying to straighten it. You really need to get that magnafluxed before you use it."

"Jim, desperate to race, pleaded with the CRA president, 'Walt I need to run tonight. Hell, that part's okay. Didn't you see me magnafluxing it while I was straightening it?"

At this point, Jim became so animated and adamant about wanting to race, that Walt relented, and agreed to let him run. "The first sign of a problem though, and you're out of here Jim," snapped Walt.

Jim ran the race that evening without incident, and though Lee doesn't recall just exactly where he finished, he does remember that Jim won the semi, and came in third or fourth in the feature.

"That was Jim's way," emphasizes Lee. "No matter what happened, he'd never let anything stand in his way. Sometimes things would get so bad that he'd become discouraged, but that wouldn't last very long at all and he'd be right back at it again."

In another LA Speedway crash, Jim wrecked the car so bad that he was unable to fix it for that night's program. Afterwards, Jim and Lee made the usual post race rounds, before ending up at a favorite hangout, the Ascot Inn. After a few more beers, and some whining about their bad luck, Jim stopped, looked across the table at Lee and said, "Damn it Lee! We've got to quit feeling sorry for ourselves. Here we are sitting around drinking beer, and we should be working on that damn race car right now."

That was Wednesday. The next race was scheduled for Sunday at El Centro. By the time they towed the car back to the NeoGlo shop in Inglewood it was already well past midnight, but, they immediately went to work on the damaged machine. Lee called in sick at National Lead, and, since work was a little slow at NeoGlo anyway, Charlie told Jim just to keep working on the race car.

At this time Jim had started dating his future wife, Jane, and Lee was dating his wife to be, Marcia. The girls kept them in coffee, milk shakes and sandwiches, and they worked, without sleep, for seventy two hours. They finished the car just as the sun was coming up on Sunday morning. By 7 AM, they had it loaded on the trailer, and were embarked on the 180 mile drive to El Centro.

Lee was so tired that he remembers little of the afternoon, other than that Jim won his heat, and ran good in the feature. By the end of that day, the adrenaline drained, completely exhausted, even youthful enthusiasm could no longer sustain them.

"I was so beat," recalls Lee, "I couldn't even talk. It was like everything was in slow motion. Jim, who always had tremendous amounts of energy, looked like he was dead. This was just Jim's third or fourth date with Jane, and just my second date with Marcia, but we were so tired that we just crawled in the car, and told the girls they would have to drive home. So, here's our dates, who had never towed a trailer before, pulling a race car for three hours back to LA while we slept in the back seat."

"But Jim's fighting spirit was just amazing," marvels Lee. "If I'd been on my own, I really don't think that I would have done all that. Went to that extent. Worked all those hours without sleep. But, his enthusiasm rubbed off, and you got caught up in that Go! Go! Go!"

Soon the results of that zealous effort were noticeable on the car. They replaced the wire spoke wheels with steel, added a quick change rear end, and installed a slick looking, professionally made, fiberglass nose piece, that Jim topped off with a new color scheme of maroon with white numbers, highlighted by a white flame that scalloped across the front, and jutted down the side of the car.

And Jim's tireless efforts were soon being demonstrated in his driving as well. He was fast gaining a reputation as one of the young lions of California racing. LeRoy Neumayer, considered one of those young lions himself, and later a good friend of Jim's, recalls the first time they met.

"It was at Gardena Stadium not long after Herk started running sprint cars," says LeRoy. "He had this car that had a set of headers on one side, and just a set of Mickey Mouse looking straight pipes on the other side. I think that he'd blown a head, and didn't have the money to replace it with another racing head, and so he was running a stock one on that side. Anyway, all the guys were just kinda' laughing and making a big joke about it. But, I'll tell you, it didn't take long to make a believer out of me. Herk blew everybody off with that old thing."

The guys Jim was blowing off weren't just a bunch of talentless hacks. Racing in the CRA in 1956 and 1957 was highly competitive, with great drivers like Roger McCluskey, Billy Cantrell, Art Bisch, Jack Rounds, Roy Prossor and Nick Valenta, plying their trade on the rough and tumble tracks of that era. Not all of them took kindly to this young, brash, upstart from New York.

"There were three groups of drivers in the CRA then," recalls Neumayer. "The old-timers. The drivers that were just filling the fields, and, then there were the Dick Tracys. Herk was one of the Dick Tracys."

"Herk really raced hard," marvels LeRoy. "He wouldn't give you a bit of room. He'd really crowd you. And, he made some of the old-timers mad, because they didn't like anybody coming in and beating them on their tracks."

Such was the case with Allen Heath.

Allen Heath had been a commanding, California racing personality for years. He first gained notoriety racing midgets just prior to World War II, and then rose to stardom during the midget racing boom that followed that conflict. The success he achieved in those diminutive speedsters earned him rides in Indy cars, and in the sprint cars of the American Automobile Association [AAA]. The AAA was the predecessor to the United States Auto Club [USAC], and with Indianapolis under its far flung umbrella, was the most respected and important sanctioning body in the nation, if not the world.

It was in an AAA sprint car race, at Illiani Speedway in 1954, that Allen crashed and brutally fractured his left arm. When the arm failed to respond to treatments, gangrene set in and it had to be amputated just below the elbow. Allen replaced his missing limb with a metal hook, and used the prosthesis to good effect, both as a device to grip a steering wheel, and as an intimidating weapon in the off track altercations that he seemed to gravitate to.

Thwarted in his attempt to drive at Indianapolis because of his handicap, Allen concentrated instead on West Coast sprint car racing. He considered Ascot, then known as LA Speedway, his own, private playground, and viewed with scorn any driver who threatened to interfere with his winning ways there. It was inevitable that Jim and Allen would clash.

That happened during one of the regular Wednesday night, LA Speedway shows. Jim and Allen lined up next to each other, near the front of the field. Almost from the drop of the green flag, Heath began nudging Jim's car with his own. He wanted this new kid to know right away just who he was dealing with and what to expect. But, Jim was having none of that. He nudged back. And Heath, caught off guard by the unexpected retaliation, went gyrating harmlessly into the wall.

Unhurt, Allen sat fuming in his stalled car while the field slowly circled the track under the yellow. Every time Jim idled by, Allen would shake his hook at him, and scream obscenities. The curses were lost to the rumble of engines, but his rage was easily discernible, even to the fans in the stands, by the livid expressions distorting his face.

When the push truck got Allen restarted and the field again took the green flag, Allen hung back at the rear of the field. He was waiting for Hurtubise. When Jim caught up, Heath got back on the gas, and, running to the inside, and slightly behind Jim, repeatedly tried to bump him into the wall. Jim managed to avoid Heath's darting car. Then Allen made a mistake. Instead of staying underneath, he pulled to the outside, and tried to slash down on Jim as they roared into turn one.

That was just the opening Jim was waiting for. He didn't back off the gas at all, but bored into the corner wide open, and leaned his car against Heath's. Again Heath went spinning into the wooden retaining wall. This time hard enough that he was unable to restart. Jim was able to continue, and as the race ran to its conclusion, excitement built in the stands. The crowd was well aware of Allen's penchant for fighting, and they knew he would not take this humiliation lightly. The post-race confrontation in the pits might well prove to be more exciting than the race they were watching on the track.

By the time the race ended, the crowd was so worked up, that they swarmed over the fence that separated them from the pits. When Allen made his way to Jim's car, several hundred people were already milling about, some shouting their encouragement to the new kid, some to the old pro.

Heath, nose to nose with Jim, led off with a predictable flurry of ranting, raving, and wild gesturing with his hook. Jim, for the most part, kept his cool, but occasionally flailed back with a few choice barbs of his own. After letting the adversaries vent their anger verbally for a few minutes, cooler heads separated them before the shouting match escalated to physical contact.

As they were being pulled apart, Lee recalls that Allen shook his hook at Jim and growled, "You crazy SOB! You keep driving like that, you dumb kid, and you're going to end up with one of these!"

Jim coldly stared back at Heath, and growled, "And, if you keep screwing with me, Heath, you're going to end up with two of those!" Despite that nasty encounter, Jim's laid back personality quickly resurfaced. "Jim was just never the type of person to stay mad," explains Lee. "He had that blowup with Heath, and a few minutes later you couldn't tell anything had ever happened. And after that him and Allen got along just fine. But, Jim was just so happy go lucky that everybody liked him."

LeRoy Neumayer agrees, "Oh, a lot of those guys would get mad at Jim because he beat 'em. And they'd rant and cuss him, but before long they'd be drinking beer together. I don't know of anybody in those days who didn't like Jim."

Jim escaped the wheel banging episode with Allen Heath unscathed. But he experienced his share of dramatic, wall pounding crashes and high flying flips that were then, and still are, very much a part of sprint car racing. Sprint cars are lightweight, high powered, evil beasts, capable of jumping up and biting an unsuspecting driver without the slightest provocation. Put twenty such twitchy, throttle sensitive machines on a dirt track no bigger than a half mile, and the results are thrilling, dangerous, and very often deadly. That was especially true in Jim's day.

By the late fifties, technology had increased the speed of sprint cars dramatically. However, advances in safety came nowhere near keeping pace. Crash helmets were, at best, rudimentary. There were no roll cages, multi-point safety harnesses, or arm restraints to secure the driver in the event of a crash. Only a simple lap belt, and a curved metal roll bar, extending no higher than the middle of the driver's head, were there to protect him in a flip.

That Jim Hurtubise, with his high sliding, throttle-to-the-floor style, was able to survive those years without being killed or seriously injured borders on the miraculous. There were many that didn't. That he not only endured, but did so with his unique, outrageous brand of humor, and his "let's have fun" attitude, created a legend.

There was the race at Manzanita Speedway in Phoenix, Arizona, for instance. Jim set fast time in qualifying, and lined up on the outside of row two for the four car trophy dash. As the cars roared into turn one at the start, the driver running inside of Jim got sideways. Trying to get out of the way, Jim's left rear wheel rolled over the other car's right rear wheel, and catapulted him high into the air. The car crashed nose first in front of a billboard perched atop the outside guard rail. The impact was so great that the car cleared the billboard on the first bounce, and began a violent series of tail over nose flips before coming to a stop, upside down, in an irrigation ditch.

Lee, watching from the first turn, grabbed a fire extinguisher and, despite the three cracked ribs he was nursing from a motorcycle accident earlier in the week, dashed to the accident scene. He took a quick look around, and didn't see Jim. He feared the worst. That his friend was still strapped in the overturned car, and on the verge of drowning in the muddy water of the ditch.

Lee jumped into the knee deep water, desperately grasping for Jim. But he couldn't find him. Puzzled he looked around, and spotted him sitting about ten feet away on the bank of the ditch, a big grin on his face. In his rush to get to the car, Lee hadn't noticed him in the crowd gathered around the overturned car.

Seeing the startled look on Lee's face, Jim broke into a laugh and said, "What the hell did you bring that fire extinguisher for, Lee? There's already more water here than you could ever use!"

"You SOB," shouted Lee in mock anger. "I ran over here with my ribs killing me, and now I'm down here, getting this dirty water in my cuts. Damn it, next time I'll just let you drown."

The crash had been so severe that the tail was completely ripped off the car during its wild, thrashing gyrations. Afterwards Jim just joked, "I guess I'll have to find another junked Cadillac, so I'll have the fenders to make a new one!"

"Wild crashes like that just didn't seem to bother Jim," insists Lee. "He'd crash out of the track and come walking back, laughing and waving at the crowd. I think he honestly believed that he was invincible."

A crash at the beautiful, half-mile dirt track in Calistoga, California, seemed to verify Lee's assessment. It was Jim's first appearance at the exceptionally fast Northern California track. Although a half mile is a half mile, Calistoga is known among racers as a big half mile because of its long straights. Even in Jim's day, straightaway speeds could approach 120 miles per hour.

Driving someone else's car that night, Jim ran the practice session while turning laps a second quicker than anyone else. The car's owner was excited and pleased. Jim was not. Whether the car was so much smoother handling than his own that Jim didn't realize how fast the strange machine was running, or he simply believed it capable of more speed, is not known. According to Lee, he rolled into the pits and complained, "I don't know, but, boy, this thing just isn't going fast."

Lee made the changes to the car that Jim directed, and they seemed to help. By the second lap of the feature Jim was leading and pulling away from the field. "Then," says Lee, "going down the back straight, it looked like Jim just disappeared down in the cockpit. I couldn't even see the top of his helmet! The owner was standing there and he looked at me and said, 'What the hell is he doing?' I was wondering the same thing myself."

"Well, up comes his head, but by then he was already at turn three. It was too late to back off, and I mean he went barreling into the turn wide open. He went in way too hot, hit the berm, flipped and bent the car up bad."

After hiking back to the pits, Jim faced the understandably distraught car owner. "The car just didn't feel like it was going fast," explained Jim. "I thought there was something underneath the gas peddle, and I was reaching down there trying to find out what it was!"

"And that's exactly the way Jim was," shrugs Lee. "If he thought about doing something like that, he didn't hesitate a minute, he'd just do it. He wasn't afraid at all, in fact, he was totally fearless in a race car."

Though his fearless nature and aggressive driving style, at times, made Jim appear to be wild, and driving way over his head, he really wasn't a reckless, unthinking driver. He just had the talent, and so much confidence in that talent, that he would try and make his car go where other drivers wouldn't. The crashes came at a time in his career when his experience lagged behind that desire.

"Herk was never afraid to extend the car," observes Don Shepherd. "He'd stick it out a little. Then stick it out a little further. Try to get a little more out of it, then a little more. He'd push it to the limit, and sometimes it would get away from him." LeRoy Neumayer, who has the unique perspective of not only having been a driver himself, but a mechanic who worked with such luminaries as Jim, A.J. Foyt, Parnelli Jones and Roger McCluskey, agrees with Don. "Herk was fearless, but not reckless," explains LeRoy. "He knew what he could do and what he could get away with. A lot of guys are brave. Anybody can stomp on the pedal, but knowing where you're going is another story altogether. Herk always knew where he was going in a race car."

"When I first realized that Herk really had something going for him," continues LeRoy, "was when he took the Kephart Offy and started winning races with it. I'd helped build that car. I'd put the Offy in it. But, I never could do anything with it. It was so stiff that it always wanted to bicycle, you had to fight it all the time. But Jim got in it and made it go."

Jim had his share of crashes early in his career. There are few drivers who don't. However, considering the number of races he ran, Jim's crashes weren't exceptionally numerous. And, they are, in fact, most remembered today not for their frequency, but because he drove so hard that they were inevitably dramatic.

Like all other men that race, Jim accepted those crashes as an unwelcome yet realistic part of racing. But Jim was also very much aware that crashes would hinder a speedy realization of his racing dreams. They would waste his energy and money on repairs. A serious injury could cost him valuable time away from racing as he recovered, and too many wrecks could earn him the reputation of a "crasher," and cost him rides in better equipment.

Jim certainly wanted no interferences, no obstacles in his headlong dash to stardom. He allowed nothing to distract him from the pursuit of that goal for long. He did, however, find time to fall in love and marry.

Walt Mahony photo -HFC

Jim in the Lee Petty coupe converted to a convertible.

Walt Mahony photo -HFC

Jim was already jacking more weight than the competition during his first year of sprint car racing.

Walt Mahony photo -HFC

Jim became a winner with one of Dempsey Wilson's cams in his Chevy.

Handprints on the nose. Handprints on the .... **Hurtubise Family Photo**

Jim's first sprint car in action. **Hurtubise Family Photo**

Life sure is fun! **Walt Mahony photo -HFC**

HURTUBISE

5

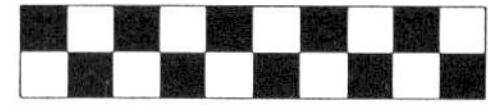

Chrysler - Plymouth photo by Dick Williford

ith his outgoing, vivacious, laugh a minute manner, Jim had little trouble meeting attractive members of the opposite sex. Not long after he arrived in California, a particular young lady, Jane Stahl, caught his eye. Jane lived with her mother in the trailer next to Jim and Lee's. "Jim spotted Jane," recalls Lee, "not long after we moved in, and he really thought she was good looking. He'd say, 'Hey, Lee! Look at her. Boy, she really looks good!"

The object of Jim's admiring glances, however, was not as enamored with him. "I really thought Jim and his friends were all a bunch of hoods," laughs Jane. "When I would leave our trailer to go anywhere, they would whistle and make all sorts of remarks when I walked by. I thought they were all obnoxious, and I certainly didn't want anything to do with Jim."

That, however, would soon change.

Jane was serving in the Naval Reserve, a rather unusual career choice for a young lady of that era. "I had wanted to be in the Navy all my life because my family was Navy, Jane explains. My uncle, brother, and sister-in-law all served in the Navy, so it was just a natural thing for me to be attracted to it."

Jim had seen Jane in her Navy uniform on many occasions, but one day, she had to make a quick dash to her car while still in her bathrobe. She wasn't quick enough. Jim intercepted her before she could get back to her trailer.

"Hey, I like this uniform much better," he laughed.

Attempting only to ignore the wise remark and make her way to the safety of her home, Jane was taken aback when he added, "You really do look nice in your uniform. I was in the Coast Guard myself."

Surprised that someone she had perceived to be only a motorcycle riding hood had actually served in the military, she stopped and allowed herself a few minutes of polite conversation with this young man with the sparkling blue eyes. Maybe he wasn't such a bad guy after all. A few more conversations followed before Jim finally convinced Jane that she had indeed misjudged him. She was impressed by Jim's charm and sincerity as he talked about his racing goals, and finally relented to his determined request for a date. They went to a movie together.

"I don't actually know of one thing in particular that attracted me to Jim," says Jane. "I really thought his friend, Lee, was cuter. But, I loved Jim's outgoing personality, his frankness, that crazy laugh of his. And, he had those beautiful blue eyes."

The physical tip off to Jim's personality was always discernible in his eyes. One admirer, after meeting Jim in person for the first time, commented to a writer:

"I've never seen a pair of eyes like those before. It's not so much a fire in them, but a real sparkle. A genuine twinkle like you read about in children's books. And he has a magnetism, a mischievousness that matches what you see in them."

Whatever the exact reason for the attraction, Jane found her thoughts turned more and more to the young man next door. One evening Jim asked her to go to a race with him, but she already had a date. Part way through that outing, however, she feigned illness, and asked to be taken home. As soon as she walked through the door, she called to her mother, "Hurry up and get dressed, Mom. We're going to the racetrack!"

"Hollywood Park?" her mother asked, thinking Jane was talking about going to a thoroughbred race at that popular Los Angeles horse track.

"No, Gardena Speedway," answered Jane. "Hurry up, let's go!"

"Gardena Speedway," replied her mother. "Why in the world would you want to go there?"

Jane's aunt and uncle were avid racing fans, and good friends with two time 500 winner, Rodger Ward, as well as drivers Eddie Haddad and Johnny McDowell. Jane had visited these men and their families many times, but before that night at Gardena Stadium she had been to a race track only one other time to watch the filming of the Clark Gable racing movie, "*To Please A Lady*," at Carrell Speedway.

"When I went to the track that night," says Jane, "I didn't know a thing about racing. I didn't even know what you were supposed to wear, so I just wore the dress and high heels that I had on from my earlier date. Then, the race didn't any more than get started, than there was this big pileup, and Jim was right in the middle of it. Jim wasn't hurt, but he was out of the race." Afterwards Jane, with her mother in tow, headed for the pits to see him. Much to her surprise, as she approached Jim's car, surrounded as usual by a crowd of admirers, she saw Jim in deep conversation with a leggy, good-looking blonde. No doubt she was offering him her considerable charms as consolation for his unfortunate evening.

As it turned out, Jane knew the other girl as a resident of the trailer court, and greeted both Jim and her with an overly cheerful, "Hello Jan, how are you? Hi Jim! Well, I made it tonight after all."

After several minutes of polite, if uncomfortable, conversation, Jane and her mother left. Jim and Jane dated steadily after that, and were married three months later.

The wedding, though not planned as such, turned into a typically unorthodox, Jim Hurtubise affair. The ceremony was set for seven PM, Saturday, January 11, 1957, at the home of Jane's brother in West Covina. But, late afternoon found Jim still at the Ascot Inn with Lee, and a couple other friends, Bill Rafter, from New York, and Jack Coonce, from the trailer court. They were sipping beers and talking about the trip to Manzinita Speedway they were to make that evening. Jim was to have his first USAC ride there in a midget owned by Gus Linhares, and it could be the break into the big time that he was longing for.

Suddenly Jim blurted out, "Hey, let's get going, we're running late!"

Surprised, Lee asked, "What's the hurry, Jim? The race is not until tomorrow afternoon, we got plenty of time to get there."

Jim nonchalantly replied, "Well, I'm getting married tonight."

Married! All three of their mouths dropped open as Jim's friends stared at each other in disbelief. This was the first time he had said anything about marriage. Surely it was just another one of his elaborate jokes. After several minutes of verbal jousting, Jim finally convinced them that he wasn't joking. He and Jane were supposed to get married at West Covina in fifteen minutes. West Covina was fifty miles, and better than an hour's drive away!

They piled in the car and sped across Los Angeles, but they already knew their headlong dash was futile. Jim was going to be late for his own wedding. The situation was so comically hopeless that their initial dismay turned to a giddy silliness, and they began joking about the whole affair.

"Jim, you can't get married," they jibed. "We didn't get to throw you a bachelor party. What kind of a guy would get married without letting his friends throw him a bachelor party?"

Jim, not to be outdone in the bantering, joined right in, "Yeah you're right. No man should have to get married without a bachelor party. Hell, we'll just have one on the way."

To the gleeful cheers of his passengers, Jim then whipped off the highway, found the nearest liquor store and returned with two six packs of beer.

"This is for the party," he merrily proclaimed.

The mood at Jane's brother's home was not as festive. Her brother, in fact, was livid. Jane, in tears, kept insisting that Jim would be there. Although it was already well past eight, she knew in her heart that he wouldn't let her down. Finally, while Jane was cloistered in a bedroom with her brother and the minister listening to one last plea to call this thing off, Jim and his partying friends made their long overdue entrance.

Lee recalls their reception rivaled the cold welcome he and Jim had received in the Juarez, Mexico bar.

"There was probably thirty people there, dressed to the nines for the wedding," says Lee. "The women were all decked out, the men in suits and ties. The minister, of course, was there. Then, here we came busting in, smelling of beer and dressed in Levis. You could have heard a pin drop. No one spoke that first word, they just stared at us."

By the time they hit the door, Jim was feeling no pain. Though normally not a heavy drinker, he'd consumed several more beers during the trip over, besides the ones he'd already downed at the Ascot Inn. Just as Jane, her brother and the minister came out of the bedroom, Jim popped through the front door with a six pack under his arm, and whooped, "Hey, when's the wedding going to start? Let's get this wedding going!"

Furious, Jane's brother grabbed her and pulled her back to the bedroom for yet another conference on the foolishness of marrying this obvious jerk. But Jane was insistent. She loved Jim and wanted to marry him. She wouldn't change her mind. Her brother relented and loaned Jim a tie and sports coat for the ceremony. It was, humorously, too large.

Considering the circumstances, the ceremony proceeded smoothly until the minister asked Jim for the rings. Dumfounded, Jim looked to Lee, who was his best man. No rings. The thought of having to buy rings had never crossed Jim's mind. Jane's sister, Margaret, came to the rescue and gave Jane her fifty-nine-cent, friendship ring as a substitute.

Jane wore that dime store ring as a wedding band for years.

When Jim escorted his new bride to his waiting car, Jane was surprised to see Lee and the rest of Jim's friends in the back seat. Jim explained that they were going along to the race in Phoenix. Jane shrugged her shoulders, and joined them in the car. This would be just the first of many times in their life together that Jane would accept Jim's impulsiveness without a fuss.

But, then, that was part of his attraction. "Jim was the most spontaneous person I've ever known," says Jane. "That's one thing I really loved about him."

As the crowd made their way outside to see the newlyweds off,

Lee heard many in the group mumble, "Well that's one marriage that won't work. I'll give that marriage about a month." Jane's brother and mother were a little more charitable; they gave the marriage six months.

That marriage, forged under such difficult and unusual circumstances lasted for thirty two years, only to be ended by Jim's death . Through the best of times, and the worst of times, Jane was always there for Jim. By his own admittance, that solid foundation carried him through his darkest days, and made the taste of success even sweeter.

Jim never offered Jane an explanation for being late for the wedding. She suspects that he was having second thoughts. However, when she questioned him he'd only answer, "Nah, that didn't even cross my mind. I was just having a good time with the guys and I lost track of the time"

Of that mystery, Lee Bruss can only say, "It was typical of the kind of things Jim would do."

No sooner had they embarked on the eight hour drive to Phoenix, than the guys began kidding Jim about where he was going to spend his wedding night. He wasn't stopping, he told them. He intended to drive straight through to Phoenix. When they insisted that he couldn't do that, that he'd just gotten married and should spend the night with his bride, he admitted he didn't have enough money for a room.

Coming to their buddy's aid, the guys offered to chip in and rent a room for the night. But, even at the little, run down motel Jim found in Paramount, California, they could not scrape together enough for Jim and Jane to have a private room, so they shared a two bedroom unit. The guys slept crosswise on the bed in one room, while Jim and Jane got the other room to themselves.

Recalling her memorable wedding night Jane says, "The only way to get to the bathroom was to go through our room. And to make sure his friends didn't barge in on us, Jim pushed a dresser up against the door. They'd drank a lot of beer, and all night long I could hear them relieving themselves in the bushes outside our bedroom window!"

Compared to Jim's wedding day, the race at Phoenix the next afternoon proved uneventful. Jim ran well in hot laps, but USAC deemed him not yet experienced enough to race at their level, and would not grant him a temporary driving permit. Disappointed, but undaunted by his failed first venture into the big leagues of auto racing, Jim returned to his apprenticeship on the CRA tracks, and his new life as a married man.

Like most newlyweds, Jim and Jane wanted to spend as much time together as possible. Uncle Sam had other ideas. Jane still had two years to serve on her enlistment in the Naval Reserve, and even though her marriage automatically relieved her of active duty, she still had to attend one more training camp in San Diego.

Married just one month, Jane was separated from Jim for two weeks. The first weekend she was gone, she had hoped Jim would be able to visit her, but he had a race to go to. So, she invited a couple of friends she worked with for an outing at the San Diego Zoo instead. When the race was rained out, Jim went on to San Diego to surprise his new bride, and wandered around the immense zoo until he found her.

"We were riding the tram that runs through the zoo," Jane recalls, "when I saw this man that looked like Jim. Then as we got closer I saw that it was Jim and I started screaming, 'It is Jim! Stop this thing, I've got to get off!' I couldn't believe that he'd come."

Her military commitment out of the way, Jane immersed herself into Jim's world. She kept him company as he and Lee worked late into the night on the car at the NeoGlo shop. She travelled with him to the races. And she shared in the sacrifices that were so necessary in order for him to race.

Despite the hardships, Jane still recalls that time with fondness, and insists that they were some of the best days of their lives.

Contributing greatly to that pleasure were the many friends Jim and Jane made within the CRA racing family. The men would hammer away at each other tooth and nail on the race track, while their wives and girlfriends sat together, held their breaths, and prayed in the stands. Though those skirmishes were often brutal to watch, there were seldom any grudges or hard feelings afterwards, and they would all gather regularly at Jim and Jane's for evenings of food, board games and cards.

There were the Neumayers, A.J. and Nancy Shepherd, Jack and Linda Rounds, Don and Sue Shepherd, Lee and his girlfriend, Marcia, and Parnelli and Grayce Jones. Though Jim considered this entire group as good friends, he would, over the course of the next few years, grow especially close to Parnelli, as Jane would to Grayce.

1963 Indianapolis 500 winner, Parnelli Jones, ranks as one of the most recognizable names in the history of American auto racing. Born in Texarkana, Arkansas, Parnelli moved as a child with his family to Torrance, California when his father migrated there seeking work in the aircraft industry.

By 1950, Parnelli was racing jalopies in the Los Angeles area, and working as a concrete finisher when he wasn't racing. Like Jim,

Parnelli was a natural behind the wheel of a race car, and soon became a consistent winner. When Jim and Lee arrived in California, Parnelli was already a local racing star, because the popular jalopy races were televised live, weekly, on Los Angeles TV, channel 5.

Jim and Parnelli were two very different and distinct personalities. Jim was relaxed and easy going, the archetypal free spirit. Parnelli, on the other hand, was tense, tough, cocky, and ready to fight at the slightest provocation. Yet, Jim and Parnelli shared a common goal. They wanted to make it big in racing.

They first met during a modified race at Gardena Stadium, and hit it off immediately. From that first meeting their friendship grew, and their careers would parallel as they pursued their dream of racing at Indianapolis.

Jane's first encounter with Parnelli wasn't nearly as auspicious as Jim's. "Jim and I hadn't been married very long," Jane recalls, "when we went to a CRA race, and Parnelli was there. I had heard that he was a rough, ornery driver, and during the race he bumped into Jim and put him out. I was absolutely furious."

However, when she criticized Parnelli's driving tactics afterwards, Jim was quick to correct her opinion, and was adamant that she not complain about the actions of other drivers. "Hey, he's a good driver," insisted Jim, "and what happened out there today was just racing. Those things happen to all of us, and there's no need to talk about another driver. It's something I just don't like to hear."

"Then, of course, after I got to know Parnelli," says Jane, "I realized that he was really a nice guy. Very serious. Very quiet, when compared to Jim, but with a very quick temper. And Grayce and I became the best of friends. We ran around together for many years. Travelled together, and sat together at the races. Grayce was the best-hearted person I think I've ever known. But she was also very outspoken and taught me a lot about racing and about standing up for myself at a time when I didn't know beans."

By the mid-point of the 1957 CRA season, Jim's hard work was beginning to pay dividends. Car owners, who previously viewed him with skepticism, began seeing Jim in a different, more positive light. "By late 1956, and certainly into 1957," insists Lee, "everybody knew that Jim was doing an outstanding job in equipment that just wasn't that good. Pretty soon owners were calling him, and he began driving other cars as well as ours."

In his short time in sprint cars, Jim had already racked up many wins in trophy dashes and heat races, but, a CRA feature win eluded him until August 31, 1957. That first sprint car feature win came at Alviso, California, when he beat Roger McCluskey, and Nick Valenta, the 1953-54 and soon to be 1957 CRA champion, to the checkered flag.

That first win seemed to open a floodgate of victories, and Jim became a consistent winner on the formidable CRA circuit. It was then, Lee believes, that Jim started thinking seriously about going to Indianapolis.

"When Jim first decided to go to California to race," says Lee, "I know Indianapolis was in the back of his mind. That was his ultimate goal. But then he got so caught up in sprint car racing that he didn't really think about Indianapolis for awhile. He loved the sprint cars. They were his life. Jim was absolutely born to run sprint cars on dirt. When he started to win regularly, and he saw he could win against good drivers, he started talking openly about Indianapolis. You could tell that's where he really wanted to be."

If that goal were to become a reality, Jim knew that his days of racing only in California were numbered. To make it to Indianapolis he would have to prove himself on a national level. That meant running in the race-rich midwest, first with the International Motor Contest Association [IMCA], and then, if he could win there, with the prestigious, United States Auto Club [USAC].

Jim would eventually make those transitions successfully, but none of it would have been possible were it not for the two years he spent racing in California. It was in California that Jim Hurtubise was molded into the exciting driver and racing personality that would capture the imagination of fans across the nation. It was in California that he learned to win. And, it was in California that he refined his distinctive driving style.

Those few times Jim slowed down enough to talk to the press about his racing, he said little about driving style. "You don't develop a style," he quipped. "Either you have one or you don't. Hell, you should either go fast or forget it!"

It's true that what is often described as driving style is nothing more than what a driver does naturally with a speeding race car. What Jim did naturally was run the car as high up on the track as he could get it.

That's called rim riding, and it is the fast way around a race track because a driver can stay hard on the throttle to maintain momentum through the corners, then shoot ahead of his competition down the straights. But, rim riding is also dangerous, for the car has to be delicately balanced on a thin, knife edge of control at all times. Only a few drivers have the guts and talent to consistently practice it. Jim was one of rim riding's most ardent devotees. According to Lee Bruss, even when Jim was racing stock cars in New York, he preferred running high on the race track, and often expressed a contempt for those who didn't share the thrill of running up there with him. "Those dab blamed pole huggers," he'd chide. "They ought to get off the pole, and get up there where they can go fast!"

Running a heavy, fully enclosed stock car up against the fence is one thing; a lightweight, jumpy sprint car is quite another. But, Jim quickly mastered that technique as well.

"I can remember," marvels Lee, "many times when Jim ran the sprint car so high that when he came in after the race, there would be splinters of wood from the fence wedged between the wheel rim and the tire."

Doing without the best equipment in those California racing days, while frustrating, also served to refine Jim's rim riding style. With his underpowered engines, he was forced to run high so he could keep enough speed through the corners not to be out horsepowered down the straights .

That made Jim constantly seek ways to make the car handle better. As he danced it across the slippery dirt and fought for traction up against the fence, he needed every bit of control he could get.

Jim always said, "The way your equipment handles is what decides who is going to be the prime dog."

In his quest to be that "prime dog" Jim became an expert at making suspension adjustments. "Jim was absolutely amazing," attests Lee. "He always knew exactly what to tell you to do to the car. He'd run a few laps, and then come in and say the car wasn't getting any bite in the corners, and that it needed this or needed that. And, every time he'd go back out and run faster."

"Jim always believed," continues Lee, "that the engine did not have to be overpowerful, as long as it didn't miss a lick, and as long as he could get every bit of that horsepower to the track. If he could make the car handle so that it would go where he wanted it to go, he could beat those guys who were running those really big engines."

Jim did that very thing many times. So often, in fact, that he became the consummate underdog. It was a role forced on him by the limits of his budget, but a role Jim relished and would continue to enjoy his entire life.

"Jim was probably the most confident person I've ever met," says Lee. "He earnestly believed that he could do anything. He loved being the underdog and he loved to beat guys who had a lot of money behind them with his own creations, and a minimum budget. That's really what made Jim tick, because he believed that when he won like that, it proved that it was his ability alone that accomplished it."

That underdog role, combined with his spectacular, rim riding style, served to make Jim an immense favorite with the fans wherever he raced. And Jim, who loved being the center of attention, fed off that adoration, and played to it with a natural flair for showmanship. The night Jim and Lee shared a pit pass at Balboa Stadium was but one example.

"When Jim whipped into the pits at Balboa with me in the trunk," says Lee, "he pulled in with the trunk towards the stands, and when I hopped out a lot of the fans saw me. You could hear them mumbling about it up in the stands, and they soon caught on to what we were doing. Whenever the pit steward came by and we were checked and got away with it, the crowd would yell and cheer. And every time they did, Jim would play right to them. He'd hold up the pass and then point to himself and to me, and they'd yell that much louder."

Then there was the show Jim put on with a trophy girl at LA Speedway. She presented him with the trophy for winning the dash, and gave him the customary kiss that went along with it. Jim returned her bashful peck with a vigorous effort of his own, bending her back, and kissing her long and hard. When they came up for air, Jim patted her on the rear, leaving his greasy hand print on her white dress. When she walked off, the crowd roared its approval at the sight of Jim's personalized brand on her derriere.

Preparing for the following week's race, Jim was touching up the maroon paint job on the car's nose, when he bent over and dropped his ever present tape measure into the pail of paint. Looking about, but not seeing any other way to retrieve it, he shrugged his shoulders and stuck his hand into the bucket. As he stood, shaking the dripping paint from his hand, he paused. A grin lit up his face. Then he turned and pressed his paint covered hand against the white flame on the nose of the car. When he pulled away, a perfect, maroon handprint remained.

Looking at Lee, who had been curiously watching the entire procedure, Jim laughed and said, "That's so we'll always remember that trophy girl from last week."

At the next race, when the fans spotted the new addition to his paint scheme, they lustily cheered his thoughtful art work.

In November of 1957, Lee received his draft notice. Rather than going to the Army, he joined the Navy, ending his heady days with Jim Hurtubise. Jim and Jane stayed in touch with Lee while he was overseas, regularly writing and keeping him abreast of Jim's racing progress with "*The National Speed Sport News*."

After his tour of duty, however, Lee didn't return to racing, rather he entered the world of business. He joined the 3-M Corporation, and travelled the world in various capacities before working his way into the position of plant manager at one of the giant corporation's struggling facilities in Chico, California. Within a year of gaining that post, Lee turned the financially floundering plant into a money making concern. So dramatic was the turnabout that 3-M produced a white paper study, for use within the corporation, extolling the virtue of Lee's procedures.

Lee insists today that the time he spent with Jim Hurtubise was an inspiration to him throughout his life. "Jim's courage and his will to succeed were unbelievable," says Lee admiringly. "Those early days of sprint car racing were grinding and intense. Most people recall Jim being on the stocky side, weighing 160, 165 pounds. But when I knew him he never weighed more than 130. The sleepless nights, constant work and little food took their toll."

"Yet, despite all the difficulties he encountered, he was totally care free and fun loving. He was a free spirit. It's very rare to see all those qualities in one individual. I'd never seen that combination in a person before I met Jim, nor have I seen it in anyone since."

"Those times with Jim, I can honestly say, changed my life. There have been many times that I've found myself in difficult circumstances. In situations that I wasn't sure I could even get through. Then, I'd think about the time Jim and I rode that truck across Georgia. Or, the times we'd go for days without sleep while working on the race car. And, I'd say to myself, 'If I was able to get through all that, I know damn well I'm going to be alright now!"

Lee's departure for the service, coincided with Jim's next career upgrade. He finished the 1957 CRA racing season tenth in points, and, in 1958, turned his attention to the midwest and the IMCA.

HURTUBISE

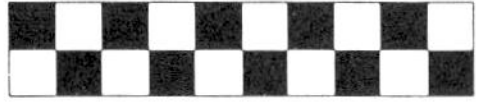

Walt Mahony photo -HFC

For years, the IMCA served as a training ground and a stepping stone to Indianapolis for many of America's greatest drivers. George Souders was not the first from that esteemed organization to successfully journey to the Speedway, but his venture there was certainly one of the most dramatic. He arrived at Indianapolis a rank rookie, and left as the winner of the 1927 500. The list of IMCA stars that followed Souders to the Brickyard and left their own indelible marks at that great track reads like a *who's who* of auto racing. Joie Chitwood, Bill Holland, Don Branson, Bobby Grim, Parnelli Jones, Jim McElreath, Johnny White, Johnny Rutherford, and Jim Hurtubise.

When Jim joined the IMCA in 1958, it was sanctioning in excess of fifty-five sprint car races a year, on tracks as diverse as Plant Field in Tampa, Florida, and the Louisiana State Fair Grounds in Shreveport. The primary stomping grounds of the IMCA, however, were the dozens of half-mile, county fair, dirt ovals that dotted the corn country of the midwest.

Jim's first race with the IMCA came in February of 1958, at what was the traditional season opener in Tampa, Florida. Held in conjunction with the mid-winter Florida State Fair, the races at Plant Field extended over a four-day period, with heat races and fifteen lap feature races held daily, culminating with a twenty five lap feature on the final day of competition.

Jim didn't win in his initial IMCA outing, but neither did he go away disappointed. Driving the Bill Leach Chevy, he scored a second, two thirds, and a sixth place finish. Quite an impressive debut for the rookie from the CRA.

The next IMCA contest wasn't scheduled until the end of May, when the midwest racing season got underway in earnest. In the meantime Jim stayed busy racing in California.

On March 1, he hopped in a midget at Gardena Stadium for the United Auto Racing [URA] season opener, and finished fifth in the feature. Two weeks later he was again racing midgets, this time at Fairmont Park in Riverside, California. In that event he blasted from his twelfth place starting spot to third in just a handful of laps, before he slid up and over the cushion, that ridge of lose dirt at the top of the track, and crashed.

Those two performances were typical of Jim's fortune in the midgets. He was never able to experience the success in those machines that he did with their bigger brothers, the sprint cars. He would usually qualify well, and run up front, only to be eliminated by mechanical problems or spins and crashes in the closing stages of the race.

In yet another midget event, Jim's bad luck continued, and he experienced the frustration of having victory snatched from his grasp at the very last moment.

The 1958 Riverside race was not held at Fairmont Park, but rather at the famed Riverside International Raceway 2 1/2 mile road course. Midgets were not designed to run on road courses, as they had no transmissions for shifting gears and their brakes were marginal at best. But, the promoters of the Riverside race believed that the nimble, short wheelbase cars with their high torque engines would provide an exciting show on the twisting, uphill, downhill course.

The May 28 race was scheduled for five hundred miles, two hundred laps. By lap 17, Jim had charged into the lead, and stayed there until he was passed on lap 137 by his old Ascot nemesis, Allen Heath. Two laps later, Jim blasted back around Heath, and led until lap 161. By that late stage of the race, the car's brakes were all but gone, and as Jim charged hard into a tight corner, with Heath right on his tail, they failed. The car whipped into a spin, and wedged itself, tail first, under the guardrail.

Jim was uninjured, but the impact of the crash was so severe that it took the rescue workers over an hour to cut the car free. Jim couldn't hide his disappointment. Interviewed after the race, he surprised many when he was obviously close to tears as he described his near win in an important, well-paying event. It was a side of Jim Hurtubise few had been privy to. Despite the devil-may-care attitude he usually displayed to the public, those tears demonstrated the intensity of Jim's desire to win.

Mixing sprint car races with his numerous midget starts, Jim travelled to El Centro on March 8 and 9 for the Imperial County Fair races. Just two years earlier, El Centro had been the site of his initiation to sprint car racing. In 1958 Jim arrived there, not as an excited kid with only a lofty dream, but as a talented driver well on the way to seeing that dream fulfilled. Driving the Leach #54 Chevy, Jim swept the program, winning both features of that prestigious two day event.

With the coming of summer, Jim made his long anticipated appearance on the midwest tracks of the IMCA. They were as dusty, rough and intimidating as he had heard, but he loved them and excelled on them. Driving the Will Kephart Offy, Jim turned in a sterling performance during his maiden venture with that highly touted organization. He racked up a feature win at Bethany, Missouri, a rare achievement for an IMCA newcomer, and added two second place finishes, five third place runs, and a pair of fifth place spots. At the end of the season he was ranked thirteenth in the 1958 IMCA standings.

While in the midwest Jim took time out from the Kephart Offy to drive the Leach Chevy in several United Speedways races. United Speedways was one of many short lived organizations that were formed in the late fifties and early sixties to capitalize on the increasing popularity of sprint car racing.

Jim won two features with that fledgling organization, the most impressive coming at Decorah, Iowa on August 15. During that race, held at the Winneshiek County Fair, Jim set fast time and won his heat by charging from sixth to first on the opening lap. He then completed his sweep of the program by handily winning the feature over second place Jimmy Jones in an Offenhauser powered car.

At the beginning of the year Jim had set the lofty goal of making a name for himself against the stiff competition of the IMCA. Having accomplished that goal, Jim returned, satisfied, to California, and finished out the year with the CRA.

Back home, Jim did not rest on his laurels, rather, from the last week of October through the first week of December, he put on a dazzling driving performance at the new Ascot Speedway that vividly demonstrated the immense scope of his talent, and left his competition stunned.

The new Ascot Speedway was inaugurated in September of 1958 when the operation of LA Speedway, located on South Vermont in Los Angeles, was assumed by a corporation headed by Tom Hayes. Hayes was an accomplished race promoter, and a seasoned track manager who also oversaw the day by day running of Gardena Stadium.

To insure that his latest acquisition was groomed to perfection for the fans as well as the competitors, Hayes put together a competent, respected maintenance team. Ralph Steck came aboard to maintain the forty acres of land, along with the assorted grandstands and buildings, while the services of "Butch" Dale were called on to prepare the track surface. Evoking the memory of the legendary California racetrack, Legion Ascot, Hayes re-named the track, Ascot Speedway.

That fast, half mile clay oval, was destined to become a legend itself, and from the beginning fan response was immense. For the first CRA sprint car race held there on October 22, 1958, every seat was quickly sold, and 1200 people were turned away at the gate. Jim was not present at that initial event, but Allen Heath was, and had the honor of winning that historic, first sprint car feature at Ascot.

Jim was there the next weekend and immediately made his presence felt. Driving the number 67, Will Kephart owned, 270 Offy, he roared to a new track record during qualifying, shattering Heath's week-old mark.

After winning the trophy dash, and finishing second in his heat, Jim shot from eighth to third going down the backstretch on the opening lap of the feature. On the next lap, he passed Heath for second, and then rode the rear bumper of racing buddy, A.J. Shepherd, for four laps before sliding by him, and into first place on lap 7. Jim never let up, and cruised to a comfortable win over Parnelli Jones, a distant second, and Allen Heath in third.

The next Saturday night at Ascot, Jim was again in the jet black Kephart Offy, and again was unstoppable. Parnelli set quick time, but once the feature was flagged off, Jim was obviously the fastest driver on the track. Buried in mid-field, he put his car up against the fence and bored straight for the front. He passed three time CRA champion, Nick Valenta for first place on lap 12 of the twenty lap race, and zipped under the checkered flag with a ten car length lead over second place, Allen Heath.

The third week of Jim's Ascot tirade found him in a different car, the Harry Abajian Offy, but he ran just as hard and again set quick time. What began as a great evening soon turned sour when he crashed while leading the trophy dash. He was able to get the badly damaged car stuck back together well enough to start the feature, but only managed to run a few laps before dropping out finishing thirteenth.

Unperturbed by his misfortune of the week before, Jim again returned to Ascot in the Abajian car. In what was an unusually wild and woolly night, even for those vicious days of sprint car racing, four cars flipped violently in separate accidents, sending three drivers, including Nick Valenta, to the hospital.

Jim only managed to qualify fifth fast, but, as usual, moved quickly to the front, and pressed Colby Scroggins for the lead, until yet another accident slowed the field on lap 15. When the wreckage was cleared, Jim jumped around Colby on the restart, and had a half a straightaway lead over second place, Parnelli Jones, at the finish.

Parnelli's crew protested the results arguing that Jim had jumped the restart and passed a car while the field was still under yellow following the fifteenth lap accident. CRA officials upheld the protest, and Parnelli was awarded the win while Jim was moved to second.

After the Thanksgiving holiday break, the sprint cars returned to Ascot for their final 1958 appearance. Jim won that race too. Once more driving the Abajian Offy, he started the feature in eighth, and swept by the leader, Allen Heath, on lap 10. With only Heath able to keep him in sight, Jim stormed non-stop to victory, shattering the twenty lap, track record in the process.

Jim's amazing five race rampage at Ascot garnered headlines in racing publications across the country and astonished many of those whom he had raced against the previous two years. While they were very much aware of his raw racing talent, most believed that he didn't yet have the patience and maturity required to be a great race car driver.

What they witnessed at Ascot, however, was a different Jim Hurtubise. There he displayed a tenacious, patient consistency. A willingness to work with, rather than just manhandle the race car.

A week later at Manzanita, he again exhibited this new found quality, honed during his summer of racing in the midwest, and demonstrated just how effective it could be.

Jim was in the Gene Richardson Chevy and struggled with the car through qualifying and the heat races, never quite able to make it handle the way he liked. Rather than trying, as he would have just months before, to force the ill-handling car to do what it couldn't, he labored on it right up until starting time. Even as the Star Spangled Banner was being played, and the other pre-race ceremonies were taking place, Jim was still making adjustments on the car. Then, once the field was pushed away for the start, he made a persistent, steady drive for the front from his twenty third place starting position and flashed across the finish line, the winner.

In 1958, Jim's personal life was changing as quickly as his professional life. After living a year in a trailer in Inglewood, Jim and Jane bought their first house, a small bungalow at Van Buren and Imperial in Lennox, California. As seemed to be the norm with Jim, even that purchase was accomplished at odds with convention. He bought the house for $8,500, complete with furniture, dishes and linen. To close the deal, Jim had to agree to let the owner, a seventy five year old widower, live with them for a month while new accommodations were found for him.

"Oh, he was really great," says Jane of their elderly house guest. "I took care of all his meals, and he didn't have to worry about a thing. He always kidded me because I made coffee on the stove, and was constantly letting it boil over. So, when he moved he left his percolator for me, telling me, 'Jane, you need it worse than I do!"

Just a week after they moved into their new home, Jim and Jane's first child was born, a daughter they named Karen. Jane remembers lying in the hospital, the day after her birth, crying. When a startled nurse asked her what was wrong, Jane sobbed, "I'm so happy! I just got a new house, and now I have a new baby."

"Jim," laughs Jane, "thought I was crazy."

While hesitant to hold Karen, because he was afraid he would break the tiny child, Jim was unabashedly proud of her and was quick to brag about her "Hurtubise" blue eyes and black hair. With his racing taking him away from home so often, the task of baby-sitting seldom fell to Jim. When it did, even that he practiced in his own inimitable style.

One afternoon while Indianapolis 500 winning car owner and West Coast promoter, J.C. Agajanian, was visiting Jim about some racing-related business, Jane was called away from home on a family emergency. She left Karen, then just a few months old, with Jim. When she returned some hours later, she found Karen in a chair on one side of the living room, while Jim stood on the other, squirting a stream of milk into her mouth by squeezing her plastic baby bottle. "I couldn't believe it," laments Jane. "Of course Karen loved it. She was lapping at the milk like a little kitten, and Jim and Aggie were just laughing their heads off."

After his initial season on the IMCA circuit proved so successful, Jim was determined to attack it even more aggressively in 1959. And, a group of his racing friends, A.J. and Don Shepherd, Jack Rounds and Parnelli Jones, seeking to advance their own careers, resolved to accompany him on the conquest.

In anticipation of that journey, Jim bought an old Pontiac station wagon, and with Don Shepherd's help pulled out the little six cylinder engine, installed a big Oldsmobile V-8, and further modified it to serve as their transportation, tow car, and sleeping quarters.

"It was a helluva' deal," laughs Don Shepherd. "We towed the race car with that old station wagon, slept in it, everything. We had a big Sealy mattress that we put in the back, and made a storage bin underneath where we kept all of the tools and spare parts. It wasn't much, but, that's all any of us could afford back in '59."

Don's brother, A.J., made the first racing trip with Jim in the station wagon. Accompanying them was Jim's latest acquisition, Prince, a huge German Shepherd pup. "You can imagine," groans A.J. "just how much fun a trip from L.A. to Florida would be with a hundred pound dog slobbering on you for two thousand miles!"

Jim had bought Prince just a few weeks before that trip, on the pretext that it would be good pet for Karen.

"Jim convinced me," says Jane, "that since he was going to be gone so much that summer, Karen, just six months old at the time, needed a dog. I thought he was going to bring home a little house dog of some kind, and then in he walked with this blonde, six month old German Shepherd that looked like it already stood six feet tall!"

From that first trip to Florida until his death in the early 1970s, Prince was Jim's constant companion at the races. "Prince would stay around Jim in the pits until the race cars started running," says A.J. Shepherd. "Then he would go get in, or sometimes crawl under the station wagon. He was afraid of all the noise from the race cars. Then, just as soon as the race was over, here would come Prince trotting through the pits, looking for Jim." Through the years Prince would become almost as well known and popular as his master. He even had his own fan following. They constantly sent him Christmas cards and gifts, and Jane remembers the time one sent Prince a postcard from Daytona Beach. On it was a photo of a bikini-clad, female German Shepherd, lounging on the beach.

That summer of '59 was an unforgettable, fun filled adventure for Jim and the California gang. Always short on money, they combined their meager resources to pay for gas and buy the hot dogs and bologna that made up the bulk of their diet. For an occasional, special culinary treat, Jim taught them how to heat a can of beans on the station wagon's engine by wiring it to the exhaust manifold. After a few miles of driving, a piping hot meal would be ready to serve.

They spent many nights in their motel on wheels. Jim would hunt for a secluded spot on a back country road, preferably alongside a stream or lake so they would have a place to bathe. After a hot, dusty day on the race track, nothing was more refreshing than a dip in the cool water.

On the very rare occasion they would splurge for a motel room, but even then the accommodations were little more than spartan. "One night," says A.J. Shepherd, "five of us went together to rent a room in this little motel. Three of us slept crossways on the bed, and the others had to sleep on the floor with their legs stuck under the bed, because the room was so damn small!"

They were young, all in their mid-twenties, and they believed passionately that racing stardom lay just around the next dusty corner. That hope let them accept even the worst of hardships as merely temporary inconveniences. They raced as though invincible, and played with the lusty exuberance of youth.

Jim, who lived by the motto, "Life's too short, you got to have fun," was usually the ring leader in their off track capers. No matter how bleak the situation, Jim's infectious laugh and crazy antics never failed to entertain them and lift their spirits.

"Once at St. Paul," recalls Don Shepherd, "a bunch of us went down on the midway including Jim, Parnelli, my brother, A.J, and myself. Jim had met this guy-who knows where Jim would meet some of these people-whose act in the carnival was riding a motorcycle in a silo.

"Well, Jim got it in his head that he could do that and was bound and determined to try. But no matter how much he talked, he couldn't convince this guy to let him do it. Finally, though, he did agree to let Jim ride with him, so Jim climbed on the back of that motorcycle, and they rode up and down the walls of that silo for a long time. When they stopped and Jim got off, he was so dizzy he couldn't stand up. He'd fall down and try to get up and fall down again. Of course, the more we laughed at him, the crazier he acted, until we were all laughing so hard we couldn't stand it!"

On another occasion Jim, Don, and Parnelli were passing through a tiny, Iowa farm town on their way from Cedar Rapids to the next race at Grand Forks, North Dakota. It was a busy Saturday morning and as they crept along in the slow moving traffic, Jim noticed a sign in the window of a corner drug store: "Harmonicas $1.50."

He wanted one.

After Jim made his purchase, they continued their journey as Jim proudly squeaked and squawked on his new mouth organ. After a couple of hours of this annoying musical interlude, Parnelli said, "Herk, let me see that thing."

"Can you play?" queried Jim.

"Nah," said Parnelli, "but I think I could do as good as you are! Let me give it a try anyway."

Jim tapped the spit from his harmonica and passed it to Parnelli. Parnelli turned it over in his hand a couple times and studied it briefly. Then, without saying a word, he flipped Jim's fine musical instrument out the window!

Most often the fun the guys took part in was the high-spirited, rowdy, young men type. Somewhat surprisingly, however, alcohol usually didn't figure into that revelry. Primarily, because they didn't have the extra money for it, but they were also serious about their racing and didn't want to be physically hampered. There's no more excruciating experience than fighting a hangover while wrestling a wild, bucking sprint car on a steamy, summer afternoon. One night though, the beer flowed freely, and Jim and Parnelli nearly came to blows because of it.

"We were in St. Paul, Minnesota," recalls Don Shepherd, "for the week long championships they held at the fairgrounds. Parnelli and I got cleaned up to go to this big party Charlie Purdue was throwing—he was one of the racers who lived in St. Paul and on the way we went over to where Herk was still working on his car. He kept it in a place across the street from the fairgrounds. We told him we were going to Charlie's, and he said, 'I'm going to work for awhile longer, I'll meet you guys over there later. Here's some money, stop on the way and put some gas in the car."

Don and Parnelli, however, in their rush to get to the party, did not stop for gas. They decided to wait and do it later. By the time Jim arrived at Charlie's, Don admits, "Me and Parnelli were drunker than a couple of hoot owls. When we were ready to go, Jim said he would drive, so we crawled in the back of the station wagon and passed out.

"Well, Herk had no sooner started down the street than we ran out of gas. And I mean he got madder'n hell! He was yelling and shaking us, trying to wake us up. And we finally did come around a little. But then Parnelli just raised up, looked around and flopped back down. Well, Jim was so mad by then, that he grabbed Parnelli and drug him out in the street.

"Parnelli was so hot headed in those days that he'd fight at the drop of a hat and I'm surprised that he didn't pop Herk right there. But, they were always real good friends and Parnelli just said, 'Aw, the hell with it, I'm walking back to Charlie's,' and he staggered off down the road."

"I wanted to go with him," continues Don, "but I'd lost my shoes somewhere, so I just laid back down. Jim ranted and raved for a while longer, then hiked after gas. When Jim drove us back to where we were staying, I was so out of it that I spent the night in the back of the station wagon. When I woke up the next morning, those huge Minnesota mosquitoes had eaten me alive! "

If Jim's spontaneous capers weren't enough to keep the guys entertained, his tunnel vision approach to racing provided ample opportunities for laughs. When Jim focused on racing, he became scatterbrained about everything else.

"Hurtubise was nuts," Parnelli Jones told the *Virginia Gazette.* "All of us were struggling to make a living and more or less lived inside Herk's Pontiac station wagon with his dog, Prince. Herk stored any prize money he won in the headliner, but he was so forgetful, I bet if you found that car today it would still have money stuffed in it somewhere."

"He would carry his money around in a paper sack, and after the race he would go to the payoff booth and throw his winnings into that sack. Well, one time we were all on the way from one race to another, and Herk suddenly said, 'Oh shit, I forgot my money!' He had gone to an office to wire money home to Jane and left his paper sack full of money on the counter. We rushed back, he ran inside, and his paper sack was still there."

"Jim was always doing things like that," continues Parnelli. "After a race he would throw his helmet into the cockpit of his race car, or lay it down somewhere, and then go celebrate. Then later, we'd be driving down the road and he'd yell, 'I forgot my helmet!' When we got to the next race track somebody, a fan or another driver, would always bring it to him."

"Jim was terrible about leaving things wherever he went," agrees Jane, shaking her head as she recalled her husband's absentmindedness. "Plane tickets, money, his billfold, you name it. I know he had these beautiful sweaters that his mother had bought for him, and he left them all over the country. But, all he ever thought about was racing, nothing else was as important."

Off track shenanigans aside, the racing was fierce and furious. The California gang, along with the rest of IMCA regulars, crisscrossed the Bible Belt, racing at fairgrounds in rustic towns with picturesque names like Oskalossa, Faribault, and Hibbing. In their garishly painted, exotic appearing machines, they generated the same romantic, exciting aura as that of the circus coming to a small town.

They drew capacity crowds wherever they went, and, as he had in California, Jim Hurtubise quickly became a favorite with those crowds. The fans fell in love with his throttle-slamming, high-sliding, dirt-slinging, style.

The IMCA, launched because the heads of several, influential county fair boards were seeking entertainment for their various venues, was always a mixture of racing and showmanship. It didn't take long for the IMCA promoters to take note of Jim's special fan appeal, and exploit it at every opportunity.

In Minot, North Dakota, at the North Dakota State Fair races, the promoter played off the Indian name of Jim's hometown, North Tonawanda, and he was billed as "The Great Sprint Car Driver From the Tonawanda Indian Tribe"

"That first night at Minot there were only a few Indians there," laughs Don Shepherd, "but the word got around, and by the second night the place was full of Indians who came to see this famous Indian race car driver! Jim just loved it."

LeRoy Neumayer recalls another time when a promoter came to Jim and him, desperate for help in soothing a crowd, that had become restless while waiting for a sloppy track to be readied.

"We were up in Rochester, Minnesota," says LeRoy, "and it had rained and rained and rained. The track was so greasy that nobody even wanted to go out and warm up. Al Sweeney, one of the heads of the IMCA, was all excited and screaming, 'We got to put on a show! We got to give 'em a show!' Then Al came to me and Herk, begging for us to run. He said, 'Why don't you two guys run a dash for me? A two car trophy dash. I'll call it a California grudge match."

"So Herk said, 'Come on, LeRoy, let's do it. Hell, it'll be fun, and maybe it'll help get the track in shape.' I was still recovering from a broken leg and couldn't use it for braking, so I didn't have a ride that day. But, I told Sweeney that I'd do it if I could find a car with a hand brake. Merle Heath had his car there, a Chevy that Rutherford and some other pretty good guys drove, and it had a hand brake. So Merle let me run it, and me and Herk put on a helluva' show."

"It was so slick you couldn't look at the track without getting sideways. We were bumping into each other, laughing and having a great time. We couldn't get going fast enough to get hurt, but the fans got a big kick out of it, and Sweeney really appreciated that. He even paid us some extra money under the table.

"But, Herk was always doing things like that. Anything to have a good time. And if it was something for the fans, something they enjoyed, then so much the better."

Jim's exploits on those IMCA tracks were often as awe inspiring to his racing buddies as they were to his multitude of fans. "Ole Herk," moans A.J. Shepherd, "was braver than Dick Tracy. If a track was slick, or dusty or rough, it didn't matter. Nothing would slow him down."

And sometimes that scared even his friends. "That crazy Hurtubise," Parnelli Jones once said, "had me ready to quit racing once at Minot, North Dakota. It was total dust. Nobody could see. But Hurtubise ran wide open anyway. He wasn't afraid of anything."

Although with his uncanny skill Jim could do remarkable things with a sprint car, even the best, on occasion, get caught out and crash. One of Jim's worst happened on July 5, at Cedar Rapids, Iowa.

The track was exceptionally rough that day, full of ruts and holes, and Jim and Jack Rounds were running close together. Whose bucking race car hit the other's first could not be determined, but the impact sent Jim's car bounding over the guardrail.

It flipped end for end five times, then slammed to a stop almost on top of the railroad track that ran through the fairgrounds just outside the track. Jim was carted off to the hospital with a slight concussion, and although he was released by the end of the day, the centrifugal forces generated during the violent rolls, burst many of the tiny blood vessels in his eyes, turning the whites a horrid, beet red.

Fortunately there was a twenty day interval between the grinding crash at Cedar Rapids and the next race at Grand Forks, North Dakota, so Jim had ample time to recover and repair the mangled race car. That layoff would prove to be eventful in many ways.

When Jim left California to race in the midwest at the beginning of the 1959 season, Jane remained at home in Lennox, pregnant with their second child. Jane had already planned to go to New York, because she was determined that at least one of her children would be born in Jim's hometown. When she began to experience what she believed were the signs of an early birth, she rushed to her doctor for permission to fly there.

The doctor's nurse politely informed her that because the birth appeared to be imminent, the forms the airline required could not be signed. Jane could be as resolute as her very determined husband, however, and told the nurse in no uncertain terms, "Either you fill out the form, or I'll do it myself. One way or the other, I'm going to have this baby in New York."

The nurse filled out the form.

Jane arrived in North Tonawanda on Friday night. Since Pete was racing that weekend, Jane accompanied Pete and his wife Shelia to the races at Merrittville and Lancaster, not telling either one of them that she was ready to give birth. But, early Monday morning they were made unmistakably aware of that situation when Jane went into labor and they had to rush her to the hospital. There, on June 22, Patricia June Hurtubise was born, six weeks premature.

Because of his hectic racing schedule, Jim was unable to get to North Tonawanda to see his newest daughter until after the Cedar Rapids crash. By then the broken blood vessels in his eyes had turned a ghastly blue/black. In phone calls Jane had proudly told him that Patricia had beautiful, blue eyes, just like his. "Then, when he got to New York," laughs Jane, " he walked in with these horrible-looking eyes. They had turned so black, that I couldn't distinguish the whites from his pupils, or even tell which way he was looking."

As if the birth of another child wasn't a significant enough event in his life, Jim, during this time, also made his first trip to the track that would elevate him to national fame, the Indianapolis Motor Speedway. Because of its central location, many of the race teams used the facilities at the Speedway as their summer racing headquarters. Driver, Elmer George, who was married to Speedway president Tony Hulman's daughter, was one who housed his race car there and told Jim that he could use his garage to repair his car. So, with time on his hands and an ideal excuse to see the fabled track, Jim towed his damaged sprint car to Indianapolis.

"I'd never seen the Speedway before," Jim once said, describing his memorable first trip there, "and I really didn't know what to make of it. The Indy guys sure didn't know what to make of me. Just some sprint car jockey with his eyes all purple from flipping, working on his tore up car.

"Well, they started telling me about how to drive the Speedway. 'Never use your brakes here,' they said. 'Back off early for the corners. Let the engine compression slow you down.' Now, I'd never driven a lap at Indianapolis, but I knew they were all crazy. 'Listen,' I said. 'This is a long track, it's a fast track, so you better use your brakes. Screw all that backing off and letting the engine slow you down. Just stand on the gas!'"

Little did those listening realize just how prophetic those words were. In less than a year's time Jim Hurtubise would indeed stand on the gas at Indianapolis. The result would make him forever a legend at that cathedral of speed.

Hurtubise Family Collection

IMCA was a great proving ground for Indy drivers. Pictured left to right are Al "Cotton" Farmer, A.J. Shepherd, Bobby Grim, Jim Hurtubise, unidentified, Gene Poulson and Parnelli Jones.

Al J. Herman photo -HFC

Jack Rounds outside Herk and Parnelli at Minneapolis.

Walt Mahony photo -HFC

The Kephart Offy.

Hurtubise Family Collection

HURTUBISE

Hurtubise Family Collection

Jim returned from the crash at Cedar Rapids with a vengeance, driving first the Kephart Offy then later switching to the Ker Mac Offy, owned by Harry Kern and Bill McDonald out of Saint Paul, Minnesota. He reeled off a string of six wins, five seconds and three thirds with the car, and by the end of August was leading the 1959 IMCA point standings. By then there were few in racing who weren't aware of the name Jim Hurtubise. That attention, combined with the misfortune of another driver, brought Jim a rare opportunity, the chance to race with USAC.

In 1959, Johnny Thomson was one of the best drivers in America. That May, he grabbed the coveted pole position at Indianapolis with a new one lap track record, led thirty-nine laps in the race, and came very close to winning the 500, before fading to third behind winner Rodger Ward and second place finisher, Jim Rathmann.

Then on September 13, Thomson crashed in a USAC sprint car race at Williams Grove, Pennsylvania. He was thrown from the car and lay stunned on the track as his still flipping race car missed him by inches. Johnny would recover from that crash to race again, but would miss the remainder of the 1959 season.

Johnny's car, The Racing Associates Special, owned by Art Lathrop and D. Coleman Glover, was a top notch machine. Once the word of his misfortune spread through the racing grapevine, Lathrop was besieged with calls from hopeful aspirants vying for the ride. Jim Hurtubise was one of those callers.

"Everybody else was calling about Thomson's ride," Jim once said, describing how his break into the big time came about. "So, I thought I might as well call too. I figured I didn't have anything to lose."

Art Lathrop, who did have a lot to lose by misjudging the talent of the driver he put in his car, displayed incredible foresight and a degree of bravery in picking the inexperienced Hurtubise over a quality group of USAC regulars.

Jim's first outing in the Lathrop car came at the September 19 Hoosier Hundred. Held on the mile dirt oval at the Indiana State Fairgrounds, the Hoosier Hundred was the most prestigious dirt track race of a prestigious racing series. Popularly known as the Championship Trail, it was, in fact a series of races with points being awarded at each event, according to the driver's finishing position, towards the USAC National Championship.

The Championship Trail was the premier open wheel racing circuit in this country and consisted of tracks scattered across the nation, all of which were at least a mile in length. Most were state fairground, dirt ovals built originally for horse racing. Only one of those dirt tracks, Langhorne, was designed specifically for auto races. The one mile ovals at Milwaukee and Trenton, and the crown jewel of the Championship Trail, the Indianapolis Motor Speedway were the only paved tracks.

There were two types of cars on the Championship Trail when Jim appeared there in 1959. The champ dirt cars, as the name implies were designed for the mile dirt tracks. They were upright, front engine, virile looking racing machines that had raced at Indy up until the mid-fifties.

The other cars were known as roadsters, and were squat, low slung, slender cars designed specifically for Indianapolis and raced occasionally at Trenton and Milwaukee.

Both types of cars were manhandled by a group of drivers with a historic lineage that stretched back to Bob Burman, Ralph DePalma and Wilbur Shaw.

When Jim got his shot at the Championship Trail, he knew he might only have the one chance to prove himself. In that era, there were no long term contracts, no guaranteed salaries. If a driver didn't perform he was replaced. Some car owners changed drivers as often as they changed tires, and, on at least one occasion, a driver was called into the pits and fired by his disgruntled car owner while the race was still in progress.

If being given this privileged opportunity put any additional pressure on Jim to prove himself, he didn't show it. Before a sold out crowd of more than 24,000, Jim rode confidently and easily on the unfamiliar Indiana State Fairgrounds track along with drivers that he had long admired and dreamed of emulating. Greats like Tony Bettenhausen, Bobby Grim, and Rodger Ward, and would be greats like Eddie Sachs and A.J. Foyt.

USAC always looked at new drivers with a degree of wariness, especially those from rival sanctioning bodies like the IMCA. They were notorious for scrutinizing rookies to the point of intimidation, but oddly, it wasn't until after the practice session that USAC officials deemed it necessary to stage a five lap test run for Jim and five other newcomers.

Though never admitted officially, most veterans observers there that day agreed that the test was a face saving gesture on USAC's part for allowing Jim, whose wide open, throttle-to-the-floor reputation had preceded him, to even be on the track. Jim, as did the other five participants, Buddy Cagle, Cotton Farmer, Herb Hill, Lee Drollinger and Leon Clum, rolled through the so called familiarization run without a hitch.

The test session out of the way, Jim qualified easily in the big, pink, Racing Associates Special, and then climbed all the way to seventh place in the race before spinning out on lap 56 while trying to get around veteran campaigner, Ralph Liguori.

Jim's smooth performance in the Hoosier Hundred assured him of the Racing Associates ride for the remaining races on the Championship Trail. If he accepted that offer to run with USAC, however, he would have to forego the remainder of the IMCA season, and although he was leading the IMCA Championship points race at that time, Jim did so without hesitation. This was the break for which he had been working so hard.

USAC meant the big time. Only the best competed in its four divisions, the champ cars, sprint cars, midgets and stock cars. Of even more importance to Jim, USAC meant the Indianapolis 500. Competing with USAC did not guarantee a young driver a shot at Indianapolis, but he certainly couldn't get there without proving himself on the USAC circuit first.

The weekend following the Hoosier Hundred found Jim at Trenton, New Jersey for another one hundred mile National Championship race. When the champ cars first ran at Trenton, in 1949, the track was dirt. In 1957 it was paved in an attempt to attract the roadsters that raced at Indianapolis, making it an ideal track for car owners to observe the pavement skills of prospective Indianapolis drivers.

With this in mind, Jim was determined to demonstrate that he not only possessed the talent needed to wrestle a race car over a rough dirt track, but also the smooth driving qualities necessary to do well on pavement. Jim put on a fine performance at Trenton. He qualified tenth quick and ran the entire one hundred miles without incident, finishing a strong seventh, ahead of such experienced Championship Trail pilots as Rodger Ward, A.J. Foyt, and Len Sutton.

After Trenton, USAC began its season ending western swing, travelling first to Phoenix, for a one hundred mile race on the Arizona State Fairgrounds, mile long, dirt track. Dirt tracks are notorious for changing drastically in the course of only a few laps of hard running, and it is not unusual for one to "go away," or get slower, with each car that makes a qualifying attempt. Pity the driver that draws a late qualifying spot on such a rapidly deteriorating surface. That is exactly what happened to Jim at Phoenix, and he missed the eighteen car cut by just tenths of a second.

Jim was disappointed but not discouraged. He knew that the same thing often happened to the best, most experienced drivers. The experience did, however, make him fiercely resolved to atone for that performance at the next Championship race.

The Golden State 100 was the final USAC champ car race of 1959 and of the decade of the fifties. Promoted by renowned racing entrepreneur and 500 winning car owner, J.C. Agajanian, the race was held on the one mile dirt track at the California State Fairgrounds in Sacramento.

Most of the USAC regulars were there. Rodger Ward, who had already clinched the 1959 National Championship, Tony Bettenhausen, Eddie Sachs, Don Branson, Len Sutton, Bob Veith, "Cotton" Farmer, and "Shorty" Templeman, all appeared. Joining these veteran stars of the Championship Trail were several west coast drivers, who were granted temporary driving permits by USAC. Among that group were Dempsey Wilson, who had helped Jim in his CRA days, and Chuck Hulse, the newly crowned 1959 CRA Champion.

Jim qualified tenth quick at Sacramento and from the start made his presence felt. Flying through the corners, the tail of his car hung out in long, smooth, dirt slinging slides, he powered his way to fourth place by lap 20. From there his progress proved to be more difficult. Ahead of him, Eddie Sachs and Tony Bettenhausen were staging a classic wheel-to-wheel duel for first place, while pole position winner, Wayne Weiler, was running a strong third.

Not intimidated by those illuminaries, the rookie from the IMCA fought his way around Weiler and began to challenge dirt track immortal, Tony Bettenhausen, for second place. Tony and Jim battled wheel to wheel for fifteen laps before Jim finally barged around him and into second place on lap 37. Now only Sachs stood between him and the lead.

Jim took after Sachs, who was far out in front and running hard. Eddie's mechanic, Wally Meskowski, had been trying for several laps to slow him down, but with Jim challenging from behind, Sachs refused to do so. Then, suddenly thick, blue smoke boiled from under the hood of Eddie's car and the engine blew with a resounding boom.

Jim was now leading.

With Sachs out, and having already shown that he could handle Bettenhausen, Jim seemed to have a lock on the win. As the race passed the halfway point, however, the track became his toughest competitor. The surface began to break up, becoming extremely rough and rutty. Before the day was over, it would be so bad that tough Bill

Homier, near exhaustion, had to be relieved by A.J. Foyt on lap 76, and Shorty Templeman had to be helped from his car at race end, his hands a mass of blisters, and near shock from the beating he had taken.

Wrestling his car around the worst holes and bouncing through the ones he couldn't miss, Jim tenaciously held onto first place. Still, Bettenhausen was hovering behind him in second, and there was no one better on a rough track.

Sure enough, the wily Bettenhausen gradually cut into Jim's lead, until he pulled right up on his tail as they flew down the backstretch on lap 61. Calling on every trick he had accumulated in his many years of dirt track racing, Tony darted low then high, trying to shove his way around Jim, but Jim was equal to the challenge and countered every crafty move from Bettenhausen with a defensive move of his own. Then on lap 72, Bettenhausen slowed, and rolled towards the pits. His engine was gone. With the pressure off, Jim cruised to the checkered flag, a full lap ahead of second place.

Jane was ecstatic when she met Jim in victory lane. Arriving unexpectedly at the track that morning, she hadn't even known if she would be able to get in. She didn't have a ticket for the sold-out event and women weren't allowed in the pits in those days. The race's promoter, old friend, J.C. Agajanian, had squeezed her and Grayce Jones in, and now they were celebrating with the winner.

"Jim's share of the prize money," recalls Jane, "was about $1700, and we thought we were rich! Jim had always told me that I could carpet the house with the winnings from his first big race, and A.J. Shepherd always kidded me about that. When we got back home, that's the first thing A.J. asked me. But, I told him, 'A.J. by the time we pay off all the bills, all I'll be able to do is carpet the bathroom!"

Jim's victory at Sacramento was a monumental achievement. Many Indy car drivers spend their entire career trying but never coming close to winning a National Championship event, yet Jim had accomplished that feat in only his third race. However, any elation he might have felt because of that special win was gone by the next day.

"That's just the way Jim was," explains Jane. "Sacramento was the biggest win of his life to that point, but a day later you would never know it. He was ready to move on to other things."

Those other things included Indianapolis.

Bob Tronolone photo -HFC

Jim on his way to victory at Sacramento in the Racing Associates Offy. This was the day he was first called "Hercules."

Jack Fox photo -HFC

Jim in the #3 Racing Associates Special passing Johnnie Tolan in the Greenman-Casale #53 at Sacramento on October 25, 1959.

Jack Fox photo -HFC

Jim in the Racing Associates Special in 1959.

Walt Mahony photo -HFC

17 Gene Force about to be passed by # 3 Jim Hurtubise at Sacramento.

HURTUBISE

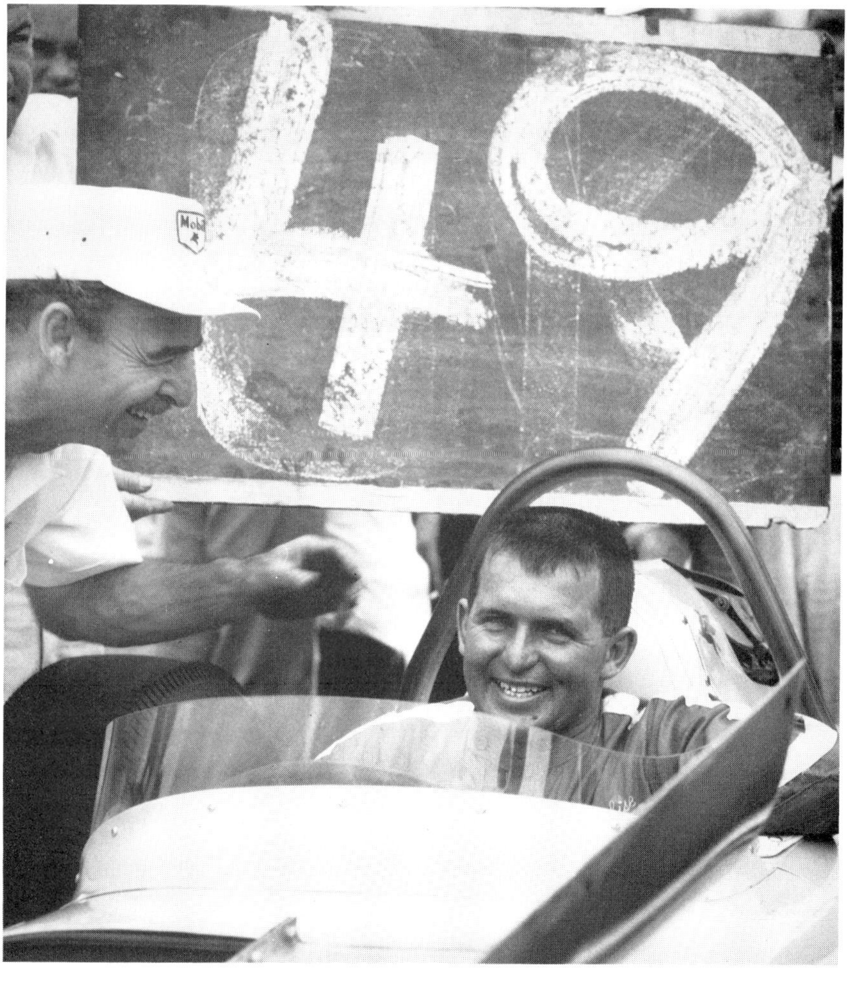

Hurtubise Family Collection

1960 loomed with an electric excitement. Indianapolis was on Jim's horizon. His performance in the champ cars had not gone unnoticed by Indianapolis car owners, and his win at Sacramento put Jim in a position of not having to go begging after a ride for the 500. Rather, car owners were calling him with offers. The chore was to chose the right one. Even though Jim knew that the seats in the very best equipment were already filled by the sport's top names, he stood firm in his resolve not to accept a ride in questionable equipment just to get to Indianapolis. Many a young driver had done that very thing, and their careers had suffered for it.

Just as it seemed that Jim would have to wait another year to go to Indianapolis, Ernie Ruiz called. Ernie owned Travelon Trailers, a company that manufactured house trailers in Modesto, California. With the mass migration to California during the economic boom that followed World War II, Ernie's business prospered and he had the money to do what he always wanted to do, own race cars.

Beginning with a team of midgets in the forties, Ernie bought his first Indianapolis car in 1953. Jim Rathmann, who would go on to win the 500 in 1960, finished seventh that year in the first Travelon Trailer Special. Ernie's fortune at Indianapolis during the next several months of May came nowhere near matching the success he had experienced his first year there, and in an attempt to rectify that situation, Ernie commissioned Barney Christiansen and Willie Utzman to a build him a new car for the 1959 500.

The car was actually designed and partially built by the highly respected A.J. Watson. Watson, who had already won back to back 500's in 1955-56 and was destined to become the most proficient car builder in Indianapolis history, constructed the car's tubular frame for Ruiz then turned it over to Christiansen and Utzman for completion. They fabricated the remainder of the framework, and running gear while the bodywork was done by sometime Watson employee, Jack Sutton.

The original A.J. Watson designed car, built for Ralph Wilke with Rodger Ward driving and Watson serving as chief mechanic, won the 1959 500. Riuz's copy, with driver "Cactus Jack" Turner, qualified a respectable fourteenth, but exited the race early with a split oil tank, a failure that would return to haunt Jim Hurtubise in 1960.

The color scheme Ruiz chose for his 1959 car was attractive but controversial. It was painted a light metallic green, complemented with a bright, fluorescent green nose. At that time green was considered an unlucky color by many racers, and most drivers would allow absolutely nothing green around themselves or their car. Those that held that particular superstition saw their beliefs justified at Milwaukee, on August 30, 1959. There the hapless Ed Elisian crashed Ruiz's car, flipped, and burned to death while trapped upside down in the flaming wreckage.

If the car's cursed past gave Jim any cause for concern about driving it, those fears were dispelled by the knowledge that the car was yet but a year old, and based on the proven A.J. Watson design. He enthusiastically accepted Ruiz's offer. Willie Utzman, one of the car's original builders was slated to be the chief mechanic, but suffered a fatal heart attack, and ace wrench, Danny Oakes, was named as his replacement.

Ruiz couldn't have made a better choice. Oakes was not only an accomplished mechanic, but also a competent driver who was the reigning USAC Pacific Coast Midget Champion. He had worked as a mechanic at Indianapolis and was familiar with the peculiarities of the Watson chassis. With his successful driving background, he related easily to the driver, and was an acknowledged expert at tutoring rookies at the often awe inspiring Speedway.

By the time Oakes got involved with the project, it was already late, just four weeks before the track opened for practice on May 1. Although most of the damage from the Elisian crash had been repaired, there was still much revamping to be undertaken.

For this effort, Oakes rented space in Al Swanson's shock absorber shop in Hollywood, and called on the considerable talents of Jack Sutton, one of the original builders of the car, to redo the aluminum body work, while he rebuilt the frame and running gear.

Once completed the car was turned over to custom car designer and builder, Dean Jeffries for painting. All the participants, Ruiz, Oakes and Jim, wanted something different. The result, which displayed Jim's artistic input, was striking.

Jeffries laid on multiple coats of hand rubbed, pearlescent lavender as the primary color. Over that he sculptured candy apple purple scallops that began at the nose, feathered to tapered lines on the hood, then flowed full length along the bottom of the car, before lapping up to graceful points on the curvaceous tail. Set off with gobs of polished metal and brilliant, chromed wheels, the car remains today as one of the most beautiful examples ever of an Indianapolis car.

Despite the long days and nights the crew had already spent on the car, when they arrived in Indianapolis, Oakes discovered that he still faced major mechanical problems. The engine leaked oil like a Texas drilling rig.

"We had a lot of engine trouble," confesses Danny. "The engine parts that Ruiz had really weren't very good. I know I had to tear the engine down at least four times in the first two weeks for oil leaks, which was highly unusual. About the time we'd think we had the leaks taken care of, we'd go out and run a few laps, and the officials would call us in for another leak, so I'd have to pull the damn thing all the way down, and start over again."

With all the engine trouble, it wasn't until Thursday, May 12, just two days before the opening day of qualifications, that Oakes finally got the oil leaks plugged enough for Jim to begin his rookie test. Proving to be an able student, Jim sailed smoothly through the session.

"I knew the Watson chassis pretty well," explains Oakes. "I knew how to set them up so you could put a green driver in and keep him out of trouble until he got through his rookie test. Then when he got to where he could go good and hang onto the car alright, I would keep adjusting it until he got fast enough to thrill himself a little bit. I started Hurtubise out like that."

Jim listened to Oakes for awhile, but his self-prevailing confidence was such that he wasn't at all intimidated by the Speedway, and after only a handful of laps was experimenting freely with a new groove around the old track.

"Jim came to me," explains Oakes, "and said, 'Danny, I've found a new way to get around this racetrack. I can take it down into the corner, give it a pitch and square it off like I would on the dirt. That way, I can shoot straight across the corner instead of having to follow the arc of the turn."

"I watched him for awhile," says Oakes, "then I called him back in and told him, 'Hey, you got to be careful with this place boy! If you lose that thing and hit the wall here, you ain't never going to forget it, so don't get too wild out there."

"But he did look like he was on to something," continues Oakes. "What he was doing was driving like we all did on the dirt tracks. But, no one had ever tried it at the Speedway, because if the car didn't handle real good and you lost it, you would really tag that wall. Jim was brave enough, and confident enough to pull it off."

Jim's racing buddy, Parnelli Jones wanted to drive in the 1960 500 and considered offers from several car owners. He turned them down however, because he believed their cars were not capable of making the race. Instead he spent the month of May with Jim in Indianapolis learning all he could to prepare himself for 1961.

Parnelli was aware that Jim was attempting to develop a radical way to get around the Speedway, and was an early observer of his new groove through the turns. In his biography, Parnelli described what he saw .

"I used to go down to the corners to study Herk's technique in the turns," stated Parnelli. "He was just a rookie, but he was doing things different from anyone else and he was going faster than anyone else. He was driving very hard and very deep into the corners, keeping his foot on the accelerator even when he braked, and he was sort of broadsliding through the turns so he'd be pointed straight when he got to the end of the turn. Then he'd just lift his foot off the brake, and wham, he'd shoot straight down the stretch, fishtailing."

"He was driving the corners sort of like you drive a dirt track" continues Parnelli, "and you're not supposed to do this on a paved track like Indy. Your tires don't get a good bite, and it's easy to get into a skid when you get sideways, which can be fatal. I couldn't quite figure out how Herk was swinging it, but he was all guts."

The official observers, stationed in observation towers around the track, weren't as impressed as Parnelli was by Jim's technique. They didn't care how he was swinging it, Jim looked out of control to them, and they complained vehemently to Oakes about his audacious rookie.

"Danny you're going to have to talk to your boy," they told Oakes. "He's wild out there, and if he doesn't straighten up, we're gonna' have to sit him down!"

"I'd tell Herk what they said," Danny says, "but he'd tell me, 'Those guys are crazy! I'm squaring the corner off, but I'm not losing it. It's not getting away from me. I can get around this racetrack, and, you wait and see, I'm really going to qualify. I'll tell you, Danny, I'm going to get that fast time away from Sachs.' Finally, I was able to convince him to ease up and practice his cornering at just one end of the track at a time. That way I just had half the officials to deal with!"

While Danny worked to keep the officials off his back, Jim's groundbreaking style was proving to be extremely quick. As he refined it, and Danny continued to adjust the car to fit his innovative method, Jim ran even faster. 145 miles per hour. Then, 146. Then, 147. Absolutely incredible speeds.

To put what Jim was doing into perspective, Eddie Sachs had grabbed the pole position the opening Saturday of qualifying with a new one lap record of 147.215 and a four lap record of 146.512. Jim was demonstrating that he had the potential to easily exceed those marks.

Jim's terrific lap times soon attracted the attention of his competitors. His speed through the corners was by far the fastest of anyone, and every time he pulled on the track, the veterans gathered in the grassy area inside turn one to determine just what this rookie was doing. Some didn't like what they saw.

Tony Bettenhausen was among a group of drivers watching when Jim cranked off a lap at over 147 miles per hour. He came roaring into the first turn, pitched the car sideways, caught it halfway through the corner, and sailed on by. Bettenhausen was livid. "There was no way a rookie should be driving that fast," he groaned. "He's dangerous in those turns!"

Jim's response to this criticism was not anger, but, typically, jokes. His sharp, verbal needles, laced with laughter, intended to ease the tension only chafed the veterans more. "Hey, old man," Jim would jab at Bettenhausen, "did you see me out there today? How'd you like that lap? Pretty good, uh?"

But, the coup de grace came when Jim and Danny Oakes approached a group of drivers on the Friday before the last weekend of qualifying. Voluble Eddie Sachs was holding court.

Danny Oakes tells what happened, "Jim strolled up to those guys and said, 'Hey Sachs, you really got around that racetrack didn't you?' Sachs was still kinda' puffed up about setting the new records and said, 'Yeah. Yeah, I guess I got around pretty good.' 'Well,' Jim said, 'I just wanted to congratulate you and tell you I'm going to blow you off that pole tomorrow!"

"I couldn't believe it" laughs Danny. "I said, 'God Almighty Jim, ease up a little bit! You're going to be about as popular as a whore in church if you don't cut that out.' He'd just laugh. I couldn't do a damn thing with him!"

"Jimmy Bryan," continues Danny, "really gave Jim a big boost one day. There were a bunch of guys standing around, Sachs, Bettenhausen and some others, trying to psych each other out, bragging about what they were going to do in the race. Bryan spoke up and said, 'You guys sound like you're gonna' be going pretty fast. But, what are you going to do when that guy in the purple race car comes up alongside and just blows you off?"

As the final weekend of qualifying began, there were eleven spots open for the 1960 500 and as bad as Jim wanted a new record, wanted to "blow Sachs off that pole," he wanted one of those even more.

Saturday morning began wet and windy, and the forecast called for more of the same. The rain finally stopped in the early afternoon and the track dried, but the high winds remained. Gusting to 35 miles per hour, they were strong enough to move the cars sideways as much as six feet on the straightaways. Despite the terrible conditions, Jim still managed several laps at over 146 miles per hour, but the rains came again, and the day ended without a single qualifying run being attempted.

Sunday, May 22 was the final day of qualifying. Rain still threatened, so Oakes rolled the Travelon car into the qualifying line early, and when the noon start time came Jim was the first out.

The pressure on him was immense. With the unpredictable weather, the odds were that this would be his only chance to qualify. The slightest speed draining bobble could cost him a starting spot. A momentary loss of control could send him crashing against the concrete wall with no time left for repairs. Faced with similar situations more than one Speedway veteran had wilted and failed.

Jim Hurtubise didn't. In the face of unfathomable stress the rookie performed with a poise unheralded in the history of the Indianapolis Motor Speedway. The result would immortalize him.

The status of the Speedway is such that a driver doesn't have to win the 500 to be entrenched in the track's history. Any number of accomplishments by a driver can catch the fan's imagination and cause him to live on in their memory. Ralph DePalma is remembered as much for trying to push his failed car to victory in 1912 as he is for the win he captured in 1915. Ted Horn, with his many top three finishes, is still known as the best driver who never won the 500. Lloyd Ruby is fondly revered for the many times he led the race yet fell short of victory in the closing laps, and Duke Nalon is still spoken of in awe because of his exploits at the wheel of the beloved, but winless Novis.

Few of the 70,000 gathered on that final qualifying day in 1960 realized as they watched this unheralded driver in the bright red driver's uniform guide his purple race car towards the green flag, that they were about to witness the birth of yet another Speedway legend. In just a little over four minutes Jim Hurtubise would rise from the ranks of the unknown to the status of an Indianapolis hero.

Jim flashed across the start/finish line with his hand in the air indicating he was ready to start his qualifying run, while his crew waited anxiously for him in turn four.

"We used a tree that was just at the entrance to turn four," explains Danny Oakes, "as a timing marker. If we clocked Herk as he passed by it, we then had time to write the speed on the blackboard, and show it to him when he passed by where we were standing. That way he knew immediately what his speed was for that lap and could adjust his driving accordingly."

A well thought out plan, but when Jim roared by on his first timed lap, Danny caught him on his stopwatch at over 148 miles per hour! Thinking his watch wrong, he compared it with another crew member's. He had the same time. The crew was so dumfounded that all they could do was look at each other in amazement and failed to display any speed at all to their driver. Jim would say later that because he hadn't seen a speed from his crew, he thought he must not be going fast enough to make the field, and tried even harder the next lap.

He needn't have. Those clocking Jim in the pits and in the stands reacted as had Danny, thinking their watches were faulty. In the film of that history making run people can be seen, as if choreographed, look at their stopwatch, shake them to make sure they are running, then turn to their neighbor in disbelief.

Then as Tom Carnegie began breathlessly spilling the news over the PA of Jim's extraordinary speed they knew their watches were right. This guy was flying!

"It's a new track record," called Carnegie in his own inimitable manner.

The crowd roared.

"The time, 1:08.81."

"The speed 148.002 mile per hour," he shouted.

The Speedway erupted in a crescendo of sound, and the cheers grew so loud that they even drowned out the bellow of Jim's powerful Offenhauser engine.

Then came the second lap. It was even faster 149.229. Another new track record. The third lap, faster still, would prove to be the fastest of the four qualifying rounds, 149.601, just sixteen one-hundredths of a second away from the then magic 150 MPH mark. The fourth lap might well have been the quickest yet. It probably would have topped 150 miles per hour if Jim had not lost the car for just an instant in turn four. Skillfully he caught it, but the bobble cost him precious time. Still the lap was 149.402, and the four lap average was an unbelievable 149.056 miles per hour, shattering Eddie Sachs' record from the week before.

The scene in the pits as Jim rolled in from his qualifying run was chaotic. Fellow drivers, mechanics, officials and guards ran almost to the side of his car, cheering, giving the thumbs up sign as Jim, a huge grin on his face, happily returned their greeting, just glad to be in the field, not yet comprehending the full impact of his run.

Former record holder, Eddie Sachs, was one of the first to greet Jim when he rolled to stop. Unflappable as always, Eddie soon had control of the microphone and the celebration. "Jim," effused Sachs, "I would have been mad at you if you had beaten my record by a little bit, but this...boy, what can I say but congratulations!"

It is difficult today to appreciate the magnitude of Jim's accomplishment. At a time when speeds were creeping up from year to year in only half mile an hour increments, Jim blasted past Sachs' four lap record of 146.512, by a phenomenal two and a half miles per hour .

His record would stand for two years, not to be broken until the rough brick front straight was covered by a smooth coat of asphalt.

That Jim was a rookie just adds to the incredibility of his feat. Drivers in their first year at the Speedway are not expected to do much more than make the field, but Jim cast aside that time-worn thinking, as he would many racing conventions with his natural ability and astounding racing savvy.

The world's best drivers had probed, tested and studied the track for fifty years in a constant struggle to pry loose a few tenths of a second of speed. Jim alone found a new, faster way around.

New technology has at times created, and will continue to create, dramatic jumps in speed at Indianapolis. But never before nor since has one driver so dramatically changed the face of speed at Indianapolis by driving ability alone.

Hours after Jim's amazing run was in the record books, many were still trying to digest and put into words the impact of what had happened.

Said Rodger Ward, "I didn't look for that. I expected him to do well, but not that well. He's a good race car driver."

1957 500 winner Sam Hanks, "They brought that car into Danny Oakes' shop at Al Sawanson's place in Hollywood, the first of April in a basket. It was a real good mechanic/driver combination. The driver is now in a class by himself. I would compare him with anybody." "It's phenomenal," proclaimed Chief Steward Harlan Fengler. "Jim has everything, youth, determination, desire. Being a rookie didn't bother him at all."

Speedway owner, Tony Hulman claimed, "It came as quite a surprise. We expected a good time from him, but not the way it developed."

Dave Cassidy, Tony's assistant and informer, described just how very surprised his boss was. "I've never seen Tony so excited. He jumped up and down, waved his arms, threw his cigarette away and rushed to meet Jim."

Of all those who offered their comments about Jim's record run, perhaps cagey, three time 500 winner Mauri Rose said it best. "Once in a while a fellow comes along—a Mays, a Lockhart, a Wilbur Shaw—with no worries. He doesn't feel like he's strapped in an electric chair. You don't get guys as smooth mentally and physically often. He enjoys it. It's fun for him. He loves it."

Jim's own assessment, coming when he was interviewed while still in his car, was simple, to the point and tinged with a bit of prophecy. "The car felt great," Jim said, "It was so good that I didn't even notice the wind. I enjoyed the ride. I really gave it heck and tried for the record. But, if you think that was fast, wait till next year. There's a friend of mine named Parnelli Jones that'll really give you something to talk about."

Jane had been confident from the beginning of the month of May that Jim would qualify well. "I knew Jim would be able to do it," she said of his new track record. "Because, when he came home after only his first day of practice, he told me, 'I like that track, and the car couldn't feel better if I was born in it.' Then when Grayce and I got to the track Sunday morning I stepped out of the car and found a five dollar bill in the parking lot. I thought that was a good omen, and as it turned out, it was!"

Jim was instantly elevated to star status. He was photographed constantly, surrounded by the press and hounded by fans. Jim's mother recalls the hectic nature of Jim's new found celebrity. "When Jim broke the record in 1960, I couldn't believe the chaos. The press kept him constantly busy. And his house was so full of people, with so much going on, that when we arrived there for the race, they had to find Jim's father, Ernie's lawyer, Ness Messing, and myself, a place to stay at a local minister's home."

John Laux, at that time a Firestone tire engineer and friend of Jim's, was standing with renowned mechanic and sage, Smokey Yunick, shortly after Jim had made his qualifying run. When Jim walked by surrounded by a cluster of reporters, Smokey cracked, "Well, John, I wonder how long it'll take him to get out of those dungarees and into a pair of them forty dollar pants?"

Jim never got out of the dungarees. Despite his popularity that would grow over the years at the Speedway to incredible levels, Jim remained fun loving, down to earth and always accessible to his fans. Jim's new found celebrity at the Speedway did serve one practical purpose. It gained Prince his freedom. Crusty Clarence Cagle, the respected Superintendent of Grounds at the Speedway, had made Jim keep Prince tied up all month. Then, when Jim broke the record, he looked the other way as Prince frolicked through the garage area with Jimmy Bryan's dog, and followed his master wherever he went.

One day Jim, with Prince right behind him, stopped by the John Zink garage. Troy Ruttman, A.J. Foyt, Johnnie Tolan and a handful of other hangers on were there.

"Come on, Prince," called Foyt, "jump in and drive this thing."

To everyone's amusement, Prince dutifully obeyed, and hopped in Zink's race car. He stayed in the cockpit only a few seconds then jumped out and trotted back to his Jim's side.

Again Foyt called, "Come on Prince, drive it!"

When Prince again obeyed, Foyt laughed and said, "That Prince is a pretty smart dog. Ruttman, I think you've lost your ride already!" Tolan, standing by watching, picked up a rag when Prince again jumped out of the car, and growled, "That dog ain't so smart, Foyt. He didn't even wipe the seat off before he left!"

While Jim passed the time between qualifying and race day by cruising the garage area with Prince, Oakes and the crew prepared the record breaking car for the 500 mile grind. There was much to be done, beginning with the leaky engine.

"On the morning we qualified," says Oakes, "we were still wiping up oil and plugging leaks just to be able to run. I told Ernie that if we got that thing qualified I was going to have to have some new parts."

After Jim's exceptional qualification run, Danny quickly got the new parts. The engine and car were torn down, all the parts checked, then it was meticulously reassembled. During routine magnaflux tests, [an x-ray type inspection for hidden defects in metal], a crack in the front axle was found. Jim and the entire crew breathed a sigh of relief at the discovery. Had it gone undetected and failed in the race, the consequences could have been deadly. However, in the rush to get the car ready, another crack was overlooked. That one would cost Jim a possible top three finish in the 500.

Jim started his first 500 with the accusation ringing in his ears that he wouldn't last a handful of laps in the race. Sure he was fast, said the so called experts, but his hard charging style was hard on equipment. This wasn't a sprint car race and if he drove as if it were he would soon destroy the car.

This was a charge that Jim had already faced many times in his racing career. It was part of the controversy that surrounded him when he was picked to replace Johnny Thomson in the Racing Associates car. Without doubt, Jim was the consummate charger. He never followed when he could lead, but the reality is that Jim was never put out of the 500 by a mechanical failure caused by his hard driving.

At the start of his first 500, Jim quickly moved from twenty third starting position, and in ten laps was in eighth place and hard after Tony Bettenhausen running directly in front of him in seventh. Their heated battle carried Jim to fifth place by his first pit stop on lap 35. That stop dropped him well back in the field, but by the fifty lap mark he was back in the top ten, and continued to advance upward in the standings throughout the course of the long afternoon. At lap 70 he was eighth. At lap 130 he was sixth. 160 laps into the race there were only nineteen cars still running and Jim's was one of them. Then with less than forty miles to go a connecting rod snapped in the engine, and Jim was out.

The culprit was not Jim's heavy right foot, rather it was the same cracked oil tank that had forced Jack Turner from the 1959 race.

"They tried to find the crack in the tank after the '59 500," explains Oakes. "But it was so small that they were never able to locate it. Then after the Elisian crash, and the rush to get the car ready for 1960, it was forgotten about. When Jim came in for his second pit stop there was oil all over the left side of the car. I couldn't see where it was coming from, so I just sent him back out and hoped we could make it to the end."

"I'll never forget standing there after Jim pulled away, and one of the guys said, 'Oh, I bet that's the same leak we had in the oil tank last year.' I could've killed him for not telling me before! We hadn't noticed it all month because the new paint had covered it up and sealed it. But then heat and vibration during the race finally opened it back up. The tank held six gallons of oil, and eventually we lost every drop. When the engine went dry, the rod broke, and we were done."

Because of his smooth, consistent performance in the race, and his outstanding qualifying effort, Jim was named the Stark and Wetzel 1960 Rookie of the Year.

More important to Jim than the award was the fulfillment of his dream of racing at Indianapolis. He had run with the best in the greatest race in the world and held his own. He knew now that he could win the 500. He had a year to wait for another try, but in the meantime he pursued yet another racing dream.

Hurtubise Family collection

Jim leads Tony Bettenhausen at Indy during the 1960 race.

Hurtubise Family collection

Danny Oakes and Jim preparing for the record breaking run in 1960.

HURTUBISE

9

Bob Scott photo - HFC

In the winter of 1959, as Jim prepared for the 1960 USAC season and his rookie year at Indianapolis, his attention was riveted on yet another project. He was building a sprint car that would use an inexpensive, stock block, Chevy engine to challenge the purpose built Offenhauser racing engine. That effort would prove so successful that it would forever change the face of sprint car racing in America.

Jim Hurtubise was unique in that he was not only an extraordinarily talented driver, but an exceptional fabricator, designer and mechanic as well. From his earliest days in racing he constantly labored to develop ideas that would gain him an edge on his competition and dreamed of one day being able to put all these ideas to work in a car he designed and built himself.

When asked, for instance, in the days following his record qualifying run at Indianapolis, who he believed was capable of breaking his record and the 150 mile per hour barrier, Jim answered, "I am. I want to build and drive the car that goes 150 here, and then win the race with it."

Jim had long been a proponent of the the overhead valve, Chevrolet V-8 as a racing engine. He was one of the first, if not the first, to use the Chevy in the CRA, and was by far, according to Lee Bruss, its most enthusiastic supporter. "Lee, this is the perfect engine for sprint car racing," Jim insisted. "One of these days you're going to see these Chevies put the Offy out of business." Parnelli Jones, who would join Jim in campaigning a Chevy powered car on the USAC circuit in 1960, and capture the National Championship with it, agrees with Lee Bruss about Jim's early enthusiasm.

"As far as California goes," Parnelli once said, "I can't say who should get credit for the 'Chivalay' engine idea. But the first person I ever heard talk it up was Hurtubise, right after he came out here to race with us. He said it was stupid to spend so much money on an Offy when a hot rodded, junk-yard 'Chivaly' would do just as well. He was right."

Ironically, despite Jim's early vocal support, it was Parnelli who would make the initial, major inroads with the stock block Chevy. First with the IMCA in 1959, and then later that same year with USAC. Both organizations were dominated by the four cylinder Offy, but unlike USAC, where the engines were limited to 220 cubic inches, there was no size restriction in the IMCA. So, most IMCA car owners chose the big, 270 cubic inch Offy, the same engine used at Indianapolis and in the champ cars. In some cases they bored the 270 out to as big as 292 cubic inches.

As much as Jim believed in the Chevy he had discovered during the 1958 IMCA season that the Chevy just couldn't match the power of those big, booming IMCA Offies. Jim had tried to take them on with the Leach Chevy, but on most tracks it was no contest.

"I'd have the lead coming out of a turn," Jim once said while talking about his experience with the Leach car, "but those guys with those big Offies would get on the gas and scream by me like I was standing still!"

That is why Jim chose to run an Offy powered machine during the 1959 IMCA season. A decision that proved to be a wise one as he finished second in points in the final IMCA standings, despite leaving the club six weeks before the end of the season to run USAC. Meanwhile Parnelli, who opted to use a Chevy, ended up in fifth place in the IMCA points race.

Parnelli, however, did have the honor of winning the first ever IMCA feature with a stock block conversion engine. That singular event occurred on August 21, 1959 when he drove to victory in Phoenix plumber Halan Fike's blue and white Chevy powered car at the Iowa State Fair in Cedar Rapids.

Then, at the end of the 1959 season, Parnelli once more vindicated Jim's faith in the Chevy with a stellar performance at Meyer Speedway in Houston, Texas. Jim didn't have a ride for that USAC sanctioned event, but he was there to cheer on his buddy who was running the Fike Plumbing car on a temporary USAC license.

Parnelli astounded the USAC regulars by setting fast time on the half mile paved oval, and winning his heat. In the feature he jumped into the lead on the first lap, but the throttle jammed and he dropped all the way to the rear of the field. Freeing the throttle, Parnelli charged hard to get back to the front, and although he ran out of time, he still finished a remarkable third behind A.J. Foyt and Don Branson.

Parnelli's impressive performance helped Jim generate interest in the Chevy powered car that he had under construction at the Neo-Glo shop. He convinced Bud Barnett who owned, with his brother, Bill, a successful San Diego, California plumbing firm, that a Chevy was the way to go in USAC. "Parnelli went through those guys like hot lead dropping through butter," Jim excitedly told Barnett. "Bud, we might not beat all those Offies with a Chevy, but we can run with them all."

Before Jim completed the car, Barnett would funnel some seven thousand dollars into Jim's stock block, racing dream. For his investment, Bud received a beautifully turned out car that would create racing history and become famous nationwide as the Sterling Plumbing Special.

As Jim pushed to get his new car completed in time for the season opener he turned to his racing friends for help. One who joined him was LeRoy Neumayer. "I had been racing IMCA," recalls LeRoy, "and during the winter of 1959, Jim asked me to help him put his new car together. He was trying to get it finished for the March race at Meyer Stadium in Houston and was running out of time."

"Jim wanted me to build the engine for him," continues LeRoy. "Now don't get me wrong, that was all Herk's idea. I just did what he wanted me to do. Herk could do it all on a car, he could build everything from the radiator cap to the rearend, to the bodywork, he really needed nobody. And he was good engine man. He knew fuel injectors and alcohol fuel, all that. I can't give him enough credit."

"The engine was a 283," explains LeRoy, "and Jim quarter stroked and bored it out to 340 cubic inches. That was about as big as he could go, because If you went any bigger than that with them, they'd break. I know that for a fact, because I'd gone to Tampa the previous February to mechanic for Parnelli on the Fike car. And, we had a bigger engine in it, 356 cubic inches I think, and it broke. That's when I began to find out what it took to keep those motors running."

Besides enlarging the displacement of the engine, Jim ported and polished the heads, added a Schneider race cam, and, with LeRoy's connections obtained a set of the latest Hilborn fuel injectors.

"I had a good relationship with Stu Hilborn," says Leroy, "so I was able to get all the good stuff before the guys back East did. I got the first two sets of the big butterfly injectors that Stu built. The first set I'd put on Parnelli's car when I was working on it, and then I got another set for Jim's."

When Jim made the trek to California in 1956, he did so knowing that the elevated level of competition there, as well as the year round racing, would enhance his own racing career. Another consideration was that in the fifties and sixties California was a hotbed of racing related technology, especially around Los Angeles where racing was a cottage industry and everything was available for the racer from wheels, to cams, to fuel injection systems.

Some of the greatest racing minds were also located in the Los Angeles area and that city became a breeding ground for the latest, most innovative racing concepts and ideas. When Jim started building his new sprint car he freely called on some of the country's leading racing experts for advice. Indianapolis 500 mechanic, Jud Phillips, was one such source of information for Jim, and he often picked Jud's brain.

"Jud would drop by the shop just about every evening," recalls LeRoy, "and he and Jim would sit and drink beer, and talk about all the latest suspension pieces and ideas. Jim would bounce a lot of his ideas off Jud, and Jud would analyze them for Jim and tell him how he might do something a different way, or a better way."

As a result, many of the mechanical ideas in the car were as innovative as the Chevy engine. To dampen the suspension movement, Jim chose the tubular type shock absorbers that were just then becoming available to the short track racer. While Jim stuck with the standard spring suspension on the front of the car, on the rear he utilized a cross, torsion bar suspension. The cross bar suspension would later became the norm on sprint cars and offered many advantages in reduced weight and more accurate suspension adjustments, but in 1960 it was still considered a bit radical.

"Looking back now, says Neumayer, "you realize that the car was really pretty simple, but back then it was pretty damn tricky! With those tube shocks and cross bars on the rear of the car, the suspension had a lot of travel, probably ten inches compared to five or six inches on most cars. And that made the car great through the ruts and holes on a rough track.

"In fact," continues LeRoy, "the car was so different that Herk had to learn to drive it. The cross bars on the rear got so much forward bite that in order to get side bite in the corner, he had to get on the throttle and use the forward bite for his side bite. It was tricky, but it worked everywhere it went. And it was especially good on a dry, slick track, which, with all their daytime races, most USAC tracks were. I'd loved to have driven that car myself, it would've made a hero out of me!"

Even though Jim was working his typical schedule of long days and sleepless nights in order to get the car built and running for the March 20 race at Meyer Speedway, he didn't spare anything in his efforts of creating an aesthetically pleasing car. The nose, tail and hood were all beautifully crafted pieces from renowned race car body fabricator Hiram Hillegass, while Jim handcrafted the aluminum side panels and belly pans himself. He sprayed his creation with the distinctive, DayGlo red paint that would eventually became his signature color, trimmed the nose and tail in white, and set off the paint scheme with gold leaf #56's.

When Jim pulled into Meyer Speedway, proudly towing his crimson and white creation, the best of USAC were there waiting for him. Foyt, Branson, McCluskey, and Elmer George. Few, if any, expected much out of Jim and his new car.

"When we got to Meyer," says Leroy, "no one really gave Jim a chance of doing any good. You know, they were thinking, 'Here's this West Coast hot dog, who's never been on an asphalt track, and he thinks he's gonna' beat us with a Chevy. He ain't gonna do crap!"

"Meyer Speedway was an asphalt track, and I kidded Jim the entire time we were thrashing, trying to get the car built, that he didn't know anything about racing on asphalt anyway, so why get in such a big rush to get there? He told me, 'I'm gonna learn, Leroy. I'm gonna' learn.' He sure did, he almost won the damn race!"

Indeed he did, but not before enduring some early race dramatics that very nearly proved his critics right. Don Shepherd joined Jim and LeRoy for the trip to Houston, and because the car was built in such a rush, they were still working on it when they got there.

"By the time I got the engine finished back in Inglewood," claims LeRoy, "all I had time to do was fire it up and just make sure it would run. When we got to Meyer, I had to fire it up in the parking lot, and run it long enough to adjust the valves, and re-torque the heads."

Jim qualified well and won his heat, but in the thirty lap feature he was never higher than seventh until lap 28. Then he caught fire. In one fell swoop Jim blew by four cars going down the backstretch, and pushed by yet another just as he took the white flag for the final lap. With only the leader Don Branson, and second place A.J. Foyt ahead of him, he roared into turn three right on Foyt's tail, then hammered by him coming off turn four.

"A.J. was so surprised," laughs Leroy, "that he jumped back on the gas so hard, he stood up in the cockpit. But all he could do was smoke his tires."

With Foyt behind him, Jim tore after Branson. He had the Chevy screaming, long blue flames licked from the tips of the chrome exhaust pipes, but, the cagey, old veteran held him off and beat Jim to the finish line by a scant three feet.

Even though Jim didn't win at Meyer, his amazing, two lap driving exhibition put the USAC establishment in a dither. Foyt growled, "Let him take the SOB to a dirt track where it really counts. Then we'll see what he does."

Elmer George was so impressed that he immediately began negotiations with driver Roger McCluskey, also a fine engine and chassis builder, to install a Chevy in his sprinter. Jud Phillips, who had watched the car under construction in California, wandered up to LeRoy and, almost sadly, said, "Leroy that Chevy really runs. It's going to be the death of the 220."

Jud was right. 1960 was the beginning of the end for the Offy in sprint car racing. Before that summer was over, Jim in his Sterling Plumbing Chevy, and Parnelli in the Fike Plumbing Chevy would make a shambles of the USAC circuit. Jim would win four features and run a close second on seven other occasions, while Parnelli won five features and the Midwest Sprint Car Championship. "The Chevy Twins," as they came to be known that simmering summer, so ingrained the Chevy V-8 into the consciousness of sprint car racing that it is still a dominate force today.

That Jim Hurtubise, in his first full season on the elite USAC circuit, had the foresight to fly in the face of the established way of doing things, as he would at Indianapolis later that year, speaks volumes about his brash confidence. Jim always knew he could win, but even more important to him than winning was being able to do it in his own way.

Just how right Jim's way was is aptly demonstrated by his performance in the car that served as a test bed for many of his creative ideas. From 1960 through 1963, Jim and the Sterling Plumbing Special won eighteen USAC features, finished second in seventeen others, and third in five more. He won the abbreviated Pacific Coast Championship in 1960, and the USAC Car Owner's Championship for Bud Barnett in 1961.

That Jim compiled this incredible record during what is considered the golden age of sprint car racing makes Jim and his car's achievements even more impressive. It was a time when any one of fifteen drivers was capable of winning a feature on a given afternoon. It was a time when drivers of the ilk of Hurtubise, Foyt, Jones, Rutherford, McCluskey, Sachs, Unser and Branson ran at Indianapolis one day [eleven 500's were won by that illustrious group] and a half mile, dirt bullring the next. It was an incredible time. The best of times. A time that will never be duplicated.

The car Jim built to challenge the men and machines of that historic era, continued to be successful long after the passing of those glorious racing days. After Jim ran his last sprint car race with the Sterling Plumbing Special at Ascot on November 3, 1963, it was parked for several years before Don Shepherd obtained it from Bud Barnett.

Don took the old machine and put a hot, young driver from Texas in it. With Jim's car, and Don's able guidance, Johnny Rutherford began his trek to the big time. When Rutherford slowed his sprint car racing activities, Don put another aspiring young driver in the cockpit, and Bobby Unser was well on his way to racing immortality.

Even after Rutherford and Unser moved to other cars, Jim's old car still wasn't ready for retirement. In 1968, eight years after Jim built the car, Don put "Scratch" Daniels in the seat at the ultra fast, high banked, paved, half mile Salem Speedway. Until then "Scratch" had been strictly a dirt track driver, but when the smoke cleared, Herk's venerable creation had won yet another USAC feature.

After the race at Houston, the stars of USAC made their way to Reading, Pennsylvania for an Easter Sunday show, and the first dirt track race of the year. Parnelli had returned to California with the Fike car after Houston. His mechanic, Joe Pitman, had discovered some serious suspension problems with the car that needed to be rectified. It would be mid-June before he returned to the USAC battles, leaving Jim to face the Offies alone. Foyt driving the blue, A.J Watson Offy, beat Jim across the finish line at Reading, making good on his boast at Houston of "... beating the SOB on dirt." But just barely, and a week later, the tables would be dramatically turned.

The next stop on the 1960 USAC sprint car circuit was April 24, at the fearsome, treacherously fast one mile dirt circle at Langhorne. This was Jim's first trip to the notorious track that many drivers, 500 winner Rodger Ward among them, refused to drive on. This was the track that before the year was out would claim the life of the legendary Jimmy Bryan.

Langhorne was a racer's track that required incredible skill and complete mental concentration. It was a track that separated the real race car drivers from the wanna' be's. Jim took to Langhorne like he was born there.

The race was scheduled for a hundred miles, but because Langhorne was so devastatingly hard on the lightweight sprint cars, the day's event was divided into twin, fifty mile features. A winner was declared for each race, and an overall winner determined by total points the drivers earned in each fifty lapper.

Jim set fourth quick time, and challenged the Langhorne track record holder, Don Branson for the lead throughout the first fifty lap feature, until a snow tire he had mounted on the left rear to help grab hold of Langhorne's oiled dirt threw a tread and forced him into the pits.

His poor finish in the first fifty lap run pushed him all the way back to the fifteenth starting spot for the second fifty lapper. But, by this time Jim had Langhorne figured out. He was in ninth place after only three laps, fourth at twenty laps, and was leading by the halfway point. With his throttle foot buried in the belly pan, the Chevy V-8 at full howl, the rear tires churning clods of dirt towards the heavens, only Foyt could keep Jim in sight. A.J. desperately hung on to second before attempting a futile charge right at the end of the race, but to no avail. The pace he had run to keep up with Jim overheated his tires, and Foyt faded to fourth at the finish.

Jubilantly and unchallenged, Jim rode on to the checkered flag fourteen seconds ahead of second place finisher, Eddie Sachs. It was Jim's first win in a USAC sprint car feature. His first win in his new car, and the first USAC win for the stock block Chevy.

After a break for Indianapolis, where Jim made his record setting qualifying run, the 1960 sprint car season rolled on through the summer. Jim ran second to Don Branson at Terre Haute, grabbed a pair of thirds, at Hidelburg, Pennsylvania and New Bremen, Ohio, then returned to the Terre Haute "Action Track" to set fast time, as well as win the feature. Jim repeated that fast time/win performance at Reading, Pennsylvania, and after a slew of seconds at William's Grove, Allentown, and Clovis, California, rolled into his home track at Ascot, on December 3, for the final USAC sprint car show of the season.

The Ascot event was promoted by J.C. Agajanian, who never spared an ounce of energy when it came to publicizing his shows. By race day a capacity crowd had packed the Los Angeles track and were in a frenzy of expectation for exciting, open wheel competition, and anxious to see Jim run against the big boys of USAC. He did not disappoint his many California fans.

Running Ascot the way he always loved to, the rear wheels bouncing off the wood fence as he fought for traction in the dark, damp clay, "Hercules" lopped an incredible two seconds off the old track record, and ran away with the thirty lap feature.

Don Shepherd, who was Jim's mechanic for that epic, 1960 sprint car season, has the trophy Jim received that night proudly displayed in the living room of his west side Indianapolis home.

"When we were preparing for Ascot," reminisces Don, as he explains why he claimed the trophy for his own, "I found out that the motor in Barnett's other car [he had one he used strictly for CRA races] had a bad motor. We had a new engine sitting in the shop, ready to go, so I said to Jim, 'Herk, Bud Starett is going to drive Barnett's other car at Ascot, and the motor's going soft. Let's pull the motor out of the 56 car, and let Starett use it, and we'll put the fresh one in our's.'

"But Herk didn't want to do that. He didn't really want to fool with it, but he told me if I wanted to change it myself, go ahead. So, I switched the motors, and that night Starett lost the rear main bearing during the heat race.

"I told Herk, 'See! If I hadn't made that change we'd have lost that engine ourselves.' Herk wouldn't have none of that and said, 'Aw, hell Don, Starett just run it out of oil or something. It'd been alright if we'd been running it.'

"Later I tore the motor down, and showed Herk that the other bearings were okay, so the engine couldn't have ran out of oil. And I reminded him that he'd been complaining about hearing a noise in that motor for the last few races. He didn't want to admit he was wrong and just mumbled something, shook his head and walked off, but I insisted that I saved that race for him, and that's how I ended up with the trophy!"

As good as the 1960 USAC sprint car season was for Jim, it was not without its striking reminders of just how dangerous and deadly these cars he loved so much could be.

Jim and the entire racing community had already been devastated by the loss of Jimmy Bryan. Then, on September 24, at Allentown, Pennsylvania, Johnny Thomson died. Besides being a friend and fellow competitor, Johnny and Jim's careers had intertwined the previous year. It was an earlier sprint car crash by Johnny that had opened the way for Jim's entry into big time racing.

When the USAC drivers and crews arrived at Allentown on that fateful afternoon, they were shocked and angered by the condition of the track. It was ill-prepared, dusty, rough, and full of holes even before the first car took to the track In that era when it came time to race, they raced. There were no driver boycotts, no briefcase carrying lawyers to threaten litigation.

So, after the usual rounds of qualifying and heat races a full field was flagged off for the feature. They got through the first two turns with no problem, but as the closely bunched cars charged down the backstretch and into the third turn, Thomson caught one of the deep holes and flipped violently. The popular little driver died instantly, leaving behind a wife and four young sons. Ironically the car that Johnny died in was the same car that had carried Bill Schindler to his death on the same track, on the same weekend, eight years before.

After the caution for Johnny's crash, Jim and an inspired Jim Packard put on as exciting two man duel as any seen that season. They raced wheel to wheel, nose to tail, with Packard barely beating Jim across the finish line for the win. A week later Packard was killed during a midget race at Fairfield, Ohio. That racing era was indeed the very best of times, but often, it was also the worst of times.

At Dayton on July 17, Jim narrowly escaped death himself, as he survived one of his most spectacular crashes. Dayton, with turns banked so high they seemed like fortress walls looming over the surrounding cornfields, had always been a fast, spectacular racing facility. In 1960 Dayton was newly paved and faster than ever.

Don Branson was the quick qualifier with a time that was not only a new track record, but a new world's record for a half mile, paved track as well. Running speeds approaching 105 miles per hour, Don shattered the old world record, set by the late Bob Sweikert at Winchester Speedway, by eight miles per hour.

Jim wasn't as fortunate in his qualifying run. On his first lap the car bottomed out and he lost control. Looping into a half spin the car slid towards the metal guardrail at an alarming rate. Whomping into the fence, the rear end of the car bound into the air, hurdled backwards over the rail, and began a thirty five foot plunge to the ground below.

An eerie silence permeated the grounds, as everyone there was certain that the crash had been fatal. In a 1952 accident that unfolded very much like this one, Jim Rigsby was killed.

After what seemed like an eternity of waiting, a roar went up from the crowd as "Hercules" was spotted climbing the embankment, a big grin on his face, waving to the fans.

Tom Hoffman, of the well known Cincinnati Hoffman racing family, was standing nearby when the crash occurred. Tom dashed towards the scene just as Jim stuck his crew cut head over the guardrail. "Heh, Heh, Heh," came the distinctive Hurtubise laugh. "How'd you like that, Tom?" was Jim's response to a concerned, startled Hoffman.

The trees bordering the track beneath the turn had miraculously served to cushion the fall, and plopped the car and driver intact, almost gently, to the ground. Jim later laughed and said, "Hell, I've slept in beds that were harder than that fall was! The worst part was the case of poison ivy I got crawling through the weeds getting out of the car."

According to Don Shepherd, the car could have been raced that same day. "There was a small dent on the hood," recalls Don. "And we had to replace a heim joint and straighten out one of the headers. Other than that the car was fine, but USAC still wouldn't let us run."

By the end of the 1960 season Jim Hurtubise had become a household name in racing circles. Nor was his exemplary season restricted to the sprint cars. He attacked the Championship Trail with the same unabashed confidence and eager enthusiasm, and the result was his record qualifying run at Indianapolis, and his second career champ car victory.

Kenneth H. Coles photo - HFC

Jim in the Sterling Plumbing Chevy leads Parnelli in the Fike Plumbing Chevy at Heidelberg, PA July 24, 1960.

Eldora in 1962. **Hurtubise Family collection**

Hurtubise Family collection

Heidelberg, PA July 24, 1960. **Kenneth H. Coles photo - HFC**

Kenneth H. Coles photo - HFC

Jim is in the middle of the pack at Salem in 1960.

HURTUBISE

10

Hurtubise Family collection

The 1960 Championship season opened on April 10, at Trenton, New Jersey. Jim qualified the #24 Koopman's Special in thirteenth place and worked his way to sixth before being forced out of the race on lap 61 with a bad clutch.

The champ cars were idle until May 1, when practice began for Indianapolis. After that month long sojourn, the National Championship season got under way in earnest with the traditional, weekend after Indy, hundred miler at Milwaukee. Jim's experience there, to say the least, was eventful.

Jim arrived for the June 5 race with high hopes and the same record breaking car and crew that he had at Indianapolis. Almost immediately, there were problems. The "Purple People Eater," as his lavender car was now fondly being called by fans and auto racing writers alike, would not handle on Milwaukee's flat mile like it had on Indy's 2 1/2 mile expanse. Jim and Danny Oakes struggled all morning trying to make the car work before finally qualifying in seventh place.

That, in itself, was quite an achievement considering that 500 winners Jim Rathmann, Troy Ruttman and Jimmy Bryan all missed the twenty two car cut, and Indianapolis pole position winner, Eddie Sachs, was added to the field only after winning the twenty lap consolation race.

Making the race would prove to be the zenith of Jim's Milwaukee weekend. He wrestled with the ill handling car all afternoon, spun with Don Branson on lap 90, and finally soldiered home in eleventh place, a lap down. Then, as if the day hadn't already been bad enough, Jim almost came to blows with Tony Bettenhausen in the pits after the race.

Bettenhausen, critical of Jim's driving since Indianapolis, claimed that Jim had blocked him on several occasions because he never bothered to look around to check traffic.

"That," said Tony, "cost me a shot at winning the race. Besides it's unsafe. Hell, Hurtubise ran right into Branson, and spun him out of the race."

Branson said otherwise. "It happened just the other way around," admitted Branson. "I tried to get under Hurtubise, and the car got away from me and I hit him. I put myself out of the race."

Speaking to the charge that Jim's driving had cost Bettenhausen a win, Danny Oakes said, "I don't know how that would have been possible. Bettenhausen was running a full second behind the leaders at that time. When Tony tried to pass Herk they were both in traffic, and short of the kid actually parking the car, there was no way Tony could have got past him."

"Besides, Jim has been used to running so far out in front of everybody else," joked Oakes about Bettenhausen's implication that Jim needed to look around more, "that he's never had to bother to look back before!"

That bit of humor defused the situation, and Jim and Tony shook hands before they left the track. The brouhaha did get Jim called on the USAC carpet back in Indianapolis. Although no official charges were brought, Branson and Milwaukee promoter, Tom Marchese, both substantiated Jim's side of the story, USAC's Director of Competition, Henry Banks, advised him to take it easy in the future.

If the incident at Milwaukee and the resulting confrontation with USAC officials afterwards troubled Jim, it wasn't evident at Langhorne just two weeks later. There, in the face of numbing tragedy, Jim won his second champ car race with one of the greatest dirt track performances of his illustrious career.

Langhorne was a track of legendary proportions. It's gone now, a victim of urban expansion and suburban sprawl. On the site of what was, "The Worlds Fastest One Mile Track," sits that monument to middle American affluence, a shopping mall. But to those who witnessed the always thrilling, often frightening, motorized combat that took place there, or read of the brave men who raced and died there, Langhorne will always be etched in their memory as an auto racing shrine.

Langhorne, located just fifteen miles outside of Philadelphia, opened in 1926 as the first dirt track in America designed specifically for auto racing. From the first race, held on July 17, 1926, until the gates were locked in 1971, Langhorne was brutally fast even though there was not a straight piece of racetrack to be found anywhere around its one mile circumference.

How the developers, a group of Philadelphia businessmen, arrived at the track's shape is not known. Best described as circular, though not perfectly round, Langhorne's unique shape was directly responsible for the high speeds that race cars were able to obtain there.

On a traditionally shaped, dirt mile, drivers blast down the two long straights, then have to get hard on the brakes and slow drastically in order to negotiate the corners. But Langhorne was a momentum track. There, a brave enough driver could slam the throttle to the floor, hang the car's tail out in one continuous, high speed slide, and never have to back off. The result was terrifyingly fast, record shattering speeds.

The fastest machines to run at Langhorne were, without doubt, the USAC champ cars. In 1958, Don Branson cranked his Bob Estes Special around Langhorne at an incredible 113.996 miles per hour. As a comparison to just how fast Langhorne was, Don also held the track record on the smooth, paved, Milwaukee mile. That mark stood at 105.603, eight miles slower than at Langhorne!

It was this same high speed that made Langhorne so fatally dangerous. With the car continually in a high speed slide, the driver never had a chance to relax. Never had a chance to lift a hand from the wheel to stretch numb fingers, or clean dirty goggles. Never had a chance to rest neck muscles tightened from trying to hold up a helmet that weighed as much as bowling ball because of the constant pull of centrifugal force. Wearied by those conditions, with dust flying, and cars roaring about him, the track's circular sameness often caused a driver to lose his bearings. The result could be deadly.

No accurate records have been compiled, but it is believed that in excess of sixty drivers died at Langhorne during its forty five year history. The most notorious section of that notorious track was in the area that would be the second turn on a normal race track. For reasons never fully understood, the car's clawing tires would dig deep, car wrecking furrows there far quicker than anywhere else on the track. So fierce and deadly were the ensuing crashes that this part of Langhorne was dubbed "Puke Hollow." On June 19, 1960, "Puke Hollow," racing's most lethal piece of real estate would claim its most fabled victim.

Jim's first appearance at Langhorne in a Champ Car came on that tragic day. Driving the #44 Peter Schmidt Special, a somewhat ancient but still proficient performer, Jim qualified third quick.

Don Branson was the day's fastest qualifier, coming within just a few tenths of a second of his 1958 record lap. Second quick that afternoon was three time National Champion, and 1958 Indianapolis 500 winner, Jimmy Bryan.

Jimmy, who had retired from the dangerous dirt tracks after his 500 win, was making his comeback in the #1 Leader Card Special normally occupied by defending National Champion, Rodger Ward. Ward, who was financially in a position to turn down any race he chose following his 1959 Indianapolis victory, saw no reward in risking his neck on a track he had always considered too dangerous.

Bryan leapt at the chance to drive the car built by and maintained by the premier race car constructor of that day, A.J. Watson. Others, however, were concerned about the wisdom of Bryan's return to the dangerous sport on its most difficult track after a two year layoff.

Writer John Sawyer questioned Bryan about this the day before Langhorne. According to Sawyer's account in his book, "*Dusty Heroes*," Bryan was relaxed and confident.

"Ward says I'm crazy," Bryan told Sawyer, "that I'll kill myself. Hell, I'm only thirty-three, and I'm in good shape too. Surely I can get around a track that I know as well as that one. I first got on that place when I was still green out of Arizona, didn't know anything at all and made it. I will this time too. Besides, I'll be careful!"

When the green flag dropped, Branson led the eighteen car field into turn one, with Bryan in hot pursuit. As Bryan stormed sideways through "Puke Hollow," his car caught one of the deep ruts already dug there, jumped skyward, then flipped wildly end for end. The tremendous centrifugal forces generated by the gyrating car stretched Bryan's lanky body three fourths of the way out of the cockpit, and thrashed him brutally against the track. Bryan was dead by the time the car bounced to a stop.

At the restart of the race, Branson again jumped into the lead and led the first ten laps before he was passed by Jack Rounds, Jim Packard and Herk. Jim rode behind Rounds and Packard for the next fifteen laps, then, in a tremendous spurt of speed, passed them both and sailed into first place. By the fortieth mile, he had a quarter lap lead on Packard in second, and seemed to be cruising to an easy victory. Then, at the halfway point, a tire shredded and he was forced into the pits.

The stop took thirty two seconds, equivalent to a half lap to make up on the track, but by lap 70 Jim was already challenging Packard for the lead, and by lap 80 was back in front. Sometimes on two wheels, sometimes completely off the ground, Jim pushed stubbornly through the ruts and holes, and by race end was a half mile ahead of Packard in second and Gene Force in third. Despite his mid-race pit stop, Jim's time for the hundred mile run was a new world record.

Bryan's death cast a pall over the racing community and struck Jim especially hard. Bryan had been one of the few veterans who encouraged him at the Speedway when he was developing his new driving style, and, ironically, they shared the same given names. Bryan's proper name was also, James Ernest.

But the specter of death is always near the race car driver and is accepted as part of the sport. For those of Jim's era this was even more true. Of the eighteen drivers who started that June 19 race at Langhorne, a third of them were destined to die in race cars.

Jim never dwelt on the dangers of racing. Only on a rare occasion would he speak on the subject, and then only half seriously, joking that it presented no more dangers than the stick and ball sports.

"You try not to think about death," Jim once said, "except when it's a friend. But I don't think racing is as bad as football or baseball or basketball. You can get hurt in them too. I sure wouldn't want to carry a football and have eleven other guys trying to tackle me and knock me down!"

Later, a little older, and after having wrestled death himself and won, Jim became more philosophical about the subject. "I console myself by saying that I never knew anyone who lived forever," Jim stated. "There are some things about racing you never understand. But if you are a race car driver, a good one, you'll send yourself to school many nights when you first climb into bed. You'll lay there and try to understand the things which you don't comprehend, and the things which seem hardest to understand."

Although Jim qualified for every race on the 1960 Championship schedule [a feat matched only by Don Branson and A.J. Foyt] after the win at Langhorne, the remainder of the 1960 Championship season was anticlimactic. He finished tenth at Springfield, twelfth at the Hoosier Hundred, after losing a wheel on lap 95 while in third, and thirteenth in the Adams Quarter Horse Special at the September Trenton race. At Sacramento, where his win the year before had opened so many racing doors, Jim led the race until a broken transmission put him out on lap 67. Then he placed second behind A.J.Foyt at the season ending event in Phoenix.

Irregardless of how the remainder of the season transpired, in an arena where many great drivers never achieve a victory, Jim, after only his first full season on the circuit, already had two National Championship wins to his credit.

When the record's of the drivers of that era are examined, most often they are compared, and rightly so, to that of A.J. Foyt. A.J. would go on to win more races in the champ cars, or Indy cars as they are now known, than any other driver in the history of Championship racing. But, when Jim won his second champ car race at Langhorne in only his sixth outing, A.J. had yet to record his first victory. Foyt's first win would not come until the DuQuoin 100 on September 9, 1960 in his thirty fourth champ car start.

In only three years, Jim's talent had taken him from being the wild man of the half mile bull rings of the CRA and IMCA, to being one of the three top drivers on this nation's best racing venues. The future did indeed bode well for Jim Hurtubise.

Louie Ensworth photo - HFC

Jim and the Peter Schmidt crew celebrating his second champ car victory at Langhorne in 1960.

Hurtubise Family collection

Winning is a family sport. Karen, Jim and Jane Hurtubise.

HURTUBISE

11

Hurtubise Family collection

The first year of the Sixties had been an excellent one for Jim Hurtubise. In the next four years of that decade, before his career was drastically curtailed by the disastrous, 1964 Milwaukee crash, Jim's racing star would climb at an extraordinary rate. No matter the form of competition he was considered a favorite to win in any race he entered. During that four-year span, only racing buddy, Parnelli Jones, and the incredible A.J. Foyt could keep pace with Jim's spectacular performance.

USAC had reacted to the Chevy's strong performance in 1960 by drastically lowering the cubic inch displacement for stock block engines from 366 cubic inches to 305. Jim and the other stock block proponents were understandably upset by these restrictions. No racer wants to lose an advantage he has fought hard to obtain.

"I just don't feel it's right," said Jim of USAC's action. "I think they went to far. I feel a reduction to about 320 inches for the stock blocks would have been more fair."

After the rule changes were announced, Jim first talked about running an Offy in 1961, but always at odds with convention, later recanted and said. "I think I'll try running a Ford next season. You don't receive much attention if you win with an Offenhauser engine," but beat 'em with a Chevy or Ford and you have 'em all talking."

Jim stuck with his Chevy, and despite being handicapped with a smaller engine displacement, it performed even better in 1961 than it had during the head-turning, 1960 season. With it Jim competed in seventeen of the twenty-four, scheduled USAC National Sprint car races, winning six, finishing second five times, third twice and setting fast time on three separate occasions.

1961 was the first year for a true USAC National Sprint Car Champion. Prior to that, USAC had crowned both a Mid-West, and an Eastern champion. Jim didn't win that initial national title tilt, he finished second to Parnelli Jones in the final point standings, but Parnelli had to run five more races than Jim to beat him.

The 1962 USAC sprint car season saw Jim again compete in seventeen feature races, and, as in 1961, he won six of them. By 1963, Jim had began to curtail his sprint car activities, as had Parnelli and A.J, in favor of stock cars, but he still managed two feature wins. He beat a hard charging Don Branson to the finish line at New Bremen, Ohio for one of them, and "cleaned house," with the fast time, a heat win, and a feature victory, at Buffalo, New York for the other.

Although the record book doesn't reflect it with a large tally of wins, Jim's performance in the champ cars during this same period was just as spectacular as in the sprint cars. When comparing Jim's champ car record with that of his sprint car record, two things must be considered. The greater number of sprint car races than champ car races, more than twice as many, and the fact that to win just one champ car race is a rare achievement for any driver. As late as the mid eighties, Jim's four wins still placed him among the top twenty drivers of all time in the history of Championship racing.

During the 1960 champ car season Jim drove seven different cars, but 1961 provided him the luxury of being able to concentrate his efforts on only one car as he prevailed upon the Barnett brothers to purchase the car he drove to victory in the 1959 Sacramento 100.

In the winter of 1960, Jim tore the car down and methodically rebuilt it, updating it mechanically with the latest racing technology, and modifying it to accept both the standard Offy or a Chevy V-8.

The rebuilding complete, Jim then painted the car in the same distinctive DayGlo red with white trim color scheme he had used on the sprint car.

With the Sterling Plumbing champ car Jim became a threat to win any race, broke numerous track speed records and led many laps. At the same time he exhibited a race-finishing consistency that might surprise many who tend to dismiss him as simply a wild charger, capable of going fast, but hard on equipment. From 1961 until the Milwaukee crash in 1964, Jim raced the Sterling Plumbing car twenty-two times, and collected two wins, three second places, three thirds, and finished in the top ten on ten other occasions.

Most drivers seem to have a particular track or type of track they take more readily to than another. A.J. Foyt, despite his four Indianapolis 500 victories and scores of other pavement track wins, was considered a better dirt track racer than a pavement driver.

Parnelli Jones, on the other hand, despite his dirt track roots, was considered the better pavement driver, especially on the high bank, half mile "hills" of Salem, Winchester and Dayton.

Jim was no different. While he was consistently fast everywhere and capable of winning on any type of track, and won back to back champ car races in 1961 and 1962 on the ultra smooth dirt at Springfield, Illinois, he did tend to excel on tracks that presented a particularly demanding challenge to most drivers. Rough tracks.

Tough tracks. Tracks where the driver's skill and daring are the most important ingredient in winning.

Langhorne was one such track. Considered so dangerous that many drivers refused to even race there, some of Jim's most memorable racing conquests took place on that fast, dirt circle. He won at Langhorne the first time he ever drove there on April 24, 1960, And later that same year recorded a champ car victory on the day Jimmy Bryan was killed.

When Jim returned to Langhorne for the June 18, 1961 champ car show, he qualified second quick, then jumped into the lead on the first lap ahead of pole sitter, Al Keller. He held the first place spot until the forty fourth lap, when he spun in the second turn and allowed A.J. Foyt to slip by him for the lead. Jim reentered the race well back in the pack, but with a monumental display of driving rarely witnessed on the tricky, Pennsylvania mile, he charged back to the front and slid past Parnelli Jones for second place on lap 80. Slashing around Langhorne in one long, beautifully controlled power slide, Jim was on the verge of catching Foyt and retaking the lead when he lost the engine on lap 93.

At the 1961 Twin Fifty sprint car race, held on August 27, Jim's luck at Langhorne proved better. In the first fifty lap feature the car's engine sputtered and ran out of fuel just as he charged down the front straight for the checkered flag. Still, Jim was able to hold off a fast closing Parnelli Jones to collect the win. Making certain his tank was well topped off for the second fifty, Jim dominated that event as well and rode home an easy winner.

USAC didn't schedule a sprint car race at Langhorne in 1962, but they did run two one hundred-mile champ car races. Jim won the pole position for the first one, scheduled for June 24, but the day was rained out, forcing the USAC champ cars to return a week later. On the July 1 rain date, Jim finished a solid third behind winner A.J. Foyt and second place Parnelli Jones, while treacherous Langhorne claimed yet another driver, up and coming young star, Hugh Randall.

The second Langhorne champ car race of 1962 was held on August 26, and Jim boosted his third place finish of the earlier Langhorne event one spot, and nabbed second place to Don Branson's win.

After a year's absence, the USAC sprint cars returned to Langhorne in 1963. Running with his usual, hard charging, high sliding style, Jim led the first feature of the April 7 race, until, as happened in 1961, he ran out of fuel on the white flag lap. But, unlike 1961, he was on the back part of track when the engine quit and could not coast to the finish line. Jim's seventh place finish in the first feature put him far back in the pack for the second fifty lap go. He beat and hammered his way through the field, but ran out of time in his pursuit of first place, and finished third, to A.J. Foyt and Parnelli Jones.

Langhorne's June 23, 1963 champ car race would be the last time open wheel racing fans would be thrilled by the sight of Jim Hurtubise bravely powering around that unique track while it was still dirt. Driving Wally Meskowski's Chevy powered car, Jim gave them something to remember, when once more he wrestled quick time from the uncompromising old racetrack, and led the first half of the race before a bad tire caused him to fade to third at the finish.

Jim's final appearance on Langhorne's dirt was on April 26, 1964, during a 150-mile, USAC stock car race. Driving a Norm Nelson prepared Plymouth, Jim proved that he could master Langhorne in any type race car as he swept to an easy win. His closest competitor was his boss, Norm Nelson, in an identical Plymouth, and he was five laps behind the incredible Hurtubise at the finish.

By the time Jim recovered from the fiery, 1964 Milwaukee crash, Langhorne had been paved in a vain attempt to tame its vicious nature. It would take more than a coating of asphalt to change Langhorne's beastly reputation, however, and until the gates were closed Langhorne would remain a wicked, yet fast and thrilling race track.

Jim returned to Langhorne to win a major stock car event and finish second in two others on the new, smooth surface, proving his mastery of truly phenomenal race track.

Langhorne was just one of the exacting tracks that Jim seemed to have a special affinity for. His performance at the famed Ascot Speedway bears testimony to his skill on that tough half-mile. His winning record there dates back to his CRA days when Ascot was known as LA Speedway, and continued with his dominating, five race rampage just after the Los Angles racing plant was renamed.

Perhaps Jim's most impressive Ascot victory occurred on November 11, 1961. That night, before a record crowd, he ran down the best USAC had to offer in a furious, forty lap, sprint car shootout.

It surprised no one when Jim set quick time in qualifying with the Sterling Plumbing car that late fall evening, but the levity of that accomplishment was muted when a heated controversy flared between several of the drivers, USAC officials, and promoter, J.C. Agajanian.

Throughout the season, USAC had started their races straight up, with the fastest qualifying cars at the front and the slowest to the rear. For this race, however, Aggie, who was always endeavoring to create an exciting, colorful show for the fans, prevailed upon USAC to invert the field and put the fast cars at the back.

When the quick qualifying teams realized how the show was going to be pushed off, tempers flared to the point that Parnelli, A.J. Foyt, Elmer George and Jim's car owner, Bud Starett threatened to load up and go home.

Jim, even angrier, shouted, "Load it up, hell. Listen, Bud, if I'm not leading this thing within ten laps then I'll pull in and help you load it up. Let's race!"

Jim wasn't leading by lap 10 as promised, but he was knocking on the leader's doors. From his last place starting spot he slashed past A.J.Foyt, Roger McCluskey, Elmer George, Bill Cantrell, Donnie Davis, and was in third place by lap 12. With only two Joneses, Dee and Parnelli, between him and the lead, Jim pressed even harder. He blasted by Dee Jones for second on lap 15 and pushed Parnelli so hard that his engine blew on lap 32. With no one left to challenge him, Jim cruised the final eight laps to the win.

Then there was New Bremen. The very name evokes images of thundering sprint cars and high speed. New Bremen with its short straights and long sweeping turns was flat and fast. Another formidable half mile stretch of dirt that Jim loved and excelled on.

Jim's first time at New Bremen in a sprint car was on August 7, 1960. On that summer afternoon, the three exciting new racing heroes, A.J. Foyt, Parnelli Jones and Jim Hurtubise, put on a show that is still talked about in Ohio racing circles today. The three ran as one the entire race before Foyt, in his Offy, out gunned the Chevies of Parnelli and Jim by only feet, right at the checkered flag.

Before he was forced from sprint car racing by the Milwaukee accident, Jim ran New Bremen four more times. In 1961, he set a new track record in qualifying and led the race until a broken sway bar caused him to spin out, and finish eighth. In 1962, Jim again set fast time and beat Parnelli for the win in the feature. 1963 saw a repeat of that performance, only this time it was the great Don Branson that chased Jim home in second. Jim's final appearance on New Bremen's black clay was on June 1, 1964. He qualified third fast, was running second in the feature and challenging for first, when his engine exploded in a billowing cloud of blue smoke.

Langhorne, Ascot, New Bremen were exacting tracks with their own demanding peculiarities and Jim excelled on them all. But, if any one track defined the bravery of Jim Hurtubise or showcased his ability to master a car on an intimidating piece of real estate, it was Terre Haute.

Illustrated Speedway News photo

Jim out of fuel after winning the 1st 50 lapper at Langhorne needs a push.

Walter T. Chernokal photo - HFC

Jim and the Sterling Plumbing Chevy challenges A. J. Foyt and his Offy.

Donald Barron photo - HFC

Jim at Reading, PA in 1962.

Kenneth H. Coles photo - HFC

The plumbers union. Jim in the Sterling Plumbing Chevy leads Parnelli Jones in the Fike Plumbing Chevy at Heidelberg, NY in 1960.

Kenneth H. Coles photo - HFC

Jim leads Don Branson in the Miricle Power Offy at New Bremen in 1960.

Kenneth H. Coles photo -Hurtubise Family collection

Three of the all time greats at New Bremen on Aug 7, 1960. #56 Jim Hurtubise leads Don Branson and #8 Eddie Sachs.

HURTUBISE

12

Kenneth H. Coles photo -Hurtubise Family collection

Ascot, Langhorne and New Bremen are all gone now. Only Terre Haute remains, a throwback to a time when tough brave men in fast cars risked their lives every other summer weekend for no other reason than what they were doing was fun.

The half mile clay oval at Terre Haute is located in the confines of the Vigo County Fairgrounds and has hosted sprint car races since 1952. The winner of that first 30 lap feature was Joe James, and the stream of winners after that includes some of racing's greatest names, Tommy Hinnershitz, Mike Nazaruk, Jimmy Bryan and Pat O'Connor among them.

Terre Haute has always had a reputation for being a rough and heavy race track, but for those brave enough to run up high, as Jim loved to do, there is always a cushion, a ledge of good dirt, to lean the car against as it slides right up to the red and white board fence. Cars bicycling up two wheels, leaping up on one wheel, sometimes bounding completely off the ground, are the norm rather than the exception at Terre Haute.

Jim loved the place. His favorite photograph of himself in a race car was an image snapped as he bounced high in the air, all four wheels off the ground, while he attempted to negotiate one of Terre Haute's tricky corners.

Today, Terre Haute is the home of two prestigious sprint car races: The Hulman Classic, named for Tony Hulman, the late owner of the Indianapolis Motor Speedway, whose home and business offices were located in Terre Haute, and the Hurtubise Classic.

Usually held in mid-July, the Hurtubise Classic, unlike other races that are named to memorialize drivers after their deaths, was initiated in Jim's lifetime as a tribute to his remarkable performance there and to recognize the contribution those feats made towards establishing Terre Haute as the legendary track it is today.

Jim's headline-capturing, fan-appealing exploits brought Terre Haute nationwide recognition and more than any other single factor, established its reputation for hard, close, fast racing action.

Jim's initial venture to Terre Haute was on June 12, 1960. Jim and Parnelli had just started raising eyebrows in USAC racing circles with their controversial, potent Chevies, but neither driver won that thirty lap feature. Parnelli finished third while Jim pushed Don Branson hard the entire race to finish a close second to the sprint car maestro.

However, the exciting display of wheel-to-wheel racing put on by

Jim and Parnelli that afternoon inspired the popular writer for the *National Speed Sport News*, Gene Powlen, to dub Terre Haute, the "***Action Track***," and the two new racing heroes in their radical engine sprint cars, the "***Chevy Twins***."

Powlen, an astute racing observer, was quick to spot and bring to the attention of the thousands of readers of his column, "Hoosier Hilites," many talented new, young racers. Gene had been one of the first to tout Jim's skill after observing him in his first champ car race at the Hoosier Hundred in 1959, but even such a perceptive follower of racing as Powlen could not have imagined what Jim was capable of accomplishing at Terre Haute. After finishing second in his maiden voyage to the track, he would not lose again there for three years.

The first of that amazing string of victories came on August 21, 1960. With his Chevy engine screaming at full tilt, Jim set fast time, then streaked to the feature win with Roger McCluskey and Don Branson in hot but futile pursuit.

June 11, 1961, marked Jim's second Terre Haute feature win in an afternoon of sprint car racing that was fraught with complications. The problems began in the heat race when Jim and Wayne Weiler came together while battling for second. The left rear wheel of Weiler's new, A.J. Watson built sprint car climbed over Jim's right rear, catapulting Wayne high into the air. He crashed down hard and began a wild series of twisting tumbles that so mangled the car that it took rescue workers fifteen minutes to free him.

Jim raced on and finished second, not fully realizing until afterwards what had happened behind him. Wayne suffered a concussion and a fractured jaw, but survived to race another day.

The heat race seemed to be a harbinger of things to come in the feature. As Jim dove into the swirling dust and dodged around or jumped over the deep ruts to grab the lead from Leon Clum on lap 12, he appeared to have the race under control.

Unknown to anyone but Jim, though, the car's oil tank had split at the start, and was spraying him with hot engine oil. The boiling lubricant so severely cooked his right leg that he had to be treated by a doctor afterwards, and the pain became so severe that at one point Jim considered pulling out of the race.

"It was so bad," Jim said later, "that I didn't think I was going to be able to finish. It hurt plenty. But when I'm leading a race I sure hate to stop!" He didn't, and went on to score yet another "Action Track" win.

The next three Terre Haute USAC sprint car races took on a stunning sameness. The winner was Hurtubise, Hurtubise, Hurtubise! Only the name of the second place driver changed. In August of 1961, it was Parnelli Jones who chased Jim home in second, after A.J Foyt blew his engine trying. A.J. and Jim had waged a lusty battle that had the fans on their feet most of the race. When A.J.'s engine expired on lap 26, he slid his car to a stop on the backstretch and dashed to greet Jim in the winner's circle.

At the next race, June 17, 1962, A.J. Foyt's engine held together for the full thirty laps, but he still finished second to Jim. In the August race of that year, Parnelli rose from the field of contenders in a vain attempt to pry the King of the Action Track crown from Jim, but he streaked to another win, and a new thirty lap record in the process.

On June 16, 1963 the sprint cars of USAC made their first appearance of the year at Terre Haute, and, as he had the past five races, Jim immediately took control. He won his heat race and was well on the way to winning his sixth sprint car race in a row when the radiator hose split. Suddenly, Jim was out, his unprecedented Terre Haute win streak finally at an end.

Besides its two prestigious sprint car races, Terre Haute is also home to one of the most important midget races in the nation, the "Hut Hundred." In a sight that can thrill the soul of the most cynical racing fan, the Hut Hundred begins when thirty three tightly bunched midgets, lined up three abreast, pour beneath the green flag and jockey for position before they even make the first turn.

From that first rumbling circuit to the end of the hundred lap grind, drivers are constantly in heavy traffic as they fight for position and overtake slower cars on the crowded half mile oval. Just to finish the Hut Hundred is, in itself, a proud achievement. To finish well there is an extraordinary feat.

When Jim ran Terre Haute's one hundred lap midget race for the first time on October 1, 1961, it wasn't yet called the Hut Hundred. It was, however, already an important, national midget event with a stellar history that extended back to 1954.

The starting field in 1961 was not thirty three cars as it is today, rather an entry list in excess of seventy machines had to be whittled down to an elite twenty four through qualifying.

Heavy rains the night before left the track a quagmire and in such terrible shape that the heat races were cancelled and the race was shortened to seventy five laps.

Jim didn't last that long. His car's belly pan became so packed with mud by the mid-point of the race, that the throttle pedal would no longer work, and he had to drop out.

That particular Hut Hundred is renowned for the driving demonstration put on by A.J. Foyt. A.J. missed the twenty four car cut because he qualified early when the track was at its worst, and it improved all afternoon. An angry Foyt bought Dick Northam's starting spot for two hundred dollars, and after having to start his own car at the tail end of the field, forced his way through the mud for the win.

Jim's luck at the Hut Hundred never quite equaled A.J.'s. He came very close to winning this major midget event the two other times he competed there, but his typical midget misfortune crept in with victory in sight.

Driving the Bob Nowicke Offy in the October, 1962 race, Jim pushed his way into first place in the opening laps, and stayed there. Just two months after his fifth consecutive Terre Haute sprint car win, Jim seemed to be on the way to an easy, consecutive feature win number six. Then on lap 98 his Offy sputtered, quit, then refired. It was running out of fuel. Jim desperately tried to keep the engine running and hold off a fast closing Ronnie Duman, but to no avail. Jim kept going, but both Duman, and Bud Tingelstad squeezed around his slowing machine as they raced down the front stretch to the checkered flag.

For the 1963 race Jim qualified the Kincaid Offy with the eighth fastest time. Then, in an argument on how to set the chassis, Kincaid fired him. Jim found a new ride in the Harry Turner car and had to start at the tail of the field. In his typical fashion he charged to the front, and dueled all afternoon with Bob Wente. The fast-paced battle, however, used up Jim's tires and Wente slipped around him in the closing laps for the win.

Few drivers have dominated a particular track like Jim dominated Terre Haute. In his ten feature starts there, Jim won five, finished second twice, and third once. His success at Terre Haute and all the other tracks aside, the track Jim wanted most to excel on was the big 2 1/2 mile oval that lies sixty miles due east of Terre Haute in the tiny town of Speedway, Indiana.

Howard Woodring photo -Hurtubise Family collection

This is how the Terre Haute track got it's name.

Bob Scott photo -Hurtubise Family collection

This is where P.J. and Herk were named the Chevy Twins by Gene Powlen.

HURTUBISE

13

Hurtubise Family collection

Jim had hoped to build his own car for the 1961 500, but it would be 1964 before he was able to undertake such a bold venture. In the meantime, there was no shortage of car owners vieing for the services of the sensational 1960 Rookie of the Year. After considering numerous offers, Jim selected a car owned by fellow North Tonawandaian, Norm Demler.

Norm had made his fortune from numerous land holdings and a proliferation of apple orchards and cider mills scattered throughout the North Tonawanda, Niagara Falls area. Appropriately, his Indianapolis car was dubbed the "Apple Cart," and sported an apple painted on its tiny tail fin, just behind the headrest.

The "Apple Cart" was a beautiful canary yellow car with the engine laid over horizontally on its side. This created an extremely low profile with the top of the hood but a scant, twenty one inches above the asphalt. Built in 1958 by master metal smith, Quinn Epperly, the car started the 500 that year in twenty fifth position with exciting little George Amick driving. George brought the car home in second place to winner Jimmy Bryan after steering through the first lap carnage that eliminated eight cars and left popular Pat O'Connor dead.

In 1959, stock car ace, Paul Goldsmith, was at the wheel of Demler's yellow, trimmed in red, #99 machine with stock car mechanic, Ray Nichles, as chief mechanic. Goldsmith, who had started the 1958 500 but never completed a full lap because he was eliminated in the first lap melee, brought the car home a respectable fifth, in his first, true 500 mile run. Goldsmith again drove the car in 1960, as Tiny Worley assisted Nichles with the mechanical chores, and for the third straight year, Demler's car completed the full 500 miles with Goldsmith finishing in third place.

Because of the car's excellent reliability record, Jim looked forward to the 1961 500 with enthusiastic expectations. Joining Jim for the first time as a mechanic at the 500 was his brother, Pete, who assisted chief mechanic, "Tiny" Worley. Pete, an excellent driver himself, had moved to California to advance his budding driving career through the sprint cars, then decided he preferred turning the wrenches.

"That interest was with me about six months," laughs Pete about his stint in sprint cars, "when I realized it just wasn't for me. I'd seen several guys get killed and hurt badly. I guess I wasn't cut out to be a race driver, because true race drivers don't even think about those things. But I was newly married and thought about it a lot. So, I decided, 'To hell with it, I'm just gonna' work on 'em!'"

A fortunate decision for Jim because while Pete was serving his apprenticeship at Indianapolis in 1961 he had already assumed the mechanical chores on Jim's sprint car, as he later would the Champ Car. It was Pete who was responsible for keeping a fast, safe set of wheels under Jim, and Jim's record in his racing heyday provides ample proof that Pete was more than capable of handling that important assignment.

Pete, who is the consummate perfectionist, and Jim, who wasn't, yet expected Pete to always prepare the cars perfectly, would at times have some rather dramatic, brotherly disagreements. Pete recalls one sprint car race in particular where Jim had been running strong and challenging for the lead when the engine blew.

"I was standing in the pits," chuckles Pete, "when Jim came rolling in. I guess he was pretty frustrated, because he had been doing real well in the race. But, just as he was coming to a stop, he jammed on the brakes and slid into my toolbox. Whether he meant it that way or not, I took it as his way of telling me what he thought of my work. I was pretty frustrated myself, so I just walked over and kicked the tail of his race car!"

Sibling disagreements aside, the Hurtubise brothers were exceptionally close, and their two very different and distinct personalities seemed to make them an even stronger driver/mechanic combination.

Unlike his first appearance at the Speedway in 1960 when he didn't get on the track until the middle of the month, Jim was on the track the day practice started in 1961, and by the second day had topped 146 miles per hour. From that point speed became much more difficult to find, however.

The problem was that the Demler car would not respond at all like the Watson roadster Jim drove in 1960. The lay down engine design, while possessing much potential with its better aerodynamics and lower center of gravity, could not be tossed through the corners like the Travelon Trailer Special.

Jim realized he would have to find a different way to negotiate the Speedway's four difficult corners. In the meantime the driver getting all the attention for remarkable speed was the venerable, Tony Bettenhausen. The 44-year-old Bettenhausen had been racing since 1938, and was a respected and popular competitor among his peers, despite his incessant needling and occasional roughhouse driving tactics.

With twenty one National Championship wins to his credit, Tony was the premier driver of that era. He had twice won the National Championship, but despite his immense talent had always fallen short in his pursuit of victory at Indianapolis. His best finish in fourteen starts was in 1955 when he finished second to Bob Sweikert.

In 1961, Tony appeared to be on the threshold of his greatest success. He was the quickest almost every practice day, and on the Wednesday prior to the opening day of qualifying turned a lap of 149.2 miles per hour. Most believed that Tony would break Jim's year old record, and many were already picking him as a favorite to win the 500 even before qualifying began.

But it wasn't to be. On the final practice day before qualifying began Tony's buddy, Paul Russo, asked him to take his ill-handling car for a test hop. Tony's car owner, Lindsey Hopkins, was adamantly against it, but finally relented to Tony's pleading to help a friend.

After a couple of warm up laps, Tony turned a lap of 143 miles per hour, followed by four more at over 145. Then he slowed, and appeared to be looking at the rear of the car as he motored down the front stretch. His chief mechanic, Jack Beckley, signaled him to come in, but instead Tony sped up. He circled the track again and as he headed down the main straight the car suddenly veered to the right, and into the retaining wall. It was later determined that a radius rod bolt had come lose, allowing the front axle to twist and jerk the car out of control.

On impact the car jumped nose first atop the wall and tumbled over and over for a hundred yards down the length of the three feet high concrete barrier. So violent was the thrashing as the car danced savagely atop the wall, that it tore six catch fence supports, made of heavy streetcar rails, from the concrete and wrapped itself in the fence and steel retaining cable. Tony, who by his own count had flipped a race car twenty eight times, had always joked, "I never worry about them as long as I can count them." Tony couldn't count number twenty nine.

Tony's death cast a pall over the normally festive opening day of qualifying. Even his fellow drivers, hardened by the commonness of death in that era, were somber. But race drivers are a tough breed, even callous, at least on the surface. When the track opened for practice on Saturday morning, May 13, every driver there was focused on only one purpose. Qualify for the 500.

And so they did. In record number. It was the busiest opening qualifying day in Speedway history. On a glorious, sunbaked May afternoon, no less than thirty six qualifying attempts were made, twenty two of those were successful.

Just an hour before his death, Bettenhausen had said, "Somebody will have to average better than 150 miles per hour to keep me from winning the number one starting spot tomorrow." And Jim's mechanic, "Tiny" Worley joked that he would, "...maybe settle for a 150 mile per hour run from Herk."

But, the much-anticipated, first 150 mile per hour lap did not materialize. Emotional Eddie Sachs won the pole position for the second year in a row with an average speed of just over 147 miles per hour, two miles off Jim's 1960 track record. Don Branson grabbed the second spot in the middle of the front row, and Jim finally found the groove he was looking for with the Demler car. Although he was slower than the year before, Jim pushed the Demler car almost four miles an hour faster than it had ever gone at the Speedway and grabbed the third starting position on the outside of row three. Indicating that he was pushing the car to the limit, Jim's first two laps were identical in speed, and his third was just three hundredths of a second slower.

Before that hectic day ended, rookie Parnelli Jones turned heads, just as Jim had predicted he would do, by qualifying fifth fastest. Qualifying on the inside of row five, was a funny looking little car driven by World Driving Champion, Jack Brabham. The car, built by Englishman, John Cooper, had the engine mounted in the rear. Within the next two years that revolutionary design was destined to change forever the face of racing at the Indianapolis Motor Speedway, but in 1961 it was derisively dubbed the "funny car."

"Were ready. Were going to win, I hope," Jim said just two days prior to the start of the 1961 500. "We've picked up quite a bit more speed with the car over what it ran last year, because we changed it quite a bit. We offset the chassis and moved the oil tank and the fuel tank to improve the balance."

"The equipment on this car is the best," praised Jim. "It should make it a strong finishing car. The car made four pit stops last year and we believe that the changes we made in weight distribution will enable us to eliminate one of those this year. And I'm satisfied with our starting spot. It's probably the best position for getting into the lead quickly, and being first is what counts."

Pole sitter Sachs vowed, "I'm going to give it all I got to lead that first lap. I know Jim Hurtubise might try for the early lead, and Ward is right behind me. That Ward is a tough competitor, and so is Hurtubise. But, I plan on leading into that first turn."

Eddie did lead going into the first turn, but Jim blew by him on the outside as they raced through that corner, and was eight car lengths ahead of Sachs as they flashed across the finish line at the end of lap one.

The first lap was a new record, and storming on at a record setting pace, Jim had a three second lead at lap 5, was four seconds in front by lap te10, and was already lapping slower cars by the twenty second lap.

Jim started the 500 with only a partial tank of fuel, as the team's pre-race strategy had been to jump into an early lead, and, with the light load of fuel run hard at the beginning. They reasoned that this would force Jim's competition to strain their engines to the breaking point as they attempted to keep up in their heavier, fuel laden cars. The plan seemed to have some merit. Front row starter Don Branson dropped out with a burned valve after only two laps, then Bobby Grim, Jimmy Daywalt and 1960 winner, Jim Rathmann, all retired quickly with mechanical problems.

This strategy, however, did force Jim into an early pit stop, and on lap 36 Jim dove into the pits from his record breaking first place run. In one of the faster stops of the day, Jim's crew had him refueled and back out in only twenty two seconds, but the time he lost dropped him out of the top ten.

Running with a full load of fuel, Jim climbed steadily back through the field. On lap 60 he was in tenth, and by lap 80 was running sixth. With his next scheduled pit stop imminent, Jim was just where he and his crew had hoped to be at this stage of the race. In the lead pack of cars, running easy enough to save the equipment, but close enough to the front that he could challenge for the lead in the latter stages of the race.

Unlike the ballet like precision of the first stop, Jim's second pit stop turned disastrous. Spilled fuel ignited as it splashed over the hot exhaust, and Jim was forced out of the car until the flames were extinguished. The costly stop consumed a valuable two minutes, way too much time to make up on the track. Jim knew his shot at victory in the 1961 500, barring a miraculous change of circumstances, had ended.

In only a handful of laps after that fateful stop, Jim realized that not only was a win in jeopardy, but the chance to complete the race as well. "I could hear things rattling when I'd back off for the turns," Jim explained after the race. "Without any gauges to give you an indication of where the trouble might be, you can only guess at what's wrong, and that's some strain. Then, just as we completed lap 99 the engine really blew up, and we were out of it."

The Speedway was celebrating its fiftieth anniversary in 1961, and the Golden 500 turned into a real donnybrook. In a race that had twenty three lead changes among seven different drivers, A.J. Foyt seemed to have the victory well in hand by his third pit stop.

Unbeknownst to A.J., however, a malfunctioning fuel nozzle had prevented him from taking on full load of fuel, and he was forced back into the pits on lap 184. The stop was quick, just six seconds, but Sachs, who was running second and pushing his car hard to catch Foyt, flew into first place. With just fifteen laps remaining, A.J.'s hopes of victory had vanished. In his frustration, all he could do was curse his fate. "It absolutely made me sick," A.J. said later.

Then suddenly, just ahead of him, Sachs slowed and dove into the pits. In the most dramatic turn of fortune in Speedway history, A.J. had the lead, and the win, back. In his desperate earlier chase of Foyt's fuel lightened car, Sachs had ruined his right rear tire and was forced to change it with just three laps remaining.

Never without something to say, even in the face of bitter defeat, Eddie was philosophical about his loss in the race he so desperately wanted to win. "He gave me the lead and all I did was give it back to him," said Eddie. "I saw the tire was wearing out on the 194th lap. I'll admit I could have slowed down and might have made it with my twenty three second lead. But, I thought it would be better to be second than dead."

Driving J.C. Agajanian's #98, Jim's buddy, Parnelli Jones, had admirably fulfilled Jim's brash prediction of the year before by leading twenty seven laps before a bolt, left on the track in the aftermath of a spectacular, five-car, front stretch crash, was kicked up by another car and pounded him just above his eye. Parnelli fought to keep control of the car while emptying blood from his goggles, and quickly dropped from contention. Still his performance was impressive enough to win him Co-Rookie of the Year honors with Bobby Marshman.

Jim joined Parnelli in his garage immediately after the race. Nice job, pop!" raved Jim, slapping Parnelli on his leg. "You made those guys know you were in the race for awhile." But Parnelli, sucking short draws from his cigarette, was inconsolable even by Jim, and sat sullenly, staring straight ahead.

For the 1962 500, Jim was reunited with the Demler team and rejoined by his mechanical mentor from 1960, Danny Oakes. After Danny prepared Jim's car for the 1960 500 they had not worked together again until the beginning of the 1961 champ car season, when Jim insisted the

Barnett brothers hire Danny as chief mechanic on the newly purchased, ex-Johnny Thomson car.

Though often at odds with each other about how the car should be set up, Oakes and Jim made a formidable team on the 1961 Championship Trail, winning the Springfield 100, and gaining a second, a third and two other top ten finishes.

"Jim was an excellent driver," says Danny, "but he could sure be bullheaded about how he wanted the car set. He was hard to please in this respect. We'd go to a race track, and Pete and I would have the car set close to what it should have been for the track, but in the first hour we'd work our butts off making changes to the car. The shocks, the torsion bars, raise them, lower them, whatever, and many times we'd end up right back where we were originally.

"Jim was hard to satisfy," continues Danny, "and was always wanting to try something different so he could get around better. Of course, that's the way you go fast. So, you can't blame Herk, or anybody, for wanting to make changes. That's how you do it."

Even when he was a rookie at the Speedway back in 1960, Jim tried to make his own setup changes to the car.

"I'd set the chassis there at the Speedway," laughs Danny, "and I'd come in the next morning and it would look different. Well, I found out that Jim was coming in at night and changing the car himself. I'd change everything back, but it got to the point where I told him, 'Listen Herk, I want you to leave the chassis alone. I've got it set a certain way for a reason. I realize you're a damn good race car driver, but you've never been here at the Speedway, and you might make a disastrous change!"

After the lecture, Jim deferred to Danny on chassis adjustments but still sought to have more control. "He left the car alone," says Danny, "but he'd argue with me all the time. He'd say, 'Jeez, Danny, I don't like the way it's doing this, or that. Lets try setting it this way and see what happens.' And I'd make some changes, and he would run a few laps and see that the car would do exactly what I told him it was going to do."

But by 1962, under the tutelage of Oakes and his 1961 Indianapolis chief mechanic, "Tiny" Worley, Jim had gained enough mechanical knowledge of Speedway cars that Demler felt comfortable turning the preparation of the his "Apple Cart" over to him. So, in the winter of 1961, Jim and Pete began work on the car at the NeoGlo shop in

Inglewood, while Danny Oakes prepared the engine. Jim's changes to the car were, to say the least, radical.

"He started by chopping a lot of weight out of the frame," explains Danny. "And the car, although it was a good one, was a little on the heavy side. But I thought he was going too far, and I said, 'Jim, I'm afraid you're taking a hell of a lot of strength out of the car. I don't think I'd take that much out.' But he went ahead, and we argued back and forth all the time about what he was doing."

"Then," continues Danny, "he took the Watts linkage, a series of bars and linkages that holds the rear axle in alignment while it moves up and down, off the left hand side and remounted on the right. I said to him, 'Herk, you know, the guy that figured all that Watts linkage out, and where it goes, was a pretty shrewd cookie. Why did you decide it would be better on the right side?'

"Oh, I just got a theory,' he said. 'And I think it's going to work out better over there.' Well, I argued with him about that and told him, 'Herk, I'd be awful careful about putting it on that side. Personally I wouldn't do it at all, but if you want to try it, it's your butt in there not mine."

So went the preparations for the 1962 Indianapolis 500. Arriving at the track early in the month of May, Jim was immediately confronted by USAC officials. Word had leaked out about the changes he had made to the car, and USAC was concerned for his safety. After they inspected it, USAC ruled that either Jim add back much of the tubing he had so painstakingly removed, or the car would not be allowed to run.

Whether it was the modifications Jim made to the car originally, or the changes to those modifications forced on him by USAC is not known. Regardless of where the fault lay, Jim could not make the car handle and he struggled to even get it to the speed he had run so easily the previous year.

Those difficulties finally came to a head on May 11, the Friday before the opening day of qualifying, when Jim lost control in turn two, spun the length of two football fields, and slammed to a rest against the concrete wall. Jim was shaken but escaped without serious injury, suffering only a small cut on his left leg. The car was not as fortunate. It sustained heavy damage, and the crew was forced on a week long binge of short nights and long days to repair the car in time for the last weekend of qualifying.

Meanwhile, Jim could do little more than pace the garage area, watch Parnelli flirt with the 150 mile per hour barrier, and test drive other cars. Two of those test hops were significant, one ironically so. Jim, who is best remembered in the latter part of his career for stubbornly trying to get a front engine car into the 500 field became one of the first, if not the first, top American driver to drive a rear engine car at Indianapolis.

Hot rodder Mickey Thompson, with the first American response to the European rear engine technology, built three Buick V-8 powered cars for the 1962 500. Two he entered himself. The other went to Jim Kimberly, of the Kimberley-Clark paper products empire. Thompson had Dan Gurney in his machine and was running well. Kimberley had English rookie, Jack Fairman, in his and was not. Kimberley called on Jim's expertise at the Speedway to help sort out the tricky machine.

Joking about the "nap" position of the reclining seat, Jim quickly had the car up to a respectable speed, while Fairman observed his cornering technique from a turn one vantage point. "There are some problems with the way the weight shifts when you're going into the turns," Jim advised Thompson, Kimberley and Fairman after his speedy run. "But, if you can get that straightened out, this thing should go really good."

The other car Jim test hopped was one of the famed Novi's. The Granatelli brothers had purchased the popular, powerful cars after the 1960 race, but had little luck in getting the cars in the race. They were still struggling in 1962 when Granatelli, acknowledging Jim's ability to analyze a troubled race car, invited him to take a test ride. Within a handful of laps, Jim had the car over 147 miles per hour, and fell in love with the powerful, brute of a machine. Climbing out of the car, a big grin on his face, Jim struck a deal with Granatelli right then and there to drive the car in 1963. That joining of man and machine would prove to be a memorable association.

The first day of qualifying opened with a flourish. 150,000 fans thronged into the Speedway on a Saturday that would prove to be the fastest in Indianapolis history, and all were expecting the 150 mile per hour barrier to be broken.

They would not be disappointed. Before that day of speed ended five drivers would surpass Jim's 1960 record, and all he could do was stand by and helplessly watch. Len Sutton was the first, with a four lap average of 149.328, but the tires on Sutton's car had no more than cooled when Parnelli Jones rolled out of the pits and on to his date with destiny.

Parnelli's first lap, almost not counted because starter Pat Vidan did not see him raise his hand to signal he was ready, was a sizzling 150.729. The first sub-one-minute lap at the Speedway was history. Parnelli's next three laps were all under the one minute mark as well, and a new Speedway legend was born.

It wasn't until Thursday, May 17, that Oakes and the Demler crew were able to get Jim's car repaired and back on the track. With the second weekend of qualifying looming, there was still something terribly amiss with the car. Jim had test driven his old Travelon Trailer Special at 149.5, in a shake down run for his former car owner, but he couldn't get past 147 in the Demler car.

"We got the car straightened out the best we could in a week's time," remarks Danny Oakes, "and the day before qualifying we were running 147. But the car was getting weird and that was as fast as we could go."

With time running out, Jim and Danny made a decision to run just fast enough to safely get in the field and hope they could find the problem with the car before race day. They set a qualifying goal of 146 miles per hour, a speed that would get them in the race but still be below the point where the car got unmanageable. Jim's first lap was 146 miles per hour, right where they wanted to be. His second was quicker just under 147, but the car still looked stable. As Jim began his third lap, Oakes and the crew were about to breathe a sigh of relief—it looked like they were going to make it. Then the yellow #99 got away from Jim, and he crashed in the short chute between turns one and two. Jim again escaped injury, but the car was too badly damaged to repair in the short time remaining.

With only one day of qualifying left, Norm Demler bought a part interest in the #47 Joe Hunt Magneto Special and installed Jim as the driver. The car appeared to be a good choice as Jim quickly had it up to 147.5 miles per hour. Then the engine blew. Demler scrambled to buy a spare from J.C. Agajanian, and the crew thrashed to install it overnight.

Temperature records had been broken throughout Indiana during the previous week, and on Sunday, the final day of qualifying, the air temperature climbed to 100 degrees, and the track temperature hit a scorching 141. Jim took one qualifying lap in the Joe Hunt car, and came back in, disappointed. The cars front end was "pushing" on the heat-slickened track. It didn't want to steer through the turns, but rather nose towards the wall.

The car was readjusted to compensate for the pushing condition, but by the time they were able to get back in the qualifying line there were twelve cars ahead of Jim, and less than an hour left. With no hope of running the Joe Hunt car, Jim headed up the line looking for a car, any car, that was closer to the front and fast enough to get him in the race.

There was no shortage of car owners willing to put the hard driving Hurtubise in their car. Jim chose the Jim Robbins Special, an old but sturdy car, and jumped in. He almost disappeared from sight! The car was originally assigned to Chuck Weyant, who stood a head higher than Jim. He stuffed the oversized cockpit with blocks of wood and foam rubber, and while leaning to one side to see around the cowling, Jim qualified a car he had never driven before at 146.963 miles per hour. Amazingly, that was the sixteenth fastest run of the entire month.

In the race, Jim held the five year old car together for the entire 500 miles, and brought it home in thirteenth place. Finishing the 200 laps for the first time won Jim entry into what was then the still exclusive Champion Hundred Mile an Hour Club, an organization reserved for those drivers who finished the 500 at an average speed of better than 100 miles an hour.

After the 1962 Indianapolis 500, Jim and Danny Oakes again parted company. Pete assumed the mechanical responsibilities on the champ car, as he had on the sprint car. Despite their differences of opinion about proper race car setup, Jim and Danny remained friends and would often join each other in their shared favorite pastime, fishing.

"Jim was one of the greatest," says Oakes, as he speaks with respect and admiration for Jim's talent on the race track. "I tell you, he could blow that A.J. Foyt off like he was standing still. That was when A.J. was really red hot, but he'd nail him. Go right by him. And that really used to tick Foyt off. Herk was the equal of anybody running at that time."

Less optimistic men would have gone home defeated by the events of 1962. Not Jim. Although he had started the month of May as one of the favorites to win the Indianapolis 500 and ended the month just struggling to get in, his confidence remained firm. He was still determined to win at Indianapolis, and he believed that the agreement with Andy Granatelli to drive one of the Novis in 1963 might just be the means to achieve that goal.

Hurtubise Family Collection

Pete Hurtubise

Jim with his fans.

Hurtubise Family collection

Bill Boggs photo -Hurtubise Family collection

The front row at Indy in 1961. Eddie Sachs, Don Branson and Jim Hurtubise.

Hurtubise Family collection

The front row at Indy in 1961. Eddie Sachs, Don Branson and Jim Hurtubise.

HURTUBISE

14

Hurtubise Family collection

Never has a race car captured the imagination of racing fans and competitors alike as did the Novi. They admired it for its vast potential, were awed by the unique, indescribable wail of its powerful, supercharged engine and mystified that it never won the race it was specifically designed for, the Indianapolis 500. It was a machine that was better known than many drivers. Steel and aluminum and iron that took on a life of its own and demanded a very special driver to control it. Many tried, a few come close and two died trying.

The heart of the Novi was its powerful engine. That sophisticated piece of engineering was conceived in the mind of renowned automotive inventor and designer, Ed Winfield, whose many contributions to American racing included the famed Winfield carburetor that he produced with his brother Bud. Designed in 1938, the Novi engine,was known then as the Winfield. It was a 183 cubic inch, supercharged V-8 with four overhead cams and was so technically advanced that many of its concepts were still being utilized forty years later.

It took three years for Ed and Bud to translate that complicated design into metal, but when they did, what a creation it was. At a time when an Indianapolis engine was considered "hot" with two hundred horsepower, the Winfield V-8 generated almost five hundred. By the early 1960's, when the Granatellis finished their refinements to the engine, horsepower numbers as high as eight hundred were seen in dynamometer tests which were twice that of any other racing engine of the day.

The Winfield V-8 first appeared at the Speedway in 1941. Installed in a six year old car sponsored by the Bowes Seal Fast Corporation, the new engine claimed a credible fourth place finish with Ralph Hepburn driving. Reportedly Hepburn drove the Bowes car with a block under the throttle so that in the heat of competition he wouldn't inadvertently unleash the V-8's tremendous power.

With the outbreak of World War II, racing was suspended in America, and development of the Winfield engine halted until after that conflict was resolved. When it was announced that the Indianapolis 500 would resume in 1946 with new owner Tony Hulman at the helm, businessman Lew Welch became involved with the engine, and for the next fifteen years Welch's fascination would bring him little but heartbreak and agony.

Welch hailed from Novi, Michigan, a small town that derived its unusual name from when it was known as toll gate No.VI on the old Grand River Plank Road. When Welch entered his Winfield powered car for the 1946 500, he did so under the name of his business, Novi Equipment Company. The press soon shortened that lengthy handle, and from that point on the popular car carried the colorful moniker, Novi.

Welch commissioned mechanical genius, Leo Goosen, whose resume included both the Miller and Offenhauser engines, to design a new, front wheel drive car to harness the powerful engine and hired California race car builder, Frank Kurtis, to build it. The sleek machine stood just three feet high at the top of the cockpit, and with its low slung, cigar shape, looked fast even standing still.

The crew struggled with the new car all month and it wasn't until the final day that driver Ralph Hepburn was able to qualify, but in those four laps, the legend of the Novi was born.

Cliff Bergere had captured the pole earlier in the month with a speed of just over 126 miles per hour. When Hepburn screamed down the front straight on his first timed lap, blue smoke rolling off his spinning tires, the clocks caught him at an unbelievable 134.288 miles per hour. Nor did he slow down. The next two laps were just as fast, the final even faster, and the Novi rolled into the history book and the hearts of racing fans.

When the race started, Hepburn powered his way into the lead from his nineteenth starting spot in just fifteen minutes. By lap 122 he was out with burned valves. That would be the Novi story for the next twenty years. Incredible speed and great promise but terrible misfortune in the race. Another Novi was built in 1947, but even with double the potential the results remained the same. To its owner and thousands of loving fans, the Novi seemed only to bring a mixed bag of joy and tragedy, with the emphasis on tragedy.

In 1948, the great Ralph Hepburn died in a Novi, when he lost control of the brutish car during a practice run and plowed head on into the unforgiving Speedway concrete wall. In 1949 Duke Nalon captured the pole in his Novi and led easily until lap 23, when the left rear axle snapped, sending the Novi pounding against the wall. Nalon just managed to jump clear as the car burst into flames, spreading a ten foot high, blazing wall of flame across the track.

Nalon recovered from his burns to sit on the pole again in 1951 with teammate Chet Miller third quick in the other Novi. Neither came close to winning. In 1952, qualifying late because of nagging, month long, mechanical problems, Miller set yet another track record with the Novi, then fell out of the race early. In 1953 the temperamental

Novi claimed another driver when Chet Miller died in a practice crash that eerily resembled the 1948 accident that had claimed Ralph Hepburn.

When the Novi missed the 500 field in 1954 and 1955 Welch commissioned Frank Kurtis to build two, lightweight, rear drive Novis for the 1956 race. The new cars were beautiful, but the results were the same. Driver Paul Russo moved from his eighth place starting position to first in ten laps, then blew a tire and crashed on lap 22. In 1957 Russo returned in one Novi, with Tony Bettenhausen as his teammate in the other. Russo was the fastest qualifier, but still a 500 win eluded the luckless Novis, as Russo rolled home fourth and Bettenhausen finished a distant fourteenth.

The Novis missed the 1958, 1959 and 1960 500s, and most believed the Novi story was over. Not Andy Granatelli. In April of 1961 he bought the remains of the once proud Novis for $111,000. Literally picking up the pieces in baskets, he began a restoration project that would consume his energy and finances for the next half a decade.

A month after the purchase, Granatelli arrived at the Speedway with one hastily rebuilt Novi sporting a huge tail fin designed to load the left rear wheel with aerodynamic generated weight. Despite the device the Novi again missed the race. For 1962 the services of Frank Kurtis were once more called on when Granatelli commissioned him to build two new Novis. The cars featured a chassis that dramatically offset the engines to the left for better weight distribution, and the engine was tuned to peak performance with the aid of Jean Marcenac, who had helped the Winfields build the original engine, and had served as the car's chief mechanic for many years. Granatelli was unable to find a suitable driver, however, and the Novis once more failed to make the race.

Then entered Jim Hurtubise. If any man alive was capable of extracting the full potential from the Novi, it was Jim. When the word began to circulate that he would drive the fabled car in 1963, shivers of anticipation ran through Novi lovers everywhere. The bravest and most exciting driver to ever turn a wheel at the Brickyard would be in the Speedway's most exciting car.

Jim made his 1963 appearance in the Novi on Monday, May 6. A huge crowd gathered as he eased the big, red car from the pits, the powerful engine growling deeply, even at low RPM's hinting teasingly of the power that was there to be unleashed. Jim's first lap was 139 miles per hour. The second, 145.5. Then came two laps at over 146, and Granatelli called him in. Andy was ready to call it a day. "That was good enough for a shake down run," he said. But Jim wasn't finished. He was just getting comfortable in the car, and was aching to push it even faster. Andy reluctantly turned him loose, and within seven laps Jim had topped 148.5 mile per hour.

The Novi was off to its best practice start in recent memory, but Granatelli remained cautious. Even in his short tenure as the Novi's owner, he had already experienced the bitter disappointment of his predecessor and had seen his high expectations shattered just as he appeared to be on the verge of success.

"I honestly think he's going too darn quick," remarked Granatelli warily about Jim's early speed. "But, Jim's capable. He knows he has to drive different in this car and he's working on it. He's really going to fly around here. There's no doubt in my mind right now that given normal conditions we will set all the speed records at the track this year."

Jim learned during his 1962 test hop that the heavier, more powerful Novi needed to be handled differently than any other car he had driven. It was certainly capable of blinding speed on the long front and back straights, but almost half the Speedway is made up of four turns connected by two, very short straights. Jim was a master at finding the best groove for a particular car through these four precarious turns and worked diligently to find the best route for the Novi.

The results were predictable. As the first day of qualifying drew near, Jim's speed rose dramatically. 149 miles per hour. Then 150. Then almost 151. Most observers had already conceded the pole to Parnelli Jones, who had run consistently over 150 all month, but few were willing to discount the threat that Jim and the Novi posed for that coveted number one starting spot.

Jim and the Novi was not the only story generating intense fan interest that year. 1963 was a time of upheaval at the Speedway. Encouraged by the impressive, 1961 run of Jack Brabham in the rear engine Cooper, and by Dan Gurney's speeds in Mickey Thompson's rear engine car in 1962, Lotus Formula One team owner and designer, Colin Chapman, joined forces with the Ford Motor Company to build two rear engine, Ford-powered cars for the 1963 race.

This was no backyard garage, hotrodder's effort. World Champion Jim Clark was assigned the driving chores in one of the Lotus Fords, Dan Gurney the other. With the chassis expertise of Chapman, and the vast financial resources of the Ford Motor Company, the Lotus Ford promised to be a serious threat in 1963. American racers were confronted with the very real possibility of not only seeing one of the "funny cars" win the 500 but of having thousands of dollars in racing equipment become obsolete overnight.

Adding to an already potentially explosive atmosphere was a tire controversy. That, too, was instigated by the Lotus/Fords. At Chapman's request, Firestone had agreed to build low profile, 15-inch diameter tires for the Lotuses. Assuming that this smaller rubber would be unsuitable for the heavier, front engine cars, Firestone had not offered them to the rest of the teams, bringing charges of unfairness and partiality.

When Jim Clark cranked off a lap of almost 150 miles per hour on the 15-inch rubber, the controversy reached the boiling point, and car owners and drivers called a meeting with Firestone. They demanded that either Firestone withdraw the smaller tires, or offer them to everyone.

Firestone said they would do neither, and a group of the top drivers that included Jim, A.J. Foyt and Parnelli Jones, stormed from the meeting and went directly to the phones. They called Goodyear and invited them to send their high speed, stock car tires to the Speedway for evaluation. Goodyear, who was already considering entering the Indianapolis fray, jumped at the opportunity. Although later in his career Jim would vehemently berate Goodyear for their negative influence on racing, he was as responsible as anyone for them being at Indianapolis to begin with, and was the first driver to use a set of Goodyear tires on an Indy car.

That occurred just a month prior to the 1963 500 during the season opening champ car race at Trenton, New Jersey. John Laux, who was a Firestone engineer in 1963, tells the story.

"I know A.J. Foyt says that he was responsible for bringing Goodyear to the Speedway," says John, "and he's not lying. A.J. was one of those who was responsible for them being there. But in reality, Herk had as much or more to do with it than anybody. Herk, Smokey Yunick, A.J. and myself were having dinner one evening at a restaurant in downtown Atlanta. We were in Atlanta for the Atlanta 500, where Herk was running one of Petty's Plymouths.

"Smokey and I got to talking to Herk and A.J. about what a crime it was that Firestone was running those skinny little hard tires at the Speedway. A.J. was a little argumentative about it, but Herk just kinda' sat there, listening, not saying a lot. The next day at the race track he asked me about getting him a set of stock car tires to run at the Trenton Championship race."

John Laux's interest in seeing the wider, smaller diameter stock car tires on an Indy car actually went back some two years prior to his conversation with Jim, A.J. and Smokey in Atlanta. He, in fact, had supplied a set of Firestone stock tires to Henry Meyer to use on the Iddlings Special that Bobby Marshman was to drive at Trenton in 1960. Meyer showed up at Trenton with the tires, but USAC would not allow him to use them because they had not been approved for Championship Car use.

After that, Firestone lost interest in the project, so when Jim asked John about obtaining a set of tires from Firestone, John directed him to Goodyear instead. He reasoned that if Goodyear became involved in champ car racing with what he believed was a superior type tire, it would force Firestone to follow suit.

"I contacted Ted Loganiger at Goodyear for Jim," continues John. "and told him what he would need to do to get USAC approval. So Ted set everything up for Jim to run the tires at Trenton. Goodyear sent Fred Gamble over to help out, but Herk was late. Hot laps came, no Hurtubise. Qualifying came, he still wasn't there. By then I was thinking, 'Why did I bother with him for? I've stuck my neck out, and he's not even going to show up!'"

Laux's disgust was soon mollified, however, for when the last car qualified, track officials opened the back gate, and Jim came flying through with the Sterling Plumbing dirt car in tow. At the last moment he had decided to switch the Offy engine for the Chevy, and the task had taken him longer than expected. Because of his late arrival, USAC would not allow him any practice laps. He was told he had one warm lap and one qualifying lap to make the race. That was all Jim needed. Without a lap of practice to set up the car or test the tires he squeezed into the field in thirteenth place.

John Laux recalls that Jim had installed the engine in such a rush that he was still trying to plug oil leaks with shop rags and feminine hygiene napkins as the pre-race ceremonies were taking place. At the drop of the green flag, Jim began a steady push for the front and though not as fast as some of the other cars down the straights, the wider, softer, Goodyear tires allowed him to pass at will, high or low, through the corners. At the end of the hundred mile run Jim was in third place, with only A.J. and Parnelli ahead of him.

"Jim's run at Trenton really impressed a lot of people," states John Laux, "and it gave Goodyear a lot of valuable information. So when the car owners and drivers started making phone calls to Goodyear after the meeting with Firestone, Goodyear was ready and sent several sets of tires similar to what Jim had used at Trenton."

A few days after Goodyear's arrival at the Speedway, Firestone decided that the smaller tires were safe for the heavier roadsters after all. The argument about whether they were faster or had better wear qualities than the standard 18-inch tires waged back and forth for days. Lloyd Ruby and Don Branson were among the first to test the new rubber, and they swore they could see no difference in speed. Eddie Sachs ran a number of endurance tests, and he saw no difference in tire wear between the two sizes. Then Parnelli ran almost 153 miles per hour on them, and the discussion was over. Most teams jumped to the 15-inch tires, and Firestone was forced to work around the clock to supply enough. Ted Halibrand, who manufactured the magnesium wheels for the Indy cars at that time did the same, while wringing his hands in despair at the fourteen thousand dollars worth of 18-inch wheels that he was stuck with.

A.J continued to test Goodyears for a few more days, then he too switched to the 15-inch Firestones. Jim also briefly tested the Goodyears, as well as the smaller Firestones, but chose to stay with the larger Firestone tires on the heavy Novi. When asked about the tire controversy, Jim cracked, "Tires? Who's worried about tires? Why, I'll bet a hundred dollars right now that I'll be on the pole in the Novi no matter what tire I use!"

The situation with tires, the excitement about the new Lola Fords, and the fan's expectations of what Jim might do with the Novi, produced a record turnout for the first day of qualifying. Over 200,000 people tried to jam into the Speedway in the early hours of Saturday morning, creating a traffic jam that stretched some five miles up 16th Street. Mild temperatures and sunny skies made the weather perfect for watching race cars, but high winds made driving them practically impossible. Eighteen drivers braved the forty mile per hour gusts to attempt qualifying runs, but only seven were successful.

Dan Gurney crashed in the high winds during the morning practice session and destroyed his new Lotus Ford. His teammate, Jim Clark, was one of the select seven to make the field as was Parnelli Jones. Parnelli was personally disappointed with his run, but broke his own one and four lap track records from the year before with speeds of 151.847 miles per hour, and 151.153 respectively.

Then the crowd sat and waited. Four hours passed at one stretch without a car venturing onto the windy, dusty Speedway, and still they waited. They knew Jim and the Novi were capable of bumping Parnelli off the pole and no one in that huge crowd wanted to miss it.

When Jim pulled the bright red Hotel Tropicana Special onto the track for his first attempt the fan's expectations rose to a fever pitch, but they and Jim were disappointed. After three laps at 147.5 mile per hour, he pulled off the track.

The crew made some crucial adjustments, and then waited with the crowd, hoping for the winds to die down. Finally, at day's end, a tremendous roar went up from the patient spectators when the big Novi V-8 again screamed to life. This was it. The day was almost gone, and there would be time for only one more run.

Tension built, and an electric excitement pulsated through the crowd as Jim pulled onto the track and slowly warmed up the Novi. Then, he was on it! Flying down the front stretch he blurred across the start/finish line, briefly hitting 200 miles per hour before he had to back off for turn one. The first lap was 151.261 miles per hour, fast enough to snatch the pole from Parnelli. The second lap was slightly slower, 150.779, but close. The crowd stood and collectively held its breath—two more strong laps like the first and the pole could still be Jim's. But, even "Hercules" couldn't hold the big car in the gusty wind. The third lap was only 150.401, and realizing that the pole was now out of his grasp, Jim wisely backed off on the last lap to a cautious 148.613.

Even with a drop in speed on the last lap, Jim's average was less than a mile an hour slower than Parnelli's, and, as he entered the pits, the powerful Novi engine now silent, the crowd erupted in a bedlam of cheers unequaled in the long history of Speedway qualifying. Never had the second fast qualifier received such an ovation. Few pole winners had experienced such a reception. The Novi was back. A hero now even more heroic.

The scene in the pits was just as tumultuous. Drivers, mechanics, and officials formed a gauntlet of greeters as Jim rolled down the pit lane. People were jumping up and down. Clenched fists shook in the air. The Granatelli's hugged and danced in a display of emotion so intense, you would have thought they had just won the 500. And, alone on the pit wall, wiping tears from his eyes, sat Jean Marcenac who had shared firsthand in the triumphs and tragedy of the Novi from its very inception.

Andy Granatelli spotted Jean on the pit wall and, in a heartfelt magnanimous gesture, brought him forward to share in the outpouring of well wishes. Then, to the wild cheers of the crowd, the Granatelli's hoisted Jean to their shoulders and victoriously carried him the length of the pits.

Later, a satisfied, but shaken Jim confided just how difficult and dangerous the run in the strong winds had been, "I'll never do that again," said Jim, shaking his head in disbelief at his own foolhardiness. "That was a scary one."

Before qualifying ended that year two more Novis joined Jim's in the starting field—rookie Bobby Unser, in the twin to Jim's front row car and another rookie, Art Malone, in the revamped 1956 car. A win for the Novi seemed to be the only fitting conclusion to this great comeback story and all agreed that if the car held together, Jim could very well pull it off.

The hoopla that surrounded Jim after he qualified the Novi in the middle of the front row equaled in intensity the attention he received after his astounding 1960 qualifying run, but Jim coolly took it with his typical, laid back manner. So laid back he missed the traditional front row starter's photo session.

"Andy called me at my garage one morning," recalls Pete, who was working with the Konstant Hot car and Chuck Rodee that year. "Andy was all excited and yelling, 'Pete! Pete, you've got to get over here right away. I need you quick!"

"Well I dropped what I was doing and rushed over to the Granatelli garage. Andy told me that the press was all ready for the front row pictures, but Jim hadn't shown up. He wanted me to pose in the car in Jim's place. I did, but I felt like a fool sitting there with Parnelli on one side, and Don Branson on the other, and the photographers yelling, 'Look this way. Now look over here.'

"While I was sitting in the car, enduring all that," laughs Pete, "I looked out into the crowd, and there was Jim! He was standing there laughing at me. I don't know if he just forgot about it, or intentionally missed it, or was trying to have some fun with Andy, but if you look closely at the photo, you'll see my ugly mug, looking real sheepish."

In the days leading up to the race, the hot topic of conversation was who would lead the first lap, Parnelli or Jim? Even the other drivers got caught up in it. "It's going to be a helluva start come race day," predicted Eddie Sachs. "And I think that Hurtubise is going to lead the first lap. He's an artist going through that first turn. High or low he can get through it in a hurry."

Publicly neither Jim nor Parnelli made any open predictions; they stuck with the routine, "...you can't win this thing on the first lap," statements. Privately, however, there was an intense rivalry between the two friends. Both were intensely competitive. Leading the first lap at Indianapolis is the world's fastest, and most dangerous, display of masochism, and neither wanted to be bested by the other. Pete insists that Jim and Parnelli had a five dollar bet on the outcome, although that was never openly admitted for fear of their car owner's reaction to the idea that their expensive equipment was being risked on such a wager.

At the driver's meeting, both Jim and Andy begged that the pace car not bring the field to the line too slowly. Slow speeds are extremely hard on finely tuned, high RPM racing engines, and this was especially true with the Novis, which were prone to load up, or have more fuel pumped into the engine than could be burned. This condition could cause the engine to misfire, quit, or, in extreme situations, destroy itself. However, despite Jim and Andy's pleading for a fast pace lap it was way too slow.

When the green flag dropped Jim hit the throttle, but nothing happened. Parnelli shot ahead of him, and while helpless to do anything about it, five other cars passed him as the field roared into the first turn. Then, suddenly, the engine cleared itself, and like a rocket slowly gaining momentum, Jim caught and repassed four cars in the short chute between the first and second turn, and then thundered past second place Rodger Ward coming out of turn two.

Calling on all the 650 horsepower at his command, Jim jammed his foot to the floor and screamed down the long backstretch after Parnelli. He caught him, pulled alongside briefly, and then dropped in behind him as they drifted through turns three and four.

Jim knew what he was going to do. Deliberately laying back until they safely exited turn four, Jim jumped back on the gas. Then, with announcer Tom Carnegie building the excitement over the PA, "It's Jones and Hurtubise fighting it out for the lead! Jones and Hurtubise fighting it out for the lead," Jim flew by Parnelli and led him by three car lengths as they crossed the start/finish line.

After the race Jim said of those first lap heroics, "All the fans expected me to lead that first lap. I just couldn't let 'em down!"

Satisfied with the intimidating demonstration of his Novi's raw power, Jim eased off on the second lap and Parnelli went back in front. Then a sudden chain of events left Jim with the only Novi in the race.

Art Malone had slipped his clutch so much on the slow pace lap that it was fried. After a brief stop in the pits, Malone labored on for several hopeless laps before retiring on lap 23. On the second lap Bobby Unser in the third Novi, jumped on the brakes to avoid another car and crashed in the short chute between turns one and two.

With the Novi hopes pinned solely on him, Jim was content to run at a measured pace, maintaining second behind Parnelli for twenty five laps. He dropped as far back as fourth by lap forty, and then pitted on lap forty nine.

After the usual reshuffling of positions following a flurry of pit stops, Jim was in seventh place at the end of 80 laps, and third behind only Parnelli and Jim Clark at the halfway point. Things could not have looked better for Jim and the Novi. The car was responding smoothly to his commands, and the engine wasn't missing a beat. Jim knew that his supercharged engine could easily out power the Ford in Clark's Lotus, and he had already demonstrated his ability to pass Parnelli. Then he pitted on lap 101.

Jim roared off the track for his second routine stop, shot down the pit lane, and slammed to a perfect stop at his pit. The crew swarmed over the car, swiftly adding fuel and changing tires.

Just as Jim was ready to pull away, he was stopped by a USAC official. Precious seconds slipped by before he was finally waved off. Then on the next circuit Jim was shown the black flag and called back into the pits. The car was leaking oil, insisted the officials. Impossible, shouted Granatelli. But to no avail. Jim was out of the race.

What had happened, as Andy futilely tried to explain to the officials at the time, was that when Jim hit the brakes to stop at his pit, oil had surged forward in the engine and sloshed out of the front mounted breather cap, leaving a pool of oil on the ground. There was no oil leak and there was nothing wrong with the engine, as Andy dramatically demonstrated after the race.

With a garage full of media people, Granatelli fired the engine, and in a fit of frustration, ran it with the throttle wide open for five minutes. The Novi's plaintive wail reverberated through the garage area, but did not miss a lick, or throw a drop of oil.

Ironically, in a race that Jim was eliminated from for leaking oil, Parnelli won despite the fact that his car had leaked oil for most of the race. His oil tank had split and gradually spread half its load, about three gallons, around the track. As he was on the verge of being black flagged, the oil level dropped below the split, and Parnelli went on to win.

That wasn't the end of the controversy. With Jim Clark in the Lotus/Ford a close second, charges of American favoritism flew about for days after the race. McCluskey and Sachs added fuel to the fire when they both claimed their late race spins were caused by the oil Parnelli's car had dropped on the track. Sachs was so adamant with his accusations that he confronted Parnelli on their way to the Victory Dinner. Jones decked him! To Sachs' credit, he took it in stride and even posed for photographers flat on his back, holding a tiny white flag.

Three exceptionally talented race car drivers had erupted onto the racing scene in the early sixties, Jim Hurtubise, A.J. Foyt and Parnelli Jones. Two of them had already won the Indianapolis 500. At that time, many believed Jim was cheated out of his chance to win the 1963 500 when the officials made a bad call and disqualified the Novi.

If Jim believed that, he never affirmed it, nor expressed any bitterness because of it. It did, however, make him more determined than ever to win the 500. And the dream of doing it with a car of his own design and construction took a step closer to reality in 1964.

Reel Racing Photos

The famous front row photo with Pete Hurtubise in the Novi. Parnelli Jones is on the pole and Don Branson is on the outside.

IMS photo - HFC

This car got it's name from a song title. "The Purple People Eater" came within sixteen one-hundredths of a second of being the first car to run 150 MPH at the Indianapolis Motor Speedway with "Rookie" Jim Hurtubise driving.

Chrysler photo

Jim Hurtubise and Andy Granatelli.

HURTUBISE

15

Hurtubise Family collection

Jim's long time dream of building his own car for Indianapolis finally came to fruition in 1964 with the backing of three Indianapolis businessmen, George Deebs, Bob Voight and Dick Sommers. Under the name DVS Racing they gave Jim the financing and a free hand to create the type of car he believed necessary to win at the Speedway.

"We signed Herk early," remarked Deebs, "because we liked his desire, and his ability to work hard. We decided he needed the chance to build his own car, just the way he always wanted it, and in our estimation, he is one of the half dozen real hot dogs out there today."

By 1964 the winds of change were blowing fiercely through the Indianapolis Motor Speedway. Goodyear, after their tentative initial venture to the Speedway in 1963, launched a concerted push to see their tire in Victory Lane at Indianapolis. Jim's friend, John Laux, had left Firestone to head Goodyear's racing division, and signed Jim as one of the first Goodyear test drivers, but despite a brace of testing and a year of preparation, not one team chose Goodyear tires for the 1964 500. Responding to the Goodyear threat, Firestone had developed an excellent Speedway tire of their own, and held off the Goodyear challenge for one more year.

The Lotus Ford performance during the 1963 race had solidified the rear engine revolution at the Indianapolis Motor Speedway. Of the sixty one cars entered for the 1964 race, twenty four were rear engine machines. Yet, Jim opted to stay with a front engine design for his new car, a decision that was not as short sighted then, as it might now appear to have been.

The rear engine Lotus Fords were potent race cars, but with the exception of a year old Lotus sold to Lindsey Hopkins, they were not available to American competitors. Several domestic constructors built rear engine cars for 1964, but their lack of knowledge of the technology was reflected in the performance of the cars they turned out.

Both Parnelli Jones and A.J. Foyt had American built rear engine cars at their disposal in 1964. Parnelli, who had never as much as skidded in three years at the Speedway, narrowly avoided disaster in his car when the right front suspension failed while practicing at over 152 miles per hour. He parked the fragile machine then and there in favor of his old, dependable roadster. Foyt eventually did the same with his after several narrow escapes of his own. As these events, and others, transpired with the rear engine cars during the month of May, Jim's choice of car design proved to have been a wise one.

Although Jim stuck with a traditional front engine design, his new car did not lack sophistication. It incorporated many of Jim's original ideas, and utilized concepts that were on the leading edge of technology for that day.

While the chassis was of standard construction with a tubular frame and solid front and rear axles, the suspension was not. In its final form the car used coil springs on both the front and rear. While this was not unheard of on a front engine Indianapolis car, it was more typical of rear engine car construction. Before Jim settled on the coil springs, he experimented with a device that incorporated the action of a spring and a shock absorber into one compact unit.

The unit was developed by Paul Taylor, a New York based entrepreneur and industrialist who built hydraulically activated shock absorbing units used for isolating vibrations on rocket launch pads and on huge naval guns. Taylor transferred this technology to automotive size pieces, that he built exclusively for Jim. Each one was labeled, "Liquid Spring Suspension Built for Jim Hurtubise."

The advantages were lighter weight, because the single piece units used fewer parts and required less mounting hardware than the traditional torsion bar and shock absorber setup used on other front engine cars. They also required less maintenance, and the suspension adjustments would be easier and more precise.

"Taylor's idea was great," says Pete, "and Jim was very interested in it. We did a lot of work with it, and we tested it early in the year, but we just ran out of time trying to develop it."

The engine was another area where Jim's creative ability was evident. While he used a standard, four-cylinder Offenhauser, he modified it to cure a constant mechanical headache of the Offy engine, magneto failure. To isolate the magneto from heat and vibration, Jim moved it from its mounting point on the front of the engine to inside the cockpit.

"Jim worked very closely with Meyer and Drake to design a system that would allow us to move the magneto away from the engine," recalls Pete of Jim's efforts in this area. "They had to modify the gear tower so Jim could run a driveshaft from the magneto and through a pilot bearing into the cockpit. He also worked with Joe Hunt, who built all the magnetos for the Offy, because the rotation of the mag had to be reversed after Jim remounted it. It wasn't a very simple setup at all, but Jim was a very inventive person, with the fabricating talent to make his ideas work."

There were no minimum weight restrictions on Indianapolis cars in 1964, and since reducing weight on a race car presents many advantages; better acceleration, more top speed, better handling and tire wear. Jim worked incessantly to reduce the weight of his car to the bare minimum.

"Jim didn't use a single piece that wasn't absolutely essential for the car," explains Pete. "And, anything that he could make out of aluminum or magnesium rather than steel he did. When the car was finished it was one of the lightest at the Speedway that year."

Jim and Pete built their very sophisticated Indianapolis race car not in a modern shop, but in an old barn on Jim's property in North Tonawanda. Jim began by laying out the dimensions of the frame with soapstone on the barn floor and warned everyone who visited, "Don't step on my race car!"

"When I look at photographs of some of today's race car shops," laughs Pete, "it's so comical when I think about us building the '64 car in Jim's barn. There we were building a car for Indianapolis, the most famous race in the world, and all the time we were pushing Jim's pony out of the way and stepping over horse turds!"

Despite the surroundings he worked in, or the amount of money he had to spend on a race car, Jim always demanded that it look good. The 1964 car was no exception. Paul Cozard, a friend of Jim's from North Tonawanda, built the bodywork with its starkly functional yet sleek lines. Like the sprint car and the champ car, when the Indianapolis car was finished, Jim wanted it painted the eye catching DayGlo red that he preferred. This task fell to Pete.

"Jim first discovered that color in California," explains Pete, "and at the time it was used on the wing tips of jet fighters to make them easily visible. The paint was hard to find and very difficult to put on. There was one particular body shop in California that I got it from. I had to paint the car with a white base first, then I sprayed five coats of the red on top of that. It was all very precise and had to be hand-rubbed between each coat. Then to get a gloss, I had to put on a clear coat, and that had to be just right as well."

In addition to the eye catching paint job, all the visible metal parts, including the side mounted oil tank, were plated in bright chrome, and gold leaf was used for all the lettering and numbers. So striking was the finished car that "*Hot Rod Magazine*" chose it as the centerfold of their pre-Indianapolis issue.

When the track officially opened for practice on May 1st, Jim had already logged many miles with his new car running tire tests for Goodyear. His plan was to slowly bring the car up to speed and be ready to run for the Pole on the first day of qualifying. Those well laid plans, however, nearly ended in disaster on the fifth day of practice when Jim lost control coming off the fourth turn. The car slid down the front stretch, bounced along the inside wall, then ricocheted across the track and slammed into the outside wall near the start/finish line.

Jim was uninjured but stunned in the crash. Helped from the car he sat in the grass along the edge of the track, his head slumped dejectedly, while Pete and Parnelli tried to console him. The beautiful new car that he had pinned his hopes and dreams on sat mangled and steaming against the wall. It was so severely damaged that it would take a week of toil to repair it. The cause of the crash was a mystery. Jim thought he might have lost control in a gust of wind, but most likely the accident was attributable to a handling problem that Jim had already discovered in the car. The front end wanted to push. That is, instead of steering around a corner, the nose of the car wanted to slide, or "push" towards the wall.

Looking back, Pete now believes that the nose-mounted air scoop was the culprit. Its shape caused the nose of the car to lift at high speed, taking weight off the front wheels. There was little known about aerodynamics and its effects on a race car in 1964, so Jim attempted to cure the pushing condition by adding weight to the right side of the car with a fifteen-gallon, reserve fuel tank he mounted in the right corner of the engine compartment.

The additional weight didn't completely cure the handling problem, but it seemed to help. On the first practice day back on the track after the crash Jim had the car above 151 miles per hour. After the quick run Jim was asked about his feelings as he passed the spot where he had previously crashed. His answer reflected the importance of a tough mental attitude in racing.

"You don't really have time to think about it," Jim said. "especially there, because you're flat footed at that point, and going as fast as you can. But, a race car usually feels about the same after any crash. The driver just has to work up his nerve again."

With the important first day of qualifying quickly approaching, Jim pushed his speed steadily upward, topping 154 miles per hour. That was by far the fastest that he had ever driven at the Speedway. Yet it wasn't Jim, or any of the drivers of the front engine cars, that were setting the speed standards. The Lotus Fords were. Jim Clark and Dan Gurney were very fast, running practice laps as high as 157 miles per hour. Bobby Marshman, in the year old Lotus reworked by Jack Beckley, was even faster. Every day he pushed the lap speeds upward, until in the cool air of the morning practice session on the first day of qualifying, Bobby recorded the first 160 miles per hour lap ever turned at Indianapolis.

When the battle for the Pole ended that day, however, it wasn't Bobby, but the exceptionally talented, personable Scotsman, Jim Clark, who was the fast man. Clark's four lap average of 158.828 broke Parnelli Jones' one year old record by seven miles per hour. Marshman was second quick at 157.867. As a sign that the rear engine revolution was complete, Rodger Ward qualified on the outside of the front row at just over 156 miles per hour in his A.J. Watson built rear engine car. It was the first rear engine front row in Indianapolis history.

Parnelli Jones and A.J. Foyt were the quickest of the conventional front engine roadsters, qualifying in first and second spots of row two respectively. Jim, still fighting a pushing condition, averaged 152.542 for his four laps, good for only for the middle spot of the fourth row, but fourth fastest of the front engine contingent.

Lining up directly behind Jim in the middle of row five was handsome, young rookie Dave McDonald. Dave was driving one of Mickey Thompson's radical, envelop bodied, Ford-powered creations, and his presence in the field on race day would prove tragically significant. McDonald, who cut his competitive teeth racing big bore Corvettes on Sports Car Club of America road courses, had endured handling difficulties with his car all month, and was overjoyed just to be in the race.

Just two days before, both MacDonald and Thompson spoke candidly of the difficulties they were experiencing. "The car doesn't feel right yet," stated MacDonald. "the front end wants to lift, and I just can't seem to handle it coming out of the turns."

With words that now seem eerily prophetic after the deadly drama that transpired on race day, Thompson explained why. "The car was designed for small, twelve inch diameter tires, but they were banned. And, that's got my suspension system messed up. The roll centers aren't in the right place, the mounting points aren't right. Anything I do to help it will be a compromise, and I'll never get it right.

"But we're making some aerodynamic changes in the car,"

Thompson continued, explaining what he was doing to correct the problem. "I'm trying to control my car with a certain amount of lift. It's still lifting too much, but I'm trying gradually to decrease it."

Jim's teammate, Eddie Sachs, crashed his rear engine, Halibrand Shrike during the Saturday morning practice session and wasn't able to qualify until the next day. In what proved to be a fatal twist of fate, Eddie was faster than several of the first day qualifiers, but because of the Speedway's unique qualifying procedure was forced to start behind them, and directly behind McDonald and his troublesome car.

To no one's surprise, Jim Clark grabbed the lead as the thirty three car field flashed under the green flag on Memorial Day, 1964. As they funneled into single file formation in turn one, Jim pulled to the outside, drove around five cars going through the corner, and was already challenging Walt Hansgen for sixth as they raced down the backstretch.

Clark was still leading at the end of the first lap but was being pressed hard by Bobby Marshman. As the front runners began their second lap, a group of about thirteen cars in the middle of the pack were jockeying for position through turn four when, suddenly, all hell broke loose.

For no apparent reason, McDonald lost control of his bright red car as the pack exited the turn. The car snapped into a half spin and slashed towards the low, concrete retaining wall on the inside of the track. On impact the car exploded into a fireball, as eighty gallons of volatile gasoline ignited.

Spewing burning fuel, MacDonald's car pinwheeled back towards the center of the track, directly in the path of the oncoming, high speed traffic. Encountering a thirty foot high wall of fire and oily black smoke from the burning fiberglass and rubber of McDonald's car, the other drivers swerved, spun and crashed trying to find a way through. Eddie Sachs could not and slammed into the flaming wreckage.

Seeing the entire southwest end of the track enveloped in broiling smoke and flame, starter Pat Vidan waved the red flag and for the first time in Speedway history, the 500 was stopped for an accident.

The accident had not been visible to everyone in the giant Speedway crowd, but few could miss seeing the dark, ominous, mushroom cloud that erupted above it. They knew anyone trapped in its eye could not have survived.

The exuberant, irrepressible Eddie Sachs had died instantly in the fiery crash. A quiet descended over the Speedway, as a half million people fell silent. The tinny babbling of transistor radios, and the rustle of flags flapping in the soft May breeze were the only sounds heard.

Often the emotional Sachs had told of how the tradition laden ceremonies leading up to the command, "Gentlemen Start Your Engines" would leave him so misty eyed that he couldn't wear his goggles for several laps. They would fill with tears had he dared. Now the tears being shed were for Eddie.

Miraculously, MacDonald survived the crash and was air lifted to Methodist Hospital in downtown Indianapolis. Dave's father and seven year old son had seen the crash in gruesome detail while watching the race on closed circuit TV in Los Angeles. They rushed from the theater to the airport, trying desperately to reach Indianapolis, but Dave died before they could arrive, his young wife at his side.

Johnny Rutherford started alongside McDonald that fateful day, but pushed his way through the burning wreckage and survived to win three Indianapolis 500's. Years later Johnny could still vividly recall the horror of that crash.

"MacDonald was loose and practically out of control going into turns one and three," Johnny said, "so, I decided to let him go. Coming off four on the second lap, there was still a lot of dirt and dust on the track, but up ahead I could see a car get sideways and smash into the inside wall."

"Then it was like you pulled a black and orange curtain across the track. I knew Sachs was an old pro and could get through the wall of flame if anyone could, so I decided to try and follow him. My most vivid recollection is Eddie's DayGlo orange helmet darting side to side searching for a hole in the smoke screen. I was on the brakes so hard my car started chattering as we plowed into MacDonald. If I hadn't been sitting upright in a big front engine roadster, I surely would have burned with Eddie and Dave."

"Somehow I went over the top of both cars. I managed to get the car out of gear, just as Bobby Unser's Novi slammed me into the outside wall so hard it ripped my uniform seams and broke my seat. Somehow I found low gear and drove away."

"Bob Veith pulled alongside me, wildly gesturing for me to pull into the infield when he saw smoke coming off my car. Entering turn one, MacDonald's fuel injector horns broke lose from my rear axle where they had become wedged. I could see my cockpit carpet flicker with sparks. My neck had second degree burns."

"Unser," continues Johnny, "had split my fuel tank or I could have continued racing. Back in the garage, the crew lifted the roadster's hood to find an enormous amount of debris. My chief mechanic discovered a lemon strung on a long shoe lace. Sachs always wore a lemon around his neck to quench his thirst."

In his biography Parnelli Jones recalls that chilling second lap crash and his fears for Jim, "When I saw that black smoke on the second lap I got sick. It was one of the most horrible sights you can imagine. I thought maybe it was Herk, because he was in a red car. But, then Jim pulled alongside me, and climbed out of his car grinning that grin of his."

"I got out of the car and waited. Jeez, it takes a lot out of you. You wonder, is it worth this? Then somebody came up and said it was Sachs and MacDonald. I asked if they had a chance. 'No way,' the guy said. I was all for parking and going home. But, I knew I'd keep racing."

As did the twenty six other drivers that came through the accident unscathed. When the race was restarted, every one of them were in their cars. An hour and forty five minutes after the crash the field sped single file through turn four for the restart. Only wispy clouds of dust from the oil absorbent compound used to clean up the mess were there to remind them of their two fallen comrades. The race was on!

Clark and Marshman resumed their pre-accident duel, and on lap 7 Marshman passed Clark for the lead. Seemingly venting his frustrations at being beaten for the Pole by Clark, Marshman continued to dramatically extend his lead, turning laps almost as fast as he had qualified. Marshman's average speed for the first thirty laps was 154.888 miles per hour, breaking Jim's record for that distance that had stood since 1961.

Marshman was soon to pay for his record speeds, however. Dipping low, all the way below the white line going through turn one, his low slung Lotus drug across a protrusion on the track and fractured the oil plug. In a few more laps Bobby rolled to a stop, the life blood drained from his Ford engine. He climbed wearily from the car, then flashed a half smile and waved dejectedly as the crowd cheered their encouragement. "You'll get 'em next year, Bobby," someone shouted.

There would be no next year for Bobby Marshman. Testing his Lotus at Phoenix that fall, Bobby crashed and died from the horrible burns he suffered.

With Marshman out, Clark inherited the lead, but that too was short lived. Within eight laps, the soft Dunlop tires that had propelled him to record qualifying speeds failed. The tread separated from Clark's left rear tire, and the thrashing rubber tore the suspension from its mounts. At almost the same time, Clark's teammate, Dan Gurney, had pitted with fuel select switch problems, and although he returned to the race, he dropped from contention.

Suddenly the three, supposedly unbeatable, Lotus/Fords were out. Dueling for the lead were the two antique roadsters of A.J. Foyt and Parnelli Jones, and in his lighter, updated version of the front engine roadster, Jim was methodically working his way up through the field to join them.

Because Firestone had developed a tire that was not only incredibly fast, but extremely durable, Jim had started the race with his fuel tanks brimming full, planning to pit only once for fuel at the mid-point of the race.

Jim passed car after car, his car becoming lighter and faster as he burned away his heavy load of fuel. By lap 50, he was fourth behind Parnelli, Foyt and Ward. Then on lap 55, Parnelli made his first scheduled pit stop, and Jim moved to third. What was supposed to be a routine stop turned disastrous, and Parnelli nearly suffered the same fate as Sachs and McDonald.

When Parnelli's crew completed refueling the car and slammed the filler cap shut, it evidently created a spark that ignited some spilled fuel. Parnelli accelerated away unaware that the tail of his car was already engulfed in nearly invisible, methanol fueled flames. In a few feet he became acutely aware of the fire himself, as he felt the flames licking at his back. Jerking his safety harness lose, Parnelli bailed out of the still moving car, and rolled on the ground to extinguish his burning uniform. He was rushed to Methodist hospital with burns to his arm and shoulder but was released that evening.

Continuing to run in third, Jim made his only scheduled pit stop on lap 100, and returned to the race without losing a position. Foyt, who was leading, and Ward, who was in second, had pitted earlier, and both were due for at least one more stop. If Jim couldn't overtake them on the track, he should be in the perfect position to take the lead when they pitted.

However, unknown to anyone except Jim and his crew, he was nursing an engine that was leaking oil. Pete explains what had happened. "Before the race Jim decided to use an experimental Offenhauser engine that had thinner bearing webs and some other modifications to the lower end that made it lighter, and supposedly produced more power. I was dead set against it and argued with Jim to use the standard Offy, knowing it would be more reliable. But, Jim was seeking every advantage he could find and insisted on using the new Offy. Then in the race it started coming apart and seeping oil. By the time he pitted, the engine had slung so much oil around the engine compartment that it was even seeping around the dzus fasteners that held the bodywork on."

The engine stayed together until lap 141, when it ran out of oil and disintegrated. Jim, normally able to deal with the disappointment of falling out of a race as easily as he accepted a win, was visibly dejected. He stayed in the cockpit, staring straight ahead, not smiling, as the crew pushed his oil covered car back to the garage. His best shot ever of winning the 500 had disintegrated with the engine.

A.J. Foyt, who went on to win the race, pitted just as Jim's engine failed. Ward, who finished second, was forced to pit twice more after Jim exited. Those stops could have put Jim into the lead, and in his fuel lightened car, he might have out raced Foyt and Ward at the end.

By the next day, Jim was able to put it all behind him and was his normal joking self at the controls of his plane as he, Jane and Prince flew back to New York. Although he had fallen out of the race early, the car he designed and built himself had displayed excellent potential. And, unlike two of his racing friends, Jim had survived to race and to enjoy the life that he had carved for himself at the top of his profession.

Hurtubise Family Collection

Jim in the car he disigned to beat the funny cars about to pass Jack Brabham during the 1964 Indianapolis 500.

Hurtubise Family Collection

Don Branson leads Herk and Jim Clark in 1964.

HURTUBISE

16

Hurtubise Family Collection

Although Jim Hurtubise had yet to win the Indianapolis 500, he was considered one of the best half dozen drivers in the country and in 1964 was at the zenith of his racing career. Fellow drivers respected his talent. Car owners sought him out. The press pursued his opinion. Fans, fueled by his magnetic charisma, adored him.

Nor was his popularity confined only to the midwest where most of his racing took place. The stature of the Indianapolis 500 is such that Jim's imagination capturing accomplishments there had propelled him to national, even international fame. Jim always purported to care little about such things, but after his death, Jim's family opened a trunk that held mementos from his racing career, and in it were fan letters not only from the United States, but from as far away as Switzerland, England, Germany, South Africa and Japan.

"It was amazing how the fans responded to Jim," recalls Don Shepherd, "It was like he was someone they knew personally. He could be walking through the pits and they'd yell, 'Hey, Herk! How ya' doing? How about a beer?' Jim would wave and yell back something like, 'I'm doing great! I'll have that beer later."

Like Don, Pete has similar memories of his brother's popularity and recalls one incident in particular.

"I was towing the race car from California with the station wagon at the beginning of the season," relates Pete, "and somewhere in the middle of Arizona, the rear axle broke. It pulled completely out of the rear end housing of the tow car and even tore up the tire. Luckily I was near a little town and limped to this small garage. I just knew I was going to be stuck there and not be able to make the first race. This little town was out in the middle of nowhere, and I didn't know how long it might take them to just get the parts."

"When the guys running the garage saw Jim's name on the race car, they got all excited and started asking me all types of questions about the car and Jim. It turned out that they were huge fans of Jim's, and they jumped right on the broken axle. They even pulled the other customer's car out of the shop so they could go right to work on mine. They pushed the axle back in place and welded the rear end housing, which turned out to be quite a job, but they got it done in a hurry and only charged me for the cost of the tire."

"People just loved Jim," continues Pete, "and he always took time for his fans. We were always the last ones to leave the pits after a race, because Jim would stay for hours talking to the fans and signing autographs for them. He never forgot how important the fans were to him and to racing."

Despite his lofty, celebrity status Jim remained the same down-to-earth, fun-loving, free-spirited person he had always been. He enjoyed people and being around them. When he and Parnelli began their assault on the USAC tracks of the midwest, Jim, Jane and their two daughters shared a tiny house on the westside of Indianapolis with Parnelli and Grayce. It was crowded, hot, and full of inconveniences, like the time Parnelli and Grayce awoke one morning to find their basement bedroom had flooded overnight. "I guess it stormed while we were sleeping, but it was the first time I ever swung out of bed and into a swimming pool!" laughs Grayce.

Jim could overlook frustrations like flooded basements, waiting for a turn in the bathroom, and having to cook army sized meals, because to him the companionship was more important than the problems. That attitude kept everyone in good spirits. "Jim was just so much fun," emphasizes Grayce, "that no matter what, no matter how bad things got, he could always make you laugh."

As Jim's racing world expanded to include USAC and Indianapolis, his circle of racing friends expanded with it. To Jim, socializing was the essence of life itself, and the place he most liked to entertain his numerous friends was at his father's island in Georgian Bay, on Lake Huron.

The racing fraternity had an open invitation to spend time there, and many took advantage of the offer to escape from the pressures of racing and the hot, steamy midwest summer, to the cool, peaceful Ontario, Canada wilderness.

On any given weekend, the island bustled with activity, as some of the best known names in racing vacationed there. John and Ginger Laux visited, as did Bobby and Janet Marshman, Jud Phillips, the Bruce Jacobis, Parnelli and Grayce Jones, Roger and Evelyn McCluskey, Danny Oakes, A.J. Shepherd and Don Shepherd and their wives. Louis Senter, the custom automotive wheel manufacturer was a regular, as were Elmer and Mari George, the parents of the current president of the Indianapolis Motor Speedway, Tony George.

A person's status mattered little to Jim. He was as comfortable with the corporate president as he was with the guy that busted tires at the racetrack, so it was not at all unusual to see sign painters, mechanics, and golfers rubbing elbows on the island with the better known racing personalities.

Getting to the Canadian retreat entailed first a flight to Parry Sound, then an hour boat ride to the island. Jane describes the scene once they arrived, "Jim's dad actually had two islands. On one he had a big two story house with enough room for everyone to stay. It had a huge screened porch that wrapped all around the house and a boat dock just out back of it. It was just beautiful there."

"My, we had such great times together," reminisces Jane. "The guys, and some of the women, would fish during the day, and then the men would play poker late into the night. We swam, water-skied, boated and the kids had a place where they could play and swim together. Jim just loved it there. Those times at the island were the best."

Grayce Jones agrees, "It was so much fun at the island. We really had a ball up there. A bunch of us would all go up together, and, depending on the racing schedule, would sometimes stay a week at a time. We'd fish, and then Jim's dad would fry all the fish we caught. It was such a great place to get away from everything for awhile."

Grayce enjoyed fishing as much as the guys and once hooked a fish so big that she didn't think she would be able to handle it. "I was fishing off the end of the pier one night," relates Grayce, "and I hooked something that I couldn't budge. So I started yelling, 'Help! Help! Somebody come and help me!' But I couldn't get Parnelli or anyone else to hear me. They were probably in the house playing cards. It took me over an hour to get that thing in, and when I finally did, it turned out to be a huge Gar. Those things aren't even good to eat!"

If that's not fish story enough, Grayce had yet another encounter with a gargantuan water adversary. "One time," swears Grayce, "Linda and Jack Rounds and myself took one of the small boats up to one end of the lake and were fishing right beneath a small waterfall. I hooked something that was so big and strong that it started pulling the boat around in a circle. I fought with it for awhile, but Linda got so scared the way the boat was being jerked around, that Jack had to cut the line."

Jim's love of the island was fed by his passion for fishing. Even when he was travelling gypsy like from race to race, trying to keep pace with a hectic racing schedule, Jim found time to fish. Anytime he spotted a likely looking body of water, or a promising stream, he would stop and try the fishing, if only for a few minutes. Most of his friend's favorite stories of Jim center around his fondness of fishing. Danny Oakes recalls one that not only emphasized that love, but to him emphasized Jim's tough, determined nature that lay just below his happy-go-lucky exterior.

"Jim loved to go fishing," says Danny. "So I took him up to the Sacramento River with me to fish for steelhead. They're big, strong fish that weigh fourteen, fifteen, sixteen pounds. They get as big as thirty eight inches long, and they're tough babies to get! The first time I took Jim up there I said, 'Now, Jim I know a little bit about fishing, so listen to what I tell you. Don't get out in that stream too far because it's swift and it's deep. If you go under there, that's the end of you.'

"Well, I got involved with my fishing and looked around and Jim was nowhere in sight. When I finally spotted him, he was all the way out in the middle of the damn river! The water was clear up under his arms. The current is really strong out there—they lose fishermen every year in it. I didn't want to alarm him and cause him to panic and slip, so I said, 'Herk, come on in. I've got a good spot here. They're really hitting.'

'No, no,' he said, 'I'm getting some good hits right here.'

"I finally conned him into coming out of there, but I really thought I'd never see him again. That he was never goanna' get out. But he was strong as a bull, and not worried at all. He was in complete charge, and just came wading on out."

Jim was the consummate, spontaneous free spirit. Always ready to try something out of the ordinary, to do something exciting. Unlike others that can be described in that manner, however, Jim took seriously the responsibility of caring for his family.

"I can honestly say," states Jane, "that I never had to worry about anything. We never went without. Jim always worked hard. Even in the beginning when he was struggling to make it in racing, he kept his job with NeoGlo. Charlie and Dave were great to him and let him go racing whenever he needed to. After he broke the record at Indianapolis, Jim got so busy with his racing that he finally had to quit, but he still worked on his cars there until we moved back to New York in 1963."

Jim and Jane had purchased fourteen-and-a-half acres of land in North Tonawanda in 1962 with the idea of someday building a house there. With the birth of their third child, Andy, on January 8, 1962, they outgrew their Lennox California home and moved quicker than planned back to New York, renting a house until they could build their own.

Jim's racing success was accompanied by substantial enough financial rewards to allow him to indulge in his, "life's too short, lets have fun" philosophy with toys like motorcycles, snowmobiles, and an eighteen foot speedboat with a 421-cubic-inch Pontiac engine. Perhaps the toys Jim enjoyed most were his airplanes. Certainly some of his most memorable exploits took place in them.

Jim learned to fly while in California and took to flying as naturally as he had driving race cars. On January 5, 1962, his flight instructor noted in Jim's logbook, "Student has excellent, natural feel for the aircraft."

Until it became prohibitively expensive for him to do so, Jim maintained and flew a variety of planes, the most well known being his ungainly looking SeaBea. As the name suggests, the SeaBea was designed to take off and land on water, but it was the highly implausible bodies of water that Jim deemed necessary to put his SeaBea down in that gained him his notoriety as a pilot.

John Laux was at Daytona Speedway one year and was anticipating Jim's arrival at any time, when he heard the distinct roar of the SeaBea. Expecting Jim to buzz the track, as was his usual practice, then land at the airfield near the track, John was about to get in his car to go pick him up, when he and the others watching were shocked to see Jim suddenly nose the plane over, and put it down in the infield lake!

John jumped into his small, motorized cart he used to get around the vast expanse of Daytona and rushed to the lake to pick Jim up. When he arrived Jim was already surrounded by irate Daytona Speedway personnel, who had been contacted by FAA officials. It seems Jim committed, to them, the minor indiscretion of crossing Daytona International Airport's landing pattern twice, without identifying himself or requesting permission. The air traffic controllers had been tracking Jim on their radar screens, when he disappeared. They assumed he had crashed.

"I mean those guys chewed Herk up one side and down the other," laugh's John. "I thought he might end up going to jail over that one, but he talked his way out of it. Then the Daytona people were really upset because that SeaBea was meant to be used on large bodies of water, where the surface was rough enough to allow the pontoons to break free. He like to never have got that thing out of that little smooth surfaced pond at Daytona!"

Pete remembers yet another one of Jim's attention getting water landings with the SeaBea. "There was a lake we fished at on occasion," says Pete, "that was so far back in the woods that the Indians had the trail laid out with stone markers. Al Krueger and I were fishing there one day when we heard what sounded like Jim's SeaBea, which had its

"We looked up, and sure enough, it was Jim. He circled around and then came back. I looked at Al and said, 'Naw, he won't try and land, he can't get that thing in here!' But, by golly he brought it down. Jim was a hell of a pilot, and to get in between the trees that surrounded the lake, he nose dived right for the lake, then at the last moment, just before he hit the water, he leveled it off and plopped it down like a duck."

"Jim stayed and fished with us for awhile, then when he was getting ready to take off, a bush pilot flew over in one of those little pontoon planes they use to get in on the lakes up there. They're so small that those guys can put down in a puddle. He saw the SeaBea and landed to see what was going on. He asked Jim, 'How the hell are you gonna' get that thing outa' there?' Jim told him that it would be no problem, but the guy hung around. He wanted to see just how Jim was going to do it. He really thought that the SeaBea was going to be a permanent fixture!"

Pete and Al began to think the same thing. The lake was surrounded by tall trees, and in order to get up enough speed to clear them, Jim backed the tail of the plane up on the shore. With Pete and Al hanging on to the plane for dear life, and the bush pilot watching skeptically, Jim revved the SeaBea's engine. When Pete and Al could no longer hold the plane back, they let go and Jim accelerated across the lake.

"We were holding our breath," laughs Pete, "it really didn't look like it was going to make it, but he picked that thing right up and out of there. Luckily the far end of the lake was kind of marshy, and so the tree line was lower than around the rest of the lake. But, even then, the leaves were flying when he flew out."

Jim loved showing off his flying expertise with aerobatic stunts. Although Jane flew with him often, she would never allow him to perform with her aboard. "Jim had a red, J-2 Piper Cub that he used to do his stunts," explains Jane. "But never with me. He knew it was divorce time if he did!"

"A neighbor of ours, Esther Stoekel, went up with him in the Piper, and while we were all standing there watching them, all at once I saw Jim jerk the plane up. I thought, 'Oh my God, no!' Well, he put it into a loop, and Esther started screaming so loud that we could hear her from the ground. She wore dentures, and while she was screaming, her teeth fell out! When they landed Jim had to hunt around under the seats to find them. It was a riot."

Although Jane would never consent to being part of Jim's aerobatics there was one occasion when she was thankful for Jim's skill with a plane and his cool thinking under pressure.

"We were coming back from the fall race at Pocono," reminisces Jane. "The children and my mother were along, and it was just beautiful. It was October, and the Pocono Mountains were a patchwork of gorgeous colors. We just flew along, all of us quitely looking at the peaceful scenery below."

That serenity was shattered once they reached the airport. Jim landed the plane with no problem, but it would not slow.

"Jim, when are you going to brake?" asked Jane.

"When are you going to brake?"

"I am, but it's not working too good. No problem though. Everything's okay. Don't worry," responded Jim.

Everything wasn't okay. The plane's brakes had failed, and Jim was quickly running out of room to stop it in. He knew that there was only one thing to do. He whipped the plane to the right, jerking it off the runway, and causing the wing tip to dig into the ground and pull the plane to a stop.

"All right, we're all okay. Hurry up and get out now," Jim calmly commanded.

Everyone swiftly obeyed. When Jane was free of the plane and stepped back to survey the scene, a cold chill ran through her body. There was fuel dripping from the crippled aircraft. She shuddered to think what might have happened to her family had that fuel ignited. Jim seemed to be as invincible in a runaway plane as he was in a race car. Then came Milwaukee, 1964.

HURTUBISE

17

Miller Brewing Company Photo - HFC

isconsin State Fair Park, located in the Milwaukee suburb of West Allis, has been the site of auto racing since 1903, making it the oldest operating raceway in the United States.

All the early races held at the one mile oval were non-sanctioned, outlaw events. It wasn't until 1933 that an AAA one hundred mile race for Championship cars was held there. The race, won by three time Indianapolis 500 winner, Wilbur Shaw, was well received, but when the depression engulfed the nation, racing slowed and there was not another AAA champ car race at Milwaukee until 1937.

With that race, won by Rex Mays, the Milwaukee 100 became an annual fixture on the prestigious AAA circuit. Like most tracks used for auto racing at the turn of the century, Milwaukee was dirt and originally built for horse racing. By 1954, however, the cars running at Indianapolis had became so specialized that they could no longer run competitively on anything but a paved track. To continue attracting the Indianapolis cars to their annual, weekend after the 500 race, the Marchese brothers, Milwaukee's astute promoters, paved the track.

In the years following the track's paving, the Rex Mays 100 rose in stature to become one of the most prestigious events on the Championship Trail. When the Indy cars arrived there for the June 7, 1964, hundred miler, most of the cars that ran the week before at Indianapolis were on hand. Foyt was there with the front engine roadster that he had driven to his second 500 win. Rodger Ward was in the same rear engine Ford he had taken second place with, and Jim was there with the car he had built for Indianapolis.

Don Shepherd, who was at Milwaukee to lend his mechanical help, recalls that Jim was still complaining about the pushing condition he had experienced at Indianapolis. So during the morning practice session, they continued to work with the Paul Taylor designed liquid suspension. When that failed to help, Jim reverted back to the coil spring set up for the race.

Evidently, it was in an attempt to gain control of the unwieldy front end that Jim had the front mounted auxiliary fuel tank filled with fifteen gallons of fuel. Neither Pete nor Don know of any other plausible reason for him doing so, since the extra fuel certainly wasn't needed for a one hundred mile race. Regardless of his reasoning, Jim's decision would prove to have tragic consequences.

Jim qualified third quick behind Ward and Foyt for the Rex Mays 100, and from the beginning the race was a battle between these three great drivers. Lap after lap they zipped around the flat, mile oval in a colorful, nose-to-tail, 120 mile-per-hour train. There have been few times when three drivers had been so evenly matched on any race track.

Then, without warning, as the trio stormed off turn four on lap 51, a puff of smoke spewed from the rear of Ward's car. A bearing in the rear end had seized, slowing him dramatically. Ward immediately shot his hand into the air to warn Foyt and Hurtubise, but they were too close.

Foyt jumped on his brakes to avoid climbing over Ward's crippled car. Jim, instantly grasping what was happening in front of him, slammed on his brakes, and instinctively jerked his car to the right to clear Foyt's fishtailing car. But at a football-field-a-second clip, it was already too late. The left front wheel of Jim's car caught the rear of Foyt's car, and vaulted itself into the air towards the retaining wall.

"I peeled over like a P-51, grabbed the wheel and crouched down," Jim recalled later. "I remember all this. When I hit, my right rear tire came off and smashed me in the chest. It broke three ribs, punctured a lung and knocked me out. That's the last I remember until they were carrying me to the ambulance."

What happened between the time Jim was knocked unconscious and the time he was loaded into the ambulance was devastating. When the car augered into the wall, the front axle twisted back and into the reserve fuel tank. The aluminum tank held intact under the force of the impact, but the pressure from the collapsing metal was so great that it popped the filler cap lose, and flooded the engine compartment and the belly pan of the car with fifteen gallons of methanol alcohol.

Either the hot engine, or a spark from the grinding metal as the car continued its slide towards the center of the track, ignited the fuel. In just seconds the heat from the flames reached almost a thousand degrees. Like a charge roaring up the chimney of a blast furnace, the fire raced through the car and surged out of the open cockpit, gobbling anything in its path.

When the car ground to a stop, Jim was helpless. Knocked out by the thrashing tire, he slumped forward in the cockpit with his unprotected hands dangling over the cauldron of burning fuel that raged below him.

That the car came to a stop on the front stretch, directly across from the pits, undoubtedly saved Jim's life. Even before the car came to a stop, emergency workers and mechanics were on their way to the burning wreckage. Pete, carrying two fire extinguishers, was the first one there, having outrun several other would be rescuers in the dash to save his brother. Surveying the scene even as he approached, Pete instantly recognized the critical situation Jim was in. Dropping the fire extinguishers, he ran to the side of the car, reached into the searing flames, and unsnapped his brother's safety harness. By then others were there to help, and while fire fighters doused the flames Jim was dragged from the flaming wreckage. Pete burned his own hands in the rescue, but his quick action prevented Jim from inhaling the lung searing fumes that kill most fire victims.

Jim was loaded into the waiting ambulance, and with sirens wailing, rushed to the hospital at West Allis. It was then that the full impact of what had transpired overcame Pete, and he dropped to the pit wall, cradled his head in his hands and wept.

Bobby Marshman, who had dropped out of the race early, jumped into the ambulance and attempted to offer some comfort to Jim, who was semiconscious and obviously in great pain.

"I remember the ambulance ride," Jim said of that trip. "I remember the siren. I remember looking at my hands, and it looked like I had gloves on, only I didn't. It was only about a half mile to the hospital, but I was already beginning to feel the burns by then."

Because going to the racetrack with three preschool age children had become increasingly difficult, Jane had not travelled to Milwaukee with Jim. Rather she and a neighbor, Mary Ann Rikered, took their children to Fantasy Island, an amusement park at Grand Island, New York.

"We were walking around," says Jane, "and we heard an announcement two or three times on the PA system for someone to come to the information office. I said to Mary Ann, 'If I didn't know better, I'd swear they were trying to say Hurtubise.' In a short time they made the announcement again, and Mary said, 'Jane I believe they are trying to say Hurtubise.' So we went to the office and sure enough they had a message for me to call home."

Through the years, Jane had trained herself not to worry about Jim when she was at home, and he was racing. "When I was at the track," explains Jane, "I prayed on every lap. But when I was not with Jim, I could block it out. It was really strange. I could give Jim a kiss goodbye, and go do my thing without thinking about the danger at all. Then about 4:30 or 5:00, what might have happened at the race would come to mind, and I would get so nervous that I would start calling anyone I could to find out how the races went. I couldn't wait for Jim to call me."

Jane had so conditioned herself with this routine, that when she was paged to the amusement park information office it didn't enter her mind that something might have happened to Jim. That changed with the call home.

Sheila answered the phone, and she had a message from Pete. Jane recalls the part of the conversation when Sheila told her that Jim had been seriously hurt, but again her mental defense mechanism kicked in, and she remembers little else of that time.

"I don't remember calling anybody," says Jane. "I don't remember anybody calling me. The next thing I knew I was on an airplane at 1:30 in the morning, and on the way to Milwaukee."

Pete's wife, Sheila recalls more of that panic filled evening. "I helped Jane get ready for the trip to Milwaukee. She was trying hard to remain calm, as if the accident didn't bother her. I can remember Jane sitting at a dressing table in the bedroom as I helped her with her hair. She was attempting to keep all the worry and pain inside her, trying not to alarm the children."

"When she was ready, we left the children with Jim's mother, and I drove her to the airport. A friend of Jim's, Mike Valley, was a corporate pilot, and he'd gotten permission from his company to fly Jane to Milwaukee."

Even as Jane was being notified of Jim's accident, the emergency room personnel at West Allis hospital were at work on Jim. They shot him with pain killers, and cut his charred uniform from him. What they found didn't look good. He was terribly burned. His legs, arms and face were broiled like a piece of meat, but it was his hands that most concerned the doctor. They had been ravaged by the inferno. Chunks of flesh had been cooked completely away.

The doctor in charge recognized immediately that Jim would require more specialized help than his hospital could provide. Aware that Jim was a veteran and would be eligible for treatment at the Brooke Medical Center, an Army hospital in San Antonio, Texas, the doctor had the presence of mind to pass this information along to the racing people who had already began to congregate.

In a demonstration of the close knit kinship that exists among racers, even though Jim was driving for the Goodyear Tire Company, it was representatives from Firestone who made the initial contacts with Brooke, and volunteered their corporate plane to fly Jim there.

However, the Firestone plane was not necessary. When Jim's military status was determined, Army personnel immediately authorized a C-131 Samaritan hospital plane with a burn team aboard to fly to Milwaukee and return Jim to Brooke.

Brooke Medical Center, was located at Fort Sam Houston and specialized in the treatment of burn trauma. Brooke's medical teams were the most knowledgable burn specialists in the world at that time, and with the Vietnam war escalating they were rapidly gaining new skills by treating the daily stream of burned helicopter and jet pilots sent there.

While the wheels were being set into motion to get Jim transferred to Brooke, the West Allis medical team rushed him into surgery to re-inflate his collapsed lung, clean his burns and stabilize him for transport.

With the race over, the hospital was soon jammed with racing people anxiously awaiting word of Jim's condition. Pete had followed the ambulance and was making calls to the family from the waiting room. Parnelli Jones arrived. Still recovering from his Indianapolis burns, Parnelli had been a spectator at the race and as he saw the crash unfold before him, he believed Jim had been killed. "I was standing on top of the Firestone tire truck watching the race," recalls Parnelli. "I had first and second degree burns under my arms and on my legs from the Indy fire. When I saw Jim crash I knew in my mind that he was dead. It was a terrible fire."

Dick Sommers, one of Jim's car owners, made his way to the hospital. His fear of what he would find there was intensified by the week old memory of seeing his other driver, Eddie Sachs, burn to death at Indianapolis.

Recalls Sommers, "When we reached the hospital, the first person we saw was Bobby Marshman. He was pretty upset, and telling the hospital staff that they shouldn't put Jim in room 213, because a lot of drivers are superstitious. 'Being in that room,' Bobby told them, 'could mean the difference between Jim's recovery or not."

"Pete was there, of course, and was trying to get in touch with Jane. Pete told us that Jim had extensive second and third degree burns and that the doctors didn't have much hope. They were doing all they could, and all we could do was sit there and pray."

"After we had been in the waiting room for an hour or so," continues Sommers, "Roger McCluskey and A.J. Foyt came in. Foyt talked with Pete and offered him his plane to fly Jim to the burn hospital. He also called his wife, Lucy, to arrange for Jane to stay at their house if she wanted."

After the accident, A.J. had gone on to easily win the race. When he climbed from his car in victory lane, he spotted the dents and black scuff marks made when Jim's car hit him. They were a dramatic reminder of just how minute the difference is between victory and tragedy in racing.

McCluskey, like Parnelli, had also been a spectator because of a racing injury. He broke his left arm in a March 29 sprint car race and would miss most of the 1964 season. After witnessing the the fire at Indianapolis, and now Jim's crash, Roger reckoned he was through with being a spectator. "I can't wait until I get this cast off and start racing again," mused Roger. "I don't think I'll watch another race unless I'm driving in it. It's too damn scary!"

When Jane arrived in Milwaukee, Jim had already endured seven hours of surgery. He was alive, but barely. Many hours would pass before the certainty of his condition was established. The doctor was not optimistic about Jim's chances of surviving, and even less optimistic about him ever regaining normal use of his hands. When Jane was briefly allowed to see him he was on the verge of delirium and showed no signs of recognizing his wife. It was then that the grim horror of Jim's accident overcame Jane, and she covered her face with her hands and fainted.

The C-131 arrived from Texas at 3:00 AM. Captain William Mills, the doctor assigned to Jim, and his assistant, Sgt. Bill Mask, immediately initiated the intravenous injections of electrolytes, plasma and dextrose that are so essential to a burn victim. Severe burns allow the vital fluids to drain alarmingly fast from the body, because the mutilated flesh is unable to contain them.

Since Jane and Pete were civilians, they were not allowed on the military aircraft with Jim. After seeing he was safely on his way to San Antonio, they rushed to the airport to catch a commercial flight to Texas. By the time they were reunited with Jim at Brooke, the battle to save his life was already well under way.

The first few hours dragged slowly by, and Jim hung on. As those critical hours stretched into a day, then two, Jim fought valiantly to live. By day three the doctors, acknowledging that Jim was winning his stubborn battle, performed their first surgical procedure, and removed much of the dead tissue from his burned body. By the fifth day, they were optimistic enough about his chances of living that they made the first skin grafts.

Jim had won the fight for his life, but for him that was not enough. From the time he was taken off the critical list, he talked of little else but racing again. Like other goals he had sought and obtained in his life, Jim would accomplish that goal as well. And with the heroics he displayed while doing it, the nickname, "Hercules," took on an entirely new meaning.

Joseph F. Lawrence Photo - HFC

Joseph F. Lawrence Photo - HFC

HURTUBISE

18

Raymond Turner Photo - HFC

Thirty days after Jim was helicoptered from the landing field at Fort Sam Houston to Brooke Medical Center, his life dangling by a mere thread, he was wheeled into a press conference. Treatments that would stretch into agonizing months had just began. He had lost thirty pounds, was very weak, and barely spoke above a whisper. To the reporters gathered there, however, he made one message startlingly clear: "I will drive again."

Though only then made public, Jim's stoic resolve to race again was obvious to his family even as they gathered about him in those first few critical days.

Jim's father had been fishing at his island in Georgian Bay the day of the accident, and several hours passed before Ernie could be located at his isolated lodge. Once notified, Ernie made his way to Texas and spent the next nine days at his son's side.

"Those were the roughest nine days of my life," admitted Ernie. "To me it looked like Jim had about a fifty-fifty chance to make it. It didn't look good. Jim, he must be part Indian or something, because he never showed any feelings. He just talked about getting well."

Pete, too, witnessed this early display of his brother's tenacity. "I remember being in the room with Jim the day he first got a good look at his hands," recalls Pete. "He lifted them up to where he could see them, and stared at them for a moment. Then he just grunted and shook his head. That was the extent of his reaction. He never made a comment about how bad they were. Never spoke a word about pain. Only about getting better. Only about racing again."

Considering the extent of his burns, Jim's attitude was amazing. His doctors had determined that he was critically burned over forty five percent of his body. Twenty five percent of those burns were second degree, the remainder were the more severe third degree. The areas with second degree burns were an angry red and ugly purple but would heal and could be restored to a semblance of normalcy with time and skin grafts.

Where the flames had burned Jim to the third degree, however, they had destroyed the nerves along with the flesh. In some places the fire had even seared into the bone. The tip of his nose was burned away, and his face would always carry the marks of the fire.

It was Jim's hands, though, that were burned the worst. They no longer resembled hands. Certainly not usable hands. What little flesh remained was burned beyond recognition, but most of it was completely gone leaving tendons and bone exposed. "I had so many leaders and tendons exposed," Jim joked, "that I looked like a walking X-ray!"

That cavalier remark masked a real concern. His doctors told him from the very beginning that he might never again be able to use his hands normally. "I knew they were in bad shape," said Jim. "The doctors told me right away, 'We're going to do the best we can, but we're not sure what we can do about your hands."

For a race driver that was devastating news. A driver's hands are absolutely essential, not only for controlling the car, but for sensing its every move, anticipating its every reaction. If Jim were to race again he had to regain the use of his hands. In the beginning, there were few at Brooke who believed that possible.

"He talked about the 500 and racing all the time," said one nurse about Jim's desire to race. "All the time racing. But none of us here really believed he'd ever drive a race car again. We wondered if he'd even be able to drive an automobile."

Jim's road to recovery began with the first skin grafts performed on his hands, just five days after arriving from Milwaukee. Those grafts were intended to be temporary only. Made partially with donated human skin and partially from the skin of animals, usually from pigs or dogs, their purpose was to cover and protect the exposed, delicate inner workings of his hands. A major setback came three days later when the grafts failed and had to be surgically removed. The painful process was repeated, and this time they took.

Ten days after his arrival at Brooke, Jim was doing well enough to be removed from intensive care, and placed in the burn ward with sixty other patients. That in itself was a victory, considering that just a few days before his chances of even living had been minimal.

Surprisingly, with severe burn cases the treatments are often more painful than the injuries themselves. The pain from the second degree burns soon subsides, and the third degree burns destroy the nerve endings, so pain in those areas can no longer be sensed.

However, the pain when the dead flesh has to be forcibly removed, or when skin is scraped from the body for grafts and newly grafted skin made to stretch and become pliable, is indescribable, and often unbearable. To recover, Jim faced months of agonizing treatments, and even those wouldn't guarantee he would be able to drive again.

At that time the Hubbard tank was the most essential, yet most dreaded tool used in the treatment of burns. Its cruciform shape allowed a person to be immersed in warm water with their arms outstretched while nurses hosed off dead skin with a high pressure spray. A few minutes in the Hubbard tank was capable of making the strongest men weep, and the screams of those undergoing treatment would often reverberate through the hospital wards. When it came time for Jim's first session in the Hubbard tank, he was determined not to cry out. Jane describes how he succeeded.

"I arrived at the hospital one day," recalls Jane, "and I heard this loud singing. I listened for a moment, and I realized it was Jim. You could hear him all over the hospital, he was singing, "You Are My Sunshine" at the top of his voice. I said to the nurse, 'What in the world is he doing?' She said, 'Jane he's in the cruciform. He told us that he was going to sing so he wouldn't have to scream. And he told the orderlies that they better sing along with him.' When the nurse described the treatment, I almost passed out thinking about it. The pain had to be terrible, but Jim never, ever screamed."

After a time the nurses and doctors of a burn ward grow hardened working with severely burned patients. They are not easy to impress, but even they were often amazed by Jim's brassy courage.

"He never said 'I'll try,' when we asked him to do something," commented one nurse. "He just did it. He never said, 'I can't.' The first time a doctor asked him to make a fist with his hand, he just closed his eyes and then tightened up those fingers as far as they would go without saying a word. Sometimes it takes a patient a full five minutes before they can make such a move, and we have to stand there and say, 'More, more, more.' But Jim just gritted his teeth and did it."

Jim approached every facet of his rehabilitation with this same steely fervor. If forcing himself to do everything the doctors asked, without regard to the painful consequences, would allow him to race again, then that is what he would do. Simple as that. Push on regardless of the pain.

"My arms and legs were bad, too," said Jim. "I couldn't bend them very much at all. I'd try, but every time I really tried, the skin would crack and bleed and I'd have to stop. I couldn't squat either. The scar tissue on my legs wouldn't let me. But I'd squat anyway and something would give a little more every time."

As impressive as the physical feats he performed was Jim's attitude as he put himself through these torturous exercises. He retained his positive, upbeat demeanor. He was never despondent.

Never negative. Never gave up hope, even in the face of the misery that surrounded him. A burn ward is not a pleasant place. It assaults the senses with sights and sounds and smells that have caused even strong men to wilt.

Grayce Jones still vividly recalls the suffering she saw during her first visit to Brooke. She arrived in San Antonio to be with Jane at the time Jim's father and Pete had to return to New York—Ernie to keep his service station operating, Pete to oversee the race team that was in the process of rebuilding.

"It was pitiful in there," recalls Grayce sadly. "I remember when I first got there, that there was a baby in one of the rooms that had been burned from its eyes all the way down its body. I came out of there crying. I just couldn't stand it."

"Then there was a young guy, his name was Rusty, that was on the other side of Jim's partition out in the ward. He had been burned in a gasoline tanker fire. I would talk to him through the walls whenever I was there visiting Jim. I remember talking to him one day, and he sounded fine. The next day I went in, and the nurse told me he had died. She said he just gave up hope."

"It was so sad. Burns are the worst, just the worst, things to see. And it's even harder to see your friends in that condition."

"Jim was absolutely amazing," insists Jane. "I wish I could convey just how heroic he was. His spirits were always up. He was always upbeat, and if he ever became discouraged or down, he never let it show."

"We used to do things like have skin peeling contests," laughs Jane. "I could hardly stand to do it, so I would just pick at the dead skin. Pull off little pieces. But Jim jerked off whole sheets of it. He'd always win! It would drive me nuts, but that's what he wanted to do. It was just his way of making it all easier."

Grayce Jones, too, can attest to Jim's positive manner. "Jim was just too mean to give up!" laughs Grayce. "Seriously, what was really amazing was that even then, laying there in the hospital, burned so terribly, with all that pain and suffering around him, he was still fun to be around. He could always make you smile."

Speaking to one writer about his rehabilitation, Jim revealed his personal feelings about how important a tough mental attitude is to the healing process.

"It was just an experience, getting burnt and worked on. Just something that happens," said Jim. "It's fun for me. I'm in a ward with sixty people, and there are a lot of other people hurting just like I am. You either make something of it, or you don't."

"Doctors working on your hands, to me it's interesting. It's a slow process and you can watch it all every day. It's not like they are cutting inside you while you're asleep. Every day you are wide awake and able to see what they're doing with your tendons and blood vessels and things. They're trying different kinds of skin on you, animal and human, to see what will work. Its a little bit like building a race car. They're learning and I'm learning too. Pain, you get used to it. It's just something that's there. Something you put up with. Pain is pain, there are no degrees of pain."

By late July the work on Jim's hands had reached a crossroads. The extension tendons of both hands were damaged beyond repair, and they had already began to shrink and draw his fingers into a claw like shape. The tendons would never be functional, but his hands could be surgically fixed into any number of permanent positions, Jim needed only to decide what shape he desired.

He took little time with that decision. If he were to drive again his hands would have to shaped so he could grip a steering wheel. "I told them that I was a guy who made a living grabbing hold of something round," Jim said. "I told them to fix my hands so I could do that."

The procedure to fix the shape of Jim's hands involved inserting long, thin, stainless steel wires through the tip of each finger and pushing them deep into the bone marrow cavity. The fingers were then bent and allowed to fuse permanently into that position.

It was later, when talking to the press, that Jim made his well known and much repeated statement about how he arrived at the position to permanently fix his hands. "I told the doctors," he said tongue in cheek, "just to shape them so I could grab a steering wheel and hold a bottle of beer."

Despite his self energizing nature, Jim needed all the encouragement he could get from Jane and others around him to keep his spirits up. The knowledge that his friends and his fans were rallying around Jane and him in their time of need certainly helped. When Grayce Jones arrived, she told Jane, "I'm here for as long as you need me." Grayce was as good as her word and spent over a month in Texas.

Driver Ebb Rose was another whose help was indispensable during that very difficult time. When Jane arrived in San Antonio, she had but one concern, to stay at her husband's side as he fought to stay alive. When those first few critical days passed, however, and Jim began what would be a nine-month-long rehabilitation, Jane realized that there were some very basic needs she had to deal with. She was stranded alone in a strange city with nowhere to stay, no way to get around, and no idea of how she would go about obtaining any of this. Then Ebb Rose called.

Besides being a race car driver, Ebb was also the owner and operator of J R Rose Trucking based in Houston, Texas. Ebb had a trucking terminal in San Antonio, along with several houses there, and answered Jane's unspoken request, when he provided her with one of those homes, rent free, for as long as she needed to be in San Antonio. He also gave her a 1963 Oldsmobile 88 to use as well.

"I don't know what I would have done without Ebb," Jane says emphatically. "God bless him. The house he let me use was furnished with linens, towels, cookware, everything. I didn't have to worry about anything. The Roses were just great to us the entire time we were there."

It was Ebb who put together a fundraising banquet in Jim's honor. Held on August 12, 1964, in the Grand Ballroom of the Sheraton-Lincoln Hotel in Houston, the event was attended by several hundred racers, and raised $10,000 towards Jim's medical expenses. A celebrity auction was held with Parnelli Jones, A.J. Foyt, Johnny Rutherford, Lloyd Ruby, Roger McCluskey and Jim McElreath serving as auctioneers for such items as autographed helmets, photographs, and Indy car tires.

Jim, of course, was unable to attend the gala, but Parnelli flew to San Antonio and picked up Jane. Ebb arranged a phone hook-up for Jim so he could listen in on the festivities, and at one point in the evening, Jim led the crowd in the singing of "Happy Birthday" to Parnelli.

A.J. Foyt was another who offered much help to Jim and Jane, although few people were aware of that because A.J. prefers to keep his charitable generosity private. Besides the support from within the racing community, racing fans from across the country flooded the hospital with thousands of cards and letters.

Jane recalls that when the first letters and cards started coming in, she bought a pack of one hundred thank-you cards with the intention of answering each one personally. When those were quickly used, Jane realized that she could not possibly respond to the avalanche of mail Jim was receiving, although she and Jim did read each piece of mail.

"I wish you'd tell all those wonderful people that I truly appreciate the cards and letters they've sent me," Jim told one newspaper. "I mean it. You don't know how much hearing from them helps. Please, tell them to keep it up."

The one thing that Jim missed above all else while being confined to the hospital was socializing with his cronies. As much as he appreciated cards, letters and phone calls, he was especially excited when his racing friends came to see him. Their antics, usually at odds with convention, didn't change when they visited a hospital.

"One day Gordon Van Liew, Duane Carter and their wives came to visit Jim," recalls Jane. "He wasn't supposed to have any alcohol, of course, but that didn't stop Gordon and Duane. They snuck a bottle of wine in for him. They also brought a little black and white TV for Jim to watch, but Jim was strapped in a Stryker bed and couldn't get into a position to see it. So, they put the TV under the bed, and rotated Jim over. Here he was, a burn patient, hanging face down in a Stryker bed, watching TV and sipping wine!"

As Jim's condition continued to improve, he was allowed to get out of bed for short periods of time. It was then that his restless nature began to reassert itself, and the staff at Brooke were hard pressed to restrain him. When sports car driver, Frank Hilton, arrived at Brooke, that already arduous task became almost impossible.

Hilton did not have a military service record, but because he was driving for the Ford Motor Company when he was severely burned in a late summer of 1964 accident, they pulled the proper strings and had him admitted to Brooke. In a major administrative misjudgment, Hilton was assigned a bed next to Jim.

Two high-strung racers together in such a constraining environment could only mean trouble. Jim was rambunctious enough on his own. Having a companion only spurred his mischievous, adventurous spirit. One day Jim convinced Hilton that after all they had been through, they deserved a night on the town. So that evening they snuck out of the hospital clad in their military issue pajamas and made their way to a nearby bar and poolroom.

While the orderlies searched the hospital room by room for the wayward patients, Jim and Frank enjoyed a cool beer and shot a leisurely game of pool. When they finally made their way back to Brooke, the institution was in an uproar. Panicked administrators had given up trying to find Jim and Frank in the hospital and were on the verge of notifying the military police. "Jim was the only civilian ever who almost got a court martial!" laughs Jane.

When Jane first arrived in San Antonio, Jim's doctors had advised her to leave the children at home. They weren't sure that Jim would even live, and if he did, Jane would need to spend many hours with him, assisting in his rehabilitation. As Jim responded well to his treatments, he and Jane began to consider the possibility of having the children join them. Then a phone conversation convinced them it was a necessity.

The children had been staying with Pete and Sheila in North Tonawanda, and doing fine. One day, however, Sheila told Jane, "Karen was talking to me yesterday, and she said, 'Auntie Sheila, I don't remember what my mother looks like!'

"Well that was it," recalls Jane. "I flew to New York that weekend and brought the kids back with me."

Their return coincided with the point in Jim's recovery that he was allowed to leave the hospital for short periods, so he went to meet Jane and his family at the airport.

Jim was afraid the children might be put off by his hideous appearance, especially after such a long separation. So, when they approached he raised his hands, with the stainless steel wires sticking from his fingers, and in a mock threat greeted them with, "Look kids, daddy's a monster!" That self-deprecating gesture broke the ice, and the children laughed comfortably with their father.

On another weekend leave, Jim decided it was time he found out if he could still drive. It wouldn't be in a race car, only the Oldsmobile that Ebb Rose had loaned them, but he had to know if he could grip a steering wheel. The stainless steel wires had yet to be removed from his fingers, and when they prevented him from operating the push button door handle, he used the toe of his shoe to push the button, while he opened the door with his hand.

"My hands were still so tender that I couldn't turn the key in the ignition," said Jim of that first tentative stint behind the wheel of a car. "I tried, but the pressure of the metal on my fingers was too much. So I wrapped the key in a Kleenex, I made a big soft ball of it, and then I could turn it to start the engine."

"It was the same with the steering wheel," Jim continued. "I could hook my hands onto it, but it felt so hard that I had to wrap more Kleenex around it to be able to hold on at all. And if I bumped one of those wires sticking out of my fingers, it hurt like hell. I didn't drive far that first day. Just far enough to know that I could still do it."

Jim's doctors were not aware that he was already testing their delicate reconstructive work, but they wouldn't have discouraged him had they known. "When a man is recovering, he can do whatever he wants to try as far as we're concerned," said Colonel Walter Switzer, the director of the burn clinic. "It's up to Jim. If he has this ambition to drive again, it isn't up to us to tell him not to try."

Jim continued to heal dramatically fast, well ahead of his doctor's preconceived time table. On September 17, although he still had five months of reconstructive surgery and rehabilitation to endure, they released him from the burn ward to live with Jane and the children in the house Ebb Rose had provided. Jim was a step closer to racing again.

The most often asked question was why? Why would Jim want to return to the sport that had almost killed him? Why would he want to take a chance of it happening again? Jim addressed this subject at another hospital press conference:

"I guess it just never struck me that people would wonder why I would want to go back. They must be people who've seen me race, but I don't believe they really know me. If they did, I don't think they would try to figure out why I'll be back.

"There's a pretty simple answer, because to return to racing isn't a complicated thing for me to decide. I guess you could reduce it to one word, profession. Racing's been mine for thirteen years, and I spent eight of them getting to Indianapolis. I'll not quit now."

"Driving race cars is the job I chose long ago. Like any job, when you're competitive, there's a lot of enjoyment in the life. And I like the competition. Racing is dangerous, sure. Who knows better than I? But there are other dangerous jobs too. How about construction work and mining? Lots of people take big chances every working day. They don't mope around thinking how dangerous their jobs are. And they don't quit."

"I definitely plan to return to racing. It won't be a comeback, I'll just be returning. I made my choice a long time ago, and it's the thing I'm happiest doing. That's why I'll jump back into racing with both feet as soon as the doctors say okay."

If Jim needed a reminder of just how dangerous the sport he wanted to jump back into was, he got a shocking one. In late November of 1964, Bobby Marshman was brought into Brooke, burned hideously over 90 percent of his body.

With skills honed on the midget tracks in and around his Pottstown, Pennsylvania, home, Bobby was one of racing's newest and brightest stars. He was Co-Rookie of the year at Indianapolis with Parnelli Jones in 1961 and by 1964 was a contender at any race he entered. As the first American to drive one of the trend setting Lotus Fords at the Speedway, he led 33 laps of the 1964 500 before dropping out with engine failure. Bobby was at the top of his game when he arrived for a series of Firestone tire tests at Phoenix on November 27.

The test was going as planned until Bobby lost control in the first turn on the eighteenth lap of a thirty lap session. The car crashed hard into the steel guardrail and burst into flames. Bobby was trapped, unconscious, in the burning wreckage for some time before rescue workers managed to free him. Taken to the Phoenix hospital from the track, Bobby was, by congressional approval, moved to Brooke the following day. The doctors there gave him little hope. One commented, "...there is no skin left that is suitable for grafting."

On December 3, six days after the crash, Bobby died. Jane was in the room with his wife Janet when he passed away. "It was just awful," says Jane sadly. "It was terrible how badly Bobby was burned. It reminded me of the photograph they ran in the paper of Eddie Sachs after that crash in 1964. Jim and I knew that Bobby wasn't going to make it."

"I was with Janet at the time," continues Jane, "and she was timing Bobby's breathing by counting off the seconds between each breath. She'd count one, two, and then he would breathe. One, two and he'd breathe. Then, suddenly, as Janet was counting, Bobby didn't take a breath. I ran out and got Betty, who was Bobby's nurse. She rushed into the room, checked Bobby, then asked us to step out. He had already died."

It was Bobby who rode in the ambulance to the hospital with Jim after his Milwaukee crash. Encouraging him, talking to him to distract him from the pain of his burns. Now Bobby was gone. Taken by the same fiery beast that Jim had so narrowly escaped. Jim's reaction to his friend's passing was, typically, unemotional. It did, however, cause Jim to speak out for the need of more safety in racing, especially in regards to protecting drivers from their worst fear, fire.

"I think," said Jim, "that they should limit the fuel load of the race car to forty or fifty gallons. You'll have to make more pit stops for fuel, but the car will be lighter and handle better."

"And when I race again," he continued, "you can bet I'll wear a lot more clothes. I might be a little warmer, but I'll be better protected.

If I had been wearing gloves, my hands wouldn't have gotten burned nearly as bad."

When Jim's doctors began to allow him brief trips away from San Antonio, these, of course, were all to racetracks. In September, he went to Indianapolis for the Hoosier Hundred, and was greeted enthusiastically by fans and fellow racers alike. Parnelli Jones, A.J. Foyt, Jud Larson, Johnny Rutherford, Danny Oakes and a host of other racing buddies surrounded him for over an hour, slapping him on the back, joking with him, welcoming him back.

Mechanic Herb Porter approached the group and shouted to Jim, "Hey, you loafer, come on over here and set this chassis up for me so we can run fast today."

"I'm not ready yet, but I will be soon," answered Jim.

Those surrounding him didn't let on, but they seriously doubted his claim. They had known, of course, that Jim had been severely burned, but most hadn't seen Jim since the accident and didn't realize just how badly he had been ravaged by the fire until they saw him at the Hoosier Hundred.

In mid-October, Jim returned to the track that almost took his life when he visited Milwaukee for a USAC stock car race. Those who saw him there were just as dismayed by his appearance as those who had seen him at the Hoosier Hundred. They thought he looked worse than he had the day they hauled him out of Milwaukee in an ambulance.

Despite appearances to the contrary, Pete assured them that with Jim, nothing was impossible. "He's really working hard," Pete said. "He wants to be ready for the next 500 Mile Race. If work and guts can get the job done, then Jim will be there."

Throughout the fall and into the winter of 1964, the operations and plastic surgery continued, and Jim worked doggedly to physically strengthen himself. He could finally see the light at the end of the tunnel. In February of 1965, Jim was discharged from Brooke and allowed to return to his North Tonawanda home.

Scheduled to return to Brooke at the end of that month for yet another operation to removal the webs of skin from between the middle and ring fingers on both hands, Jim never went back.

"I don't need another operation," he told the doctors. "I can use my hands like they are, as good as you can use yours."

He was finished with hospitals. Forever as far as he was concerned. Besides he knew that if he were to compete in the next 500, he would first have to prove himself to USAC officials at the season opening champ car race to be held at the end of March in Phoenix. If he were operated on, he would not be healed in time for that important event.

Free from the regimen of the hospital, Jim continued to push himself relentlessly at home. Construction had started on the new house he and Jane had always dreamed of building, and he spent hours preparing the site himself. He operated a bulldozer, working the landscape and preparing the foundations. He bought a pickup truck and hauled materials to the job site. Jim's ramrodding of the job sped the construction of the house along, but his real intent was to strengthen himself and toughen his hands.

"I still couldn't handle small tools," Jim said, "but I could drive some and there were days when I'd just get in the truck and spend all day looking for a place to go and something to do. I got a rowboat, too, and I would row for hours to toughen my hands and increase my grip. While I was rowing I'd keep telling myself over and over that I wanted to race again and that if I kept working, I could get my hands tough enough to do it."

Come March, Jim deemed himself ready for that racing return. USAC, however, desired something more official, and demanded a release from his doctor before they would allow him in a race car.

"The day Doctor Mills got the letter from USAC asking for a statement that Jim was fit to drive, he called me," says Jane. "He told me that if it was up to him, he wouldn't let Jim race, but he knew how strongly Jim felt, and wanted to know what I thought. I told him I wouldn't be able to live with Jim if he didn't let him drive!"

Doctor Mills granted his approval and wrote USAC: "I don't know what it takes to drive a race car, but from what I know of Jim Hurtubise, he can drive anything with four wheels."

Incredibly, just nine months after he almost lost his life, and had little hope of ever being able to use his hands again, Jim Hurtubise was set to climb back into a race car.

Hurtubise Family Collection

Driving on the recovery road.

Hurtubise Family Collection

Jim with Nurse Walters at Brooke

Swede Photo - HFC

Jim at Terre Haute Oct 11, 1964. Chuck Rodee is in the car. Howard Linne and Bud Tingelstad are to his left.

HURTUBISE

19

Hurtubise Family Collection

While Jim had been enduring his nine month ordeal at the Brooke Medical Center, Pete had been busy keeping the racing team operating. In less than a year, DVS had seen one of their drivers burn to death and had almost lost the other to a fire, but they still wanted to race.

The car Jim and Pete had built for the 1964 500 had been destroyed in the Milwaukee crash, and when it looked like Jim might very well make good on his vow to return to racing, his car owners began to shop around for a new car.

Even though A.J. Foyt had won the 1964 500 with a front engine car, it didn't require a crystal ball to see that the roadster was a thing of the past. Had it not been for Jim Clark's tire problems, the broken oil plug on Bobby Marshman's car, or Rodger Ward's fuel select valve difficulties, one of the rear engine cars most likely would have won. If Jim were to continue his winning ways, he knew it would have to be in a rear engine car.

At that time Ted Halibrand was the only American builder offering a rear engine car to the mass racing market. Called the Shrike, it was a solidly designed and sturdily built car, if not as sophisticated as the Lotuses of Colin Chapman. Since Chapman still was not making new Lotuses available to other teams, Jim settled on a Shrike.

"DVS sent me to California to pick up the car in late 1964," explains Pete, "and when I got to the Halibrand shop, it was practically still on the drawing board. So I ended up sticking around, and helping assemble the car myself. Then I took it over to Inglewood and painted it at Bob Carter's shop."

Pete got the car ready in time for the November 22, 1964 champ car race at Phoenix. Bob Veith filled in for Jim in the two hundred mile event, and finished an unimpressive eighth, eight laps off the pace of winner, Lloyd Ruby. That next time the car ran it would again be at Phoenix, but both the driver and the results would be dramatically different.

On March 25, 1965, the attention of the racing world was riveted on the mile oval in Phoenix, Arizona. For there, in a 150 mile Championship race, Jim Hurtubise would make his racing comeback. There were many questions to be answered. Could Jim make the race in one of the rear engine cars? The only time he had been in one was at the Speedway during the short test drive he had performed for Mickey Thompson in 1962. If he got in the race, would he have the stamina to endure a hundred and fifty miles of close competition under the hot, Arizona sun? Were his hands really ready for such a grueling ordeal?

Performing as if he had never been away, Jim easily qualified his unfamiliar car in the eighth starting position and calmly awaited the start of the race. What thoughts were cascading through Jim's mind at such an important time in his life can only be speculated on. As he sat in his car on the starting grid, helmet on, isolated from the turmoil around him, surely the events of the past year came to mind. Jim had survived his fiery ordeal and was again seated in a race car. There were others who hadn't.

Most certainly there were anxious thoughts about the day ahead. Jim had worked hard for this and was confident of his capability to get the job done, but the only true test would be the race. Any lingering doubts would be answered once the green flag fell.

When the command to start engines was given, Jim gave a nod to Pete and Don Shepherd, then pulled away with the rest of the field. The stomach tightening waiting was over, the race was on!

As of old, Jim began an early push for the front, running consistently and smoothly, each lap completed a personal victory.

"Look at that little SOB," yelled Don Shepherd to Pete, "he's really getting it done out there!"

Jim was getting it done. He could have gone out and just stroked along to finish the race. No one would have thought less of him for it. But Jim was a racer. He hadn't endured nine months of torturous rehabilitation to stroke. He went to Phoenix to race, and was soon running among the leaders until his brakes began to fail, and he was forced to back off. Quieting the skeptics, and perhaps quelling some of his own inner doubts, Jim raced on despite the mechanical problems and finished the 150 mile race in fourth place.

The ovation Jim received as he rolled into the pits at the end of the race exceeded even that of the race winner, Don Branson. Grinning, but obviously exhausted, he lifted himself from the car and was swarmed by a multitude of happy, tearful greeters. Most of his family had travelled from New York for this long awaited occasion, and several of the staff who had treated him at Brooke were there as well. Jane grabbed him, her eyes brimming with tears, and hugged him long and hard. His children jumped and squealed for his attention, and someone grabbed Andy and plunked him atop his father's shoulders. When asked about his comeback and how he felt physically, Jim responded, "Comeback? What comeback? I just went to work after my accident. I was sick and I started racing again, it's my job."

"No, I was never really worried about my eventual return to racing," he continued. "No matter how dark things looked in the hospital, I was always optimistic. When you think about the alternative, I wasn't so bad off. I never felt sorry for myself. I was alive. I had my friends and family. Jane knows racing is my life, and she's always been right by my side."

"I proved everyone wrong, and now that I've done it I feel pretty good, really. I was real tired at the finish, which is only natural. But, I'll be okay now. I'm sure of it."

"My rear end is hurting more than my hands," he laughed. "I lost my brakes about half way through the race, and I had to pump them the rest of the day."

Jane differed with Jim's cryptic attempt at humor. "His hands were a mess after that race," she insists. "They were swollen, red and absolutely killing him, although he tried not to let on."

Jim had taken his first step back to racing, but with Indianapolis only two months away, there were many who still questioned whether Jim would be ready. One hundred fifty miles was one thing, five hundred was quite another.

Jim had planned to run only two more races before Indianapolis, and the first of those did little to still his doubters. At the Trenton 100 champ car race, held on April 25, Jim's clutch failed, and he fell out of the race after only twenty laps. The Yankee 300, however, was quite a different story.

Contested on the 2 1/2 mile road course at Indianapolis Raceway Park, the Yankee 300 was a USAC sanctioned stock car race held on the first Saturday in May. Slinging a three thousand pound stock car for three hundred miles around a tight, twisting circuit with one hand, while shifting gears with the other, would be the supreme test of Jim's physical endurance.

Jim was to drive one of the 1965 Plymouths campaigned by USAC Stock Car Champion, Norm Nelson. Jim had driven for Norm on several occasions before the Milwaukee accident, and Nelson had kept in touch with Jim while he was recovering at Brooke. Nelson never doubted that Jim would make his return to racing and saved one of his cars for the hard charging Hurtubise.

"I had no doubt in my mind that I wanted Jim to drive for me again, nor that he could do the job," said Nelson. "I never really considered who I might ask if Jim hadn't felt up to driving. With his spirit and determination I knew he would make it. And, now that he's pulled through that terrible accident, he's gotta' race."

Norm did ask Lloyd Ruby, who had raced the car in Jim's absence, to stand by in case Jim needed relief during the long afternoon. Lloyd wasn't needed. Jim drove the three hundred miles unaided, and although he lost the clutch, making shifting next to impossible, he brought the car to the finish in third place.

After the grueling four hour grind, Jim was mobbed in the pits. "I was really getting tired at the end," sighed Jim, "I thought once I'd have to give up, but then my crew showed me the board and it said there were only ten laps to go. I thought I could surely tough out ten laps. Then a little later they showed me the board again, and I still had ten laps to go! I didn't know what was going on, but I decided, 'What the hell, I can finish now."

Pete arrived at the Indianapolis Motor Speedway on May 10 with the Halibrand rear engine car, revamped after Phoenix. As befitted Jim's status as one of the country's top drivers, his team had been selected by the Ford Motor Company to use one of their potent, double overhead cam racing engines. Pete was sent through Ford's intensive training program and had installed the new engine after the race at Trenton.

Jim's return to the Speedway was highly heralded but uneventful. He took a few slow warm up laps to break in the Ford engine and pulled back in. With the first day of qualifying less than a week away, Jim was not concerned about the theatrics of his return. Instead he concentrated on working his car up to speed, while Pete continued to learn the idiosyncrasies of the Ford engine. By Pole day, Jim was displaying solid practice speeds. Not as fast as the 160 mile per hour laps being cranked out by Foyt and Clark in Lotus Fords, but quick enough to qualify within the first three rows, where, statistically, most of the 500 winners start from.

Then, during the Saturday morning practice session, the throttle stuck open as he entered turn four. Jim later surmised that the fuel injectors had iced up, a condition sometimes created when the air/fuel mixture is driven through the injector passages at high speed.

With the engine screaming, the car shot across the track and slammed into the concrete wall. Big chunks of the bodywork broke off and were slung high into the air. The magnesium wheels exploded in a shower of sparks, as the car scraped along the wall for three hundred feet, grinding through the side-mounted fuel tank. A collective gasp went up from the crowd as cloud of dust and smoke poured from the car.

There was no fire. The car was destroyed, but the rubber and foam fuel cells, mandated by USAC after the rash of fatal fires in 1964, held. Jim joked that he was going to have to get his sponsor to change their name. "Tombstone [the Tombstone Life Insurance Company was his car's sponsor] might not be such a good name to carry on a race car after all," he laughed.

Joking aside, the situation Jim faced was serious. With just a week of practice and only two days of qualifying remaining, he was without a car. Lindsey Hopkins offered him a ride in one of his cars, as did A.J. Foyt and Parnelli Jones, both of whom had rear engine, Lola Fords. Jim turned them all down, however, when Andy Granatelli pulled out the Novi he had qualified so well with in 1963.

Granatelli, in his ongoing obsession for winning the 500 with the Novi, had built a state of the art, four wheel drive chassis to harness the powerful engine. Bobby Unser was the driver and had practiced among the fastest all month. On the Friday before the opening day of qualifying, Bobby tangled with Ebb Rose and his new Novi was destroyed. Unser then jumped in the back up, year old Novi and qualified solidly in the middle of row three the next day.

When Jim agreed to drive the remaining Novi, Granatelli pulled the highly tuned engine from Unser's wrecked car and installed it in Jim's. The work wasn't completed until midweek, so when Jim roared out to qualify on Saturday morning, he only had a handful of practice laps in the car.

Regardless, Jim possessed the special skill required to tame the Novi, to make it do things other drivers couldn't, and when his qualifying run ended, Jim had averaged 156.863 miles per hour. He was the fastest qualifier of the final weekend, and the tenth fastest in the thirty three car field. Afterwards, Jim could hardly contain his excitement.

"Man that tiger was really roaring," Jim whooped. "It was doing some sputtering, and I never did get the RPMs I should have. But when it took hold-vrooooom-it really roared! It's a hell of a race car, and I'm glad to be back in it. And I'm glad to be back in this race. I finally feel like a race car driver again."

Granatelli was no less excited. "There's no doubt about it," exclaimed Andy, "Hurtubise just has to be the story today. He's a brave driver. A great driver. He's a super human being. If he had been driving that car since he got here at the beginning of the month, he would have been doing 160 in it by now."

When asked about his chances of winning the 500 in the Novi, Jim answered, "I'd like to have gone a little faster, but we'll have it running by race day and those other guys better watch out. I'm starting so far back that I might not lead that first lap on Memorial Day, but watch out for the second!"

There would have been no more fitting end to Jim's courageous comeback at Indianapolis than for him to have won the 500 in 1965. To see him in victory lane, the winner's wreath draped across his shoulders, that Hurtubise grin filling his scarred face, waving to the crowd with his disfigured hands. It didn't happen. The overpowered Novi engine destroyed its clutch, and Jim was out on the first lap.

Dejected by such an early exit, Jim climbed remorsefully from his car, and made his way slowly down pit lane to his garage. As he did, the crowd in the packed grandstands rose to its feet and saluted the brave man passing before them. The ovation brought a smile. He visibly brightened and turned and acknowledged the cheers. Two small boys stopped him and he posed, smiling, for a photo with them. Nothing, it seemed, could erase for long Jim's cheerful optimism.

It was for this attitude, as much as his heroic physical accomplishments, that Jim earned nine different awards for valor following his 1965 comeback. At the Indianapolis 500 Victory Banquet, Jim was presented with the Angelopolous Sportsmanship Award. As he made his way forward to accept the prestigious award, the crowd rose and gave him a standing ovation, an honor usually reserved for the race winner. In making the presentation, *Indianapolis News* Sports Editor, Wayne Fuson said, "Jim, you might have run just a short distance in Monday's race, but you have travelled a long, long road back to racing."

In the next months, The Ford Motor Company made Jim the recipient of their new award honoring the person who had contributed most to the image of auto racing. Along with a plaque they presented Jim with a 1966 Thunderbird and Jane with a silver tea service.

Perhaps the most impressive award, however, came from the Philadelphia Sportswriters Association, who named him the most courageous athlete of 1965. In the long, tradition-laden history of this particular award, Jim was the first race car driver to be so honored.

Indianapolis was, without doubt, the most visible race of Jim's comeback year, but it would be on the lower profile tracks, where a driver was required to hammer out a living week by week, that Jim's perseverance would be put to the complete test.

Although racing sprint cars on dirt with his delicate hands seemed to be out of the question, in late summer Jim did attempt to run two champ car dirt races—DuQuoin on September 4 and the Hoosier Hundred two weeks later. At DuQuoin, he had to be relieved by Bobby Unser, and at the Hoosier Hundred Roger McCluskey took the wheel for him. Afterwards Jim sat staring at his hands and repeating, "They're getting better all the time. They're really getting better all the time."

The other races Jim ran on the Championship Trail produced similar results. He returned to Milwaukee almost a year to the day after his fiery crash, and missed the race when the brakes failed on the Vita Fresh Orange Juice roadster.

A week later the champ cars ran at Langhorne, where Jim had enjoyed some of his greatest success. Langhorne had been paved by then, and in what looked like a repeat of Milwaukee the previous year, Jim was locked in a three-car duel, this time with Mel Kenyon and Ralph Lugori. They were running as though roped together when Kenyon's engine blew and they tangled in a crunching, fiery accident.

Jim and Lugori escaped uninjured, but Kenyon was trapped in his burning car. Mel lost his left hand to the flames, but, inspired by Jim's ordeal, he too made a courageous comeback. Using a special glove designed by his mechanic brother, Don, that locked the stub of his hand to the steering wheel, Mel returned to race at Indianapolis, and went on to become one of midget racing's greatest competitors. He has won the USAC National Midget Championship seven times and continues his distinguished career today.

When the Indianapolis cars made their debut at the high banked stock car track in Atlanta, Georgia, Jim was again at the wheel of the Novi. In its only appearance on an American track other than Indianapolis, Jim pushed the big car to sixth fast qualifying time, and finished the 250 mile race in fourth place.

Jim was pleased with his comeback, thrilled to be racing again, but he wanted to do more than just return, he wanted to win. In an impressive drive at Trenton, on July 18, he came close.

Starting sixteenth in the Dupont Golden 7 rear engine Ford, Jim moved to fourth by lap 20. Then, while battling Jim McElreath and Roger McCluskey for third, he spun on lap 35 and dropped back to mid-pack. Again he worked his way to the front, then while running second he promptly spun again! Lloyd Ruby had vacated the car earlier in the year when he couldn't make it handle, and now Jim understood why. Not to be deterred, Jim, for the third time, worked his way back to the front, and finished second to winner, A.J.Foyt.

Jim's illusive, first comeback victory finally occurred in 1965 at the track that had put his promising career into a fiery tailspin. On July 11th Jim had finished second to his boss, Norm Nelson, when Norm passed him on the last lap of the Milwaukee 200. The fans thought it was a put-up deal with the "boss" having to win and they were quite angry until Jim got on the PA and calmed them down. During the September 19, 250 miler it was a different story. No one could catch Jim and he triumphantly rolled to victory.

With his trip to the winner's circle Jim's comeback was complete. One driver put it simply, but accurately, "Herk's not making a comeback, he's here!"

Dick Williford Photo - HFC

Jim at Indianapolis Raceway Park in 1965.

Dick Williford Photo - HFC

If the engine was up front I could see what they were doing.

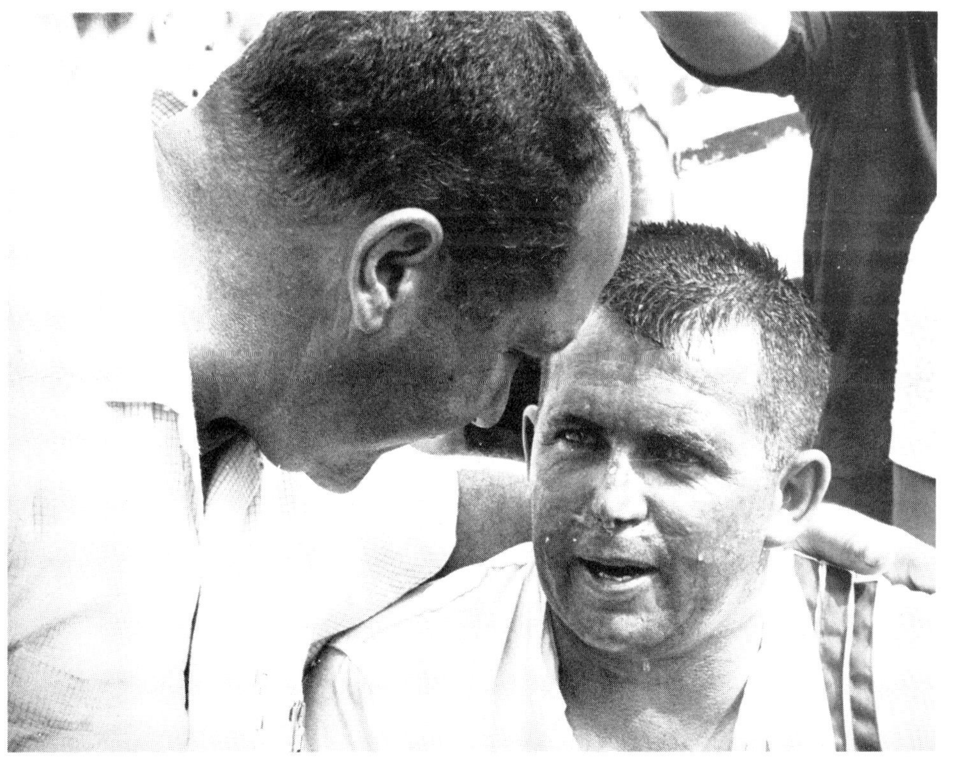

Hurtubise Family Collection

Andy Granatelli and Jim at Indy in 1965 after he qualified.

Hurtubise Family Collection

Taken at Phoenix, this photo shows just how bad Jim's hands were as he made his comeback to auto racing.

HURTUBISE

20

Chrysler-Plymouth Photo by Dick Williford

After proving to himself and the racing world, in 1965, that the Milwaukee fire had not eroded his ability or desire, Jim looked to 1966 with high expectations. Although he had lost a year to his debilitating injuries, his amazing comeback gave him the confidence that he could return to his winning form on the Championship Trail and capture that elusive 500 victory.

What Jim had not anticipated, however, were the monumental changes in technology that had transpired in Indy car racing during the ten months he was absent from the sport. In 1963, the year Jim sat on the front row at Indianapolis with the Novi, there were only three rear engine cars in the field. By 1965 that ratio had drastically flip flopped, with only six front engine cars having made the field. In 1966 there would be but one.

Jim attempted to keep abreast of the rapidly changing technology by joining forces with car owner, and race car builder, Fred Gerhardt. Gerhardt's rear engine cars were the latest offering by a domestic constructor, and while technically behind the Lotus and Lola cars from the English manufacturers the Gerhardt was a solid performer, as evidenced by the fact that there were more Gerhardt cars in the 1966 500 than any other make.

Unfortunately, in his constant quest to be innovative, Jim and his team's choice of a turbocharged Offy engine was not as astute as their choice of cars. The turbocharged Offy was designed as a response to the threat offered by the powerful Ford double overhead cam engine.

A turbocharged Offy would power Bobby Unser to his first 500 win in 1968 and a turbocharged engine of one make or another has won every 500 since, but in 1966 turbochargers on racing engines were still experimental and were plagued with mechanical problems.

As a result, what had begun as a year of high expectations for Jim, turned to disappointment. The first race on the 1966 champ car circuit was a March 20, 150 mile event at Phoenix. Jim qualified a mediocre eleventh and exited the race early when the turbocharger failed.

At Indianapolis, Jim qualified twenty third, one of only three turbocharged cars in the thirty three car field. He escaped the first lap melee that eliminated eleven cars, including several of the favorites, but dropped out after only twenty nine laps. The turbocharger was again the culprit.

Jim had learned during his 1965 comeback that his damaged hands would not allow him to run the dirt tracks of the Championship

Trail. Limited, therefore, to the paved tracks, the pattern established in the first two races continued throughout the year, and for the first time since he joined the champ car circuit in 1959, he was not competitive.

The weekend after Indianapolis, Jim was twenty second at Milwaukee. At Atlanta he finished twenty sixth. In the fall race at Milwaukee he was twenty sixth. He fell out and was seventeenth at Trenton, and fifteenth at Mount Fugi, Japan.

1966 would have been a dismal year, indeed, for Jim had it not been for his performance in the stock cars. Jim was no stranger to stock car racing. His earliest racing experiences were in modified stock cars in Florida and New York. Then there was the Plymouth convertible he ran at San Diego in his early California racing days. And even as his career advanced to the champ cars and Indianapolis, Jim stayed involved in stock car racing.

Although Jim had dabbled in USAC stock car racing from the time he joined the club in 1959, he did not really get seriously involved until 1964 when Norm Nelson invited him to replace Paul Goldsmith in one of his factory backed Plymouths.

Norm had long been an admirer of Jim and his throttle-to-the-floor style. "Herk doesn't know what it is to slow down," he once remarked. "Wide open is the only pace he knows."

Jim demonstrated the accuracy of Norm's statement in the opening race of the 1964 USAC stock car series at Langhorne on April 26. The condition of the track that day was typical of Langhorne, dusty and rough. By the time the field got to the second turn on the first lap, the was so much dirt being thrown into the air that the drivers, literally, could not see where they were going.

Curtis Turner spun directly in front of Jim in the dust storm, but Jim, relying on his instinctive knowledge of Langhorne, honed from hundreds of miles in sprint and champ cars, found his way through, and slid past the gyrating Curtis and into the lead.

As the race progressed, the track worsened. The spinning tires of the heavy stock cars dug crater size holes in the turns, and flung fist size stones with rocket like force. One such projectile shattered Jim's windshield.

Despite the abysmal conditions, Jim took his Plymouth up to the high groove he loved to run, planted the tail of the car against the wall, and stuck his foot to the floor. At one point, Jim was running so high and hard that a deep rut pitched his speeding Plymouth out of control, and he hit the wooden barrier with such force that it shattered, and impaled his car's quarter panel with a four foot long splinter. Still, he raced on. By the end of the 150 mile race Jim had a five lap lead over second place, and a new track record to his credit.

The crash at Milwaukee ended Jim's racing for 1964, but Norm Nelson stayed in touch with him during his long rehabilitation and reserved a spot for him on his 1965 team. Explaining why he saved the first class ride for Jim, when many were wondering if he could even race again, Nelson said, "Jim has more guts and go than any man I've ever seen in my lifetime. I have no doubt he will race, and race hard again."

Jim rewarded Nelson's confidence by winning the 1965 USAC Car Owners' Championship, with six top three finishes in the thirteen USAC stock car races he ran, including his dramatic comeback win at Milwaukee.

So formidable was the Hurtubise/Nelson Team on the 1965 USAC circuit, that Plymouth offered them factory backing to run a few NASCAR races in 1966. The first was at Riverside, California on January 23, where Jim finished sixth behind Dan Gurney, and NASCAR regulars David Pearson, Curtis Turner, Dick Hutcinson and Paul Goldsmith.

A month later, Jim ran the Daytona 500 in Nelson's Plymouth and again finished sixth in a race he might have easily won. Winner Richard Petty admitted afterwards that Jim had the fastest car on the track and expressed doubts about his ability to catch him had Jim's tires not blistered in the closing laps of the race.

NASCAR racing was so popular by the mid-sixties that many of the top Indianapolis drivers would compete at Daytona and several other major NASCAR races on their FIA international racing licence. Only two of these interlopers were taken seriously by the "good 'ole boys" of NASCAR, A.J. Foyt and Jim Hurtubise. At the Atlanta Motor Speedway, on March 27, Jim proved why.

Atlanta Motor Speedway is a high banked, 1.522 mile long, superspeedway oval that annually hosts the prestigious Atlanta 500. In 1966, the Atlanta 500 was, next to Daytona, the most important race on the NASCAR schedule. As he had at Daytona earlier in the year, Jim ran with the leaders from the start of the race and took the lead when Richard Petty dropped out with engine failure at the midway point of the race.

With Petty out of the picture, first Curtis Turner, and then Fred Lorenzen moved up to battle Jim for first place. Turner's challenge was short lived, falling out after only a few laps with engine trouble. Lorenzen, on the other hand, fought with Jim all afternoon. In one fifty lap stretch they swapped the lead five different times. When Lorenzen made his last pit stop, Jim put him a lap down, and in a fortunate turn of events, the yellow caution lap flashed on just as Jim made his final pit stop on lap 295. With the field slowed under the yellow, Jim came out of the pits with his lead intact and finished the 328 lap race a full lap ahead of Lorenzen in second.

"Herk deserved to win," complimented Lorenzen after the race. "That guy was running the last five laps as fast as the first five."

Jim's car owner, whose own car had dropped out early, watched anxiously in the pits as Jim raced to victory. "Those last ten laps were just pure suffering," admitted Norm Nelson. "I've never been so nervous in my life."

Had Nelson known that Jim's car had developed a mysterious vibration, he would have been more nervous yet. "The car felt good," explained Jim, "but it started vibrating about two-thirds of the way through the race. I slacked off for awhile, but it vibrated at both high and low speed, so I decided to tromp on it and get the show over with."

Much later, Jim confided that a bit of mechanical skullduggery aided him in his most important racing victory. NASCAR has recently tried to clamp down on the practice, but cheating within the ranks of NASCAR has been the norm rather than the exception for years. Unlike other sports, however, this practice is not necessarily considered dishonorable. Rather, depending on the creativity of their efforts, the practitioners are looked upon with a degree of respect.

Few NASCAR racers, especially in those early years, didn't bend the rules some, but perhaps the most ingenious example was the Chevrolet that Smokey Yunick built for the Daytona 500 one year. Everything appeared to be in order with the car as it passed through pre-race technical inspection, but, closer examination revealed that in actuality the car was a 3/4 scale model!

Jim's friend, John Laux, who worked closely with NASCAR as a tire engineer, insists that the reason Jim didn't win more NASCAR races is that he didn't know how to cheat good enough. "Herk was always too obvious with his cheating," laughs John. "One time I remember they were running restrictor plates on the carbs, and Jim just drilled a bunch of little holes in his to override it. Hell, they caught that right away!"

For the 1966 Atlanta 500, though, Jim had it down pat. He discovered during practice that if he lowered the car's front end below the minimum specified in the NASCAR rule book, it was faster and more stable through Atlanta's high banked turns.

To get by the NASCAR inspectors, the car was set at the proper ride height before the race. Then on the pace lap, Jim flipped open a hidden access panel that the crew had installed above the adjusting nut that controlled the ride height. With a socket wrench he sneaked aboard the car in his boot, he cranked the nut seventy times, a number predetermined by his crew to gain the optimum setting.

After he got the checkered flag, Jim pulled the wrench from his boot, furiously cranked the nut back to its original position, and tossed the wrench out the window on the backstretch, where he was out of sight of NASCAR officials. That took him so long to accomplish, he told Al Krueger years later, that he had to take an extra lap to get it done. "I guess those NASCAR guys thought that the crazy Yankee wanted an extra lap to wave at the crowd," laughed Jim.

Jim ran one other NASCAR race in 1966, the Firecracker 400 held at Daytona on the Fourth of July, where he finished fifth. Returning to the USAC circuit, Jim finished an excellent year in the stock cars with seven top five finishes, including a win in the 250 mile race held at Langhorne Speedway September 11.

Jim continued to be enamored with stock car racing throughout the remainder of his career and in 1967 he even announced that he was withdrawing his USAC membership to run NASCAR exclusively.

"I like the stocks, and I've been pretty successful on the NASCAR tracks," explained Jim. "I know I'm not physically capable of driving the dirt anymore. It tears up my hands. In stocks I feel a little racier, because they steer easier. I think I can be more competitive in NASCAR and make more money."

When asked whether this meant he would give up running at Indianapolis, Jim quickly responded, "Oh, no, I'll not give up the 500. I'll be there next year."

Jim was there that next year, and the next year, and the year after that. For, despite the disappointments, the near misses, and his growing lack of confidence in the rear engine cars that were dominating there, he would not give up his dream of winning the Indianapolis 500 Mile Race.

Chrysler-Plymouth Photot by Dick Williford

Jim on his way to victory in the Atlanta 500 in 1966.

Dick Williford Photo - HFC

Jim, Ronnie Householder and Norm Nelson.

Dick Williford Photo - HFC

Jim at Milwaukee Sept. 19, 1995

Jim at Indianapolis Raceway Park in 1965.

Dick Williford Photo - HFC

HURTUBISE

21

Hurtubise Family Collection

Jim shocked the racing world in late 1966 when he announced that he was designing and building a front engine car for the 1967 500. Some thought it was just another one of Jim's outlandish jokes, but he was serious. Not only would he build it, but he continued to refine it and campaign it for thirteen years.

Jim's logic for running the car long after even he knew it was uncompetitive is difficult to understand, but when he originally built the car, he was convinced that it was the ideal design for Indianapolis. It combined the best ideas of the rear engine and the front engine car designs into a hybrid that he believed eliminated the weaknesses of each.

The engine, although mounted in the front, sat further back in the chassis than in a traditional front engine car providing a mid-engine location that, theoretically, creates better weight distribution than that found even on a rear engine car. Jim copied the semi-monocoque type design of the rear engine cars for a rigid, yet lightweight chassis. At the same time the front and rear axles were the solid type used on the old roadsters to provide a strong, stable base to maintain the precise tire alignment that is critical with the high speeds generated at Indianapolis.

"I want to beat the trend," said Jim at the Speedway press conference when he unveiled his car. "When Jimmy Clark almost won with his rear engine car in 1963, everybody started to build rear engine cars. They were lighter than the old roadsters, and the overhead cam Fords were putting out more horsepower. Soon the roadsters were obsolete.

"I want to start the trend back to the roadsters this year at Indianapolis. They said you couldn't build a roadster as light as the rear engine cars. I have. My car weighs only 1350 pounds. It's a semi-monocoque design with magnesium body panels riveted to the thin wall steel tubing frame contributing greatly to the strength and rigidity of the chassis. The car is very low and narrower than any of the rear engine cars. I still believe that the solid axles I'm using can work better at the Speedway. They keep the tires flat against the track and let them run in a straight line, which allows them to run cooler than on a rear engine car.

"My cockpit is way back in the chassis where I get much more precise feel and control than I've ever felt with a rear engine car. It's going to be great fun for me to race at Indianapolis against all those rear engine cars."

Jim dubbed his new car the Mallard, because with its short upturned tail it resembled the duck of that same name. "Dan Gurney calls his cars Eagles, and we've got Coyotes, too," said Jim. "So I named my car the Mallard, after the ducks that swim on my pond back on Shawnee Road in North Tonawanda."

As he had with his innovative 1960 Chevy sprint car, Jim called on the racing expertise of his friends to help him with his new Indianapolis car. Don Shepherd agreed to prepare the turbocharged Offy engine. Jim, though a competent welder, had difficulty practicing this craft after the fire because the skin on his hands was so thin that the heat from the welding torch would cause third degree burns. A friend, Bill Henderson, was called on to weld the chassis, and Paul Cozard, who had done the bodywork on the 1964 car, was assigned the same task on the Mallard.

Jim was not only the car's designer and builder, but the owner as well and without the financial backing he enjoyed when he built his 1964 Indianapolis car, he was forced to be innovative on a limited budget. His intention was to build three cars, one for himself, and the other two to be sold to help finance his project. He did manage to manufacture enough parts for three Mallards, but only two were built. His own, and another which he sold to Ebb Rose.

Aware of Jim's tight financial situation, the men working with him volunteered most of their time or worked for a minimal wage. "I actually lost money during that time," says Don, ungrudgingly, today. "I was running Bobby Unser in my sprint car, and there were times I didn't even have a chance to wash it between races. But, Jim was a friend, and I promised him I would stick with him through the month of May."

Don did, but even his bountiful racing savvy was not enough. New race cars are notoriously difficult to develop and few come out of the box ready to race. From the time Jim arrived in Indianapolis on May 2, he experienced fuel injection problems with the still developmental turbocharged Offenhauser engine.

Jim and the crew worked desperately with the car, but because of the recurring engine problems, he was never able to get the suspension of the car working to his satisfaction. "There are just too many things I don't know about the car," sighed Jim at one point. "And I'm running out of time to find out."

Jim's comments proved to be true and for the first time since he arrived at the Speedway as a record breaking rookie in 1960, he missed the 500. Jim did qualify his new creation at a four lap average of 162.411 miles per hour, but that run was less than a half mile an hour too slow, and he was bumped from the field in the waning hours of qualifications. The other Mallard was destroyed in a practice crash caused when Ebb Rose was hit in the head with a valve churned up by another car.

When Jim returned to the Speedway with the Mallard in 1968, he was better prepared than he had been the year before. He had worked out many of the handling problems he had experienced in 1967 during a series of tire tests run at the Speedway that October. He comfortably ran many laps in excess of 165 miles per hour, a speed that would have put him near the front of the field in 1966, had he been able to obtain it then.

With the great lap times in tire tests, and the finances provided when he picked up Pepsi and one of its snack food firms, Frito Lay, as a major sponsor, things looked promising for the 1968 500. That is until the track opened for practice on May 1st. Immediately the car's engine started burning pistons. The problem was so severe that it was impossible for Jim to string more than two or three practice laps together. Desperate, Jim called Pete.

Pete had grown weary of the rigors of life on the road and retired from racing at the end of the 1966 season. He didn't relish being gone from his wife and family, or that his children were growing up with an absentee father. Despite his decision to turn the direction of his life away from racing, Pete was always there when Jim needed him.

Al Krueger, a captain on the North Tonawanda fire department and soon to be friend of Jim's, was at Pete's home when Jim called from Indianapolis.

"I knew Pete and Jim's father, Ernie, very well, but I didn't know Jim at that time," says Al. "Of course I knew of him. I was at Pete's for a cookout when Jim called and wanted Pete to go to Indianapolis to help him with his car. When Pete got off the phone, he turned to me and said, 'I've got to go to the Speedway right away. Jim needs help. You want to go and give us a hand, Al?' I said, 'Sure!' I made arrangements at the fire department, and Pete and I took off the next day. That's how I first started working with Jim."

Arriving at the Speedway, Pete and Al quickly realized they had their work cut out for them. "I think it was seventeen engines that we blew that year," states Al. "I didn't know anything about engines. I just did what Pete told me to do and gave him a hand anyway I could."

"We lost so many engines that we had a routine worked out. When Jim blew an engine, the crew would pull it out of the car while Pete and I were back at the motel getting a couple hours sleep. They'd call us, and we'd go and work on the engine all night, rebuilding it, getting it all set, and then we'd call them. They'd come out, put the engine back in, do all the plumbing and get back out on the track while we were sleeping. Then another engine would blow and we'd start all over again."

In between the blown engines, Jim searched frantically for the speed that had come so easily in the October tire tests. The first weekend of qualifying came and went, and Jim was no nearer making the thirty three car field than he had been the year before. On May 18, searching for those elusive, extra miles per hour, he brushed the wall twice and spun one-and-a-half times at over 160 miles per hour. Fortunately both Jim and the car were unscathed.

He switched from Goodyear to Firestone tires, but even that didn't help until Al Clark, assigned to Firestone's stock car division, made the observation to Jim that the Mallard with its front engine and A-frame suspension really resembled a stock car more than an Indianapolis car, and should be set up that way.

Acting on that advice, Jim replaced the skinnier front tires with a set of wide rear tires and his speed jumped three miles per hour. He found the speed he needed, but with the final weekend of qualifying at hand, Jim was still blowing engines and running out of time to rebuild them. That is when his racing friends stepped in. Former car owner, Fred Gerhardt, loaned him an engine. When that one blew, John Laux, who had quit the tire companies and was running the Gene White racing team with Lloyd Ruby as a driver, loaned him another.

Quipped Jim of the situation, "I may not be able to run very fast, but I sure can borrow engines! We borrowed an engine from Fred Gerhardt, and blew it Saturday. Then we got one from Gene White and blew it too. So my crew and I stayed up all night and had the original engine rebuilt and running by nine o'clock Sunday morning."

That all night session proved to be futile. Rain that had plagued the Speedway all month came again on the final Sunday of qualifying, and time trials, for one of the few times in Speedway history, had to be extended to the next day.

In a tension filled Monday afternoon qualifying session, two drivers crashed. Rick Muther suffered a mild concussion after hitting the turn one wall. Bob Hurt crashed in the same turn and suffered spinal injuries that left him a paraplegic. Eight drivers managed to qualify for the race, and Jim was one of them.

Fans had been following the saga of the popular Hurtubise all month. They knew of the problems he had encountered. They knew his chances of making the race in a front engine car were virtually nonexistent. Yet that knowledge just caused them to pull for Jim all the harder.

He was their record breaking champion. Their comeback hero. And when he rolled out to qualify, they rose to their feet and didn't sit down until he returned to the pits, safely in the race.

Once more Jim had thrilled them by accomplishing what seemed to be the impossible. It had been two years since a front engine car had qualified at Indianapolis, and in the years after, no other has made it. Only a driver of Jim's extraordinary talent could have pulled it off.

"Boy this has been a long month," Jim sighed afterwards. "All I wanted to do was get in the race. Even my sponsors have been going nuts. They kept calling me up and asking to help. They told me to order whatever I needed and they'd pay for it."

Then Jim revealed that there were other mechanical troubles even as he tried to qualify. "When we were rolling the car to the starting line," Jim explained, "I pushed the brake pedal and it went right to the floor. I must have had some air in the brake line. I had brakes, but I had to go to the floor for them and that sure wasn't comfortable!"

Of the run itself he said, "We've had trouble all month getting four laps in succession without anything going wrong. I knew this was it. I was going through the turns so slow I didn't think I was moving. When my pit crew gave me 161 on my first lap, I thought, 'My gosh man, you'd better push it a little bit!' And when I got into the 162's I just stayed there."

"But we're in the race. If we can get everything put back together the way it should be by race day, we'll race with them all."

Jim wasn't able to race with them at all. The problem that had plagued him all month cropped up again, and after only nine laps he was out with a burned piston. But he had made history. Jim's name is still in the record books as the driver of the last front engine car to run in the Indianapolis 500. That he designed and built the car himself was an accomplishment that Jim looked on with pride the rest of his life.

On July 6, 1968, Jim proved just how sound the design of the Mallard was, when at the urging of NASCAR president, Bill France Sr., he took the car to Daytona's high banked 2 1/2 mile oval and set a new world closed course record of 191.938 miles per hour.

His Mallard was indeed fast. The trouble was, Jim couldn't obtain that speed on the track that was most important to him, Indianapolis. In 1969, after another difficult month of practice, he made one attempt to qualify the Mallard. He was running fast enough to have made the race, but blew an engine. In 1970, he made two qualifying attempts, but neither were fast enough. In 1971, he crashed and ran out of time before he could repair the damage, and wasn't even able to make a qualifying attempt.

Jim's narrow window of opportunity, when the technology of his front engine car overlapped that of the rear engine cars, had closed. Development of the rear engine machines accelerated at an astounding rate. Advancements in suspensions, engines and aerodynamics pushed qualifying speeds towards two hundred miles an hour, while Jim struggled to get into the mid 180's.

Regretfully, in 1972 Jim gave up the battle against the rear engine cars and joined them. "I'm switching to a rear engine car for Indy," said Jim, "because I believe one of the 'pushers' will win, and I want to be in it."

The "pusher" Jim chose was a year old Coyote/Foyt purchased for him from A.J. Foyt by Jim's former car owner, Dick Sommers. Proving that he had lost little of his special touch at the Speedway, and despite not having driven a rear engine car in six years, Jim easily qualified in thirteenth place.

During the race he moved into the top ten in the first twenty laps, was eighth at the end ofsixty laps, and ten laps later had moved into seventh place. Just when it seemed Jim was in position for a strong finish, he ran out of fuel on lap 94. Coasting to a stop on the backstretch he was helped back to the pits by a group of track attendants and over zealous fans who pushed him through the infield to the garage area. Jim's crew took the car back out to the pits, refueled it, and Jim was back in race. Although the USAC officials allowed him to rejoin the race and run the remainder of the race, a ruling after the race dropped him from sixteenth place to twenty third. The seventy seven laps he recorded after being pushed through the infield were disallowed.

Although his emphasis had been directed to the Coyote in 1972, Jim did enter the Mallard as part of his Miller Beer sponsored team. After he safely qualified the Coyote, he took the time to run practice laps with the Mallard and got the six year old car going pretty fast. On May 17, he cranked off a lap at 176.991 miles per hour, and rumors ran rampant that he would withdraw his Coyote, and requalify in the roadster.

That didn't happen, but in 1973, Jim again returned to the Speedway with his venerable old car, and, except for 1974 when he qualified a rear engine McLaren, stuck with it for the next seven years.

When Jim made that decision, he threw away any realistic chance of winning the 500.

Why a driver of his obvious talent would do so has been a source of mystery to Jim's admirers for years. It has been argued that Jim didn't feel comfortable in a rear engine car. That is true, but not surprising since most of the drivers of Jim's era did not like that first generation of rear engine Indianapolis cars. However, they adapted, and Jim, who had driven and won in every type of race car he ever sat in could have too.

It has been suggested that Jim's fire-ravaged hands were a hindrance with the rear engine cars, and there is some credence to that. No less an authority than Al Unser Jr. attests to this. "A sprint car or a stock car," says Al, "you feel with your rear end. But, a rear engine car, an Indy car, you have to feel through your hands. You anticipate what it's going to do through the steering wheel."

Even that obstacle Jim could have overcome had he chose, and in fact there is much to suggest that he had. There was his masterful drive in an ill handling rear engine car at Trenton in 1965. The car was of some renown, having appeared on the cover of the May 31, 1965 issue of *Sports Illustrated*. When driver Lloyd Ruby was fired because he couldn't make it handle, Jim was called as his replacement, and had his first laps in the car during the morning practice session at Trenton.

He soon realized what Ruby had to contend with.

One experienced observer said of Jim's rear engine mount, "It's the kind of car that spins out as soon as it gets a little out of control. One slight error, and it's gone."

Jim fought the car all afternoon. Three times he moved into contention for the lead, and three times he lost control and spun out before finally finishing second to A.J. Foyt.

Afterwards, Jim said of his hairy ride, "I was driving the heck out of it. It took a lot of work to steer, but I just wanted to finish. With a few adjustments, I think we could have kept up with A.J."

As late as 1967, Jim competed on the Championship Trail with a rear engine car. Driving for the Bob Wilke team, with legendary mechanic A.J. Watson turning the wrenches, Jim ran ten champ car events. The car was not a good one, but Jim turned in several solid performances with it. He finished eighth on the road course at Mosport, Canada. At Indianapolis Raceway Park, he had the ninth fastest lap time of the thirty four cars that attempted to qualify. He finished seventh at Mt. Trembant, Canada, and tied the track record in qualifying it at Milwaukee.

Jim was a race car driver, and a great one. He was more than capable of doing well in any type car he desired to race. Therein lies the key. Very simply, Jim Hurtubise had no desire to race the rear engine cars. That had less to do with the type of car than the climate that was introduced to racing with the advent of those machines.

Hurtubise Family Collection

Hurtubise Family Collection

Reel Racing Photos

HURTUBISE

22

Hurtubise Family Collection

When the rear engine technology proved to be successful at Indianapolis and on the remainder of the Championship Trail, thousands of dollars of American oval track equipment was obsoleted. Not only did car owners have to bear the expense of new cars, but new engines as well. First the Ford displaced the Offy as the engine of choice. Then turbocharged Offys replaced the Fords, only to be replaced by turbocharged Fords. Costs escalated to astronomical levels and car owners, who up until the early sixties consisted primarily of sportsmen who raced as a hobby, were financially hard pressed to keep up.

Coincidentally, just as the financial crunch was beginning to wreak havoc, the tire companies stepped in with a seemingly bottomless coffer of cash. When Goodyear made its appearance at the Speedway in 1963, it instigated a bidding war with Firestone for the services of the best teams and drivers. No longer did teams have to buy tires, rather, they were paid for using them.

When Goodyear made the 500 starting field for the first time in 1965, the stakes went even higher. There is an old racing adage that goes: "What wins on Sunday, sells on Monday," and the two, giant tire companies dumped money by the basketful into Indianapolis racing to insure that their tire was the one that sold on Monday.

The prosperity the racing teams reaped, however, was not without a price. To keep that stream of money flowing in, teams had to maintain their competitive edge. To do this, more and more money had to be invested in more and more sophisticated, expensive machinery.

Simple suspension systems were replaced by complicated, intricate designs. When these designs reached their cornering potential, wings were added to increase downforce and stick the cars to the track through the turns. To gain more downforce, the wings became larger and the accompanying aerodynamics grew more refined and more costly. To power these cars that had evolved into nothing more than inverted airplane wings, simple engines gave way to sensitive, touchy turbocharged powerhouses that were expensive to buy, and even more expensive to maintain.

Teams that once had been willing to loan a part to a competitor, even if it meant they were beaten in the race by the recipient, became secretive and their garages closed to visitors. Those virtues that had attracted Jim, and many others, to racing; the fun, the satisfaction derived from beating another driver by skill alone, and the sense of accomplishment derived from obtaining a goal by hard work, were gobbled up by greed, and political backbiting.

Jim first noticed this changing climate when he made his comeback in 1965. Maybe it was because he had been forced away from the sport for awhile that he was more sensitive than others to those changes, regardless, what he saw affected his attitude towards racing.

Don Shepherd, an astute racing observer and a friend of Jim's from his earliest racing days, caught a glimpse of this during Jim's comeback race at Phoenix.

"Herk changed," says Don. "I could see it in him. I was with him the first time he ran at Phoenix after the accident. He had that Halibrand car, and he was running up front. He was right there, getting the job done."

"But, I noticed after that race that something happened. He just didn't have the same outlook towards racing he had before. I would ask Jim about it from time to time, but he would avoid it. He wouldn't even answer me. He'd just look at me and not say anything."

Jim wasn't silent with his views on the state of racing for long, and began to speak out on what he saw as wrong with the sport. "Racing no longer involves skill, except in kissing the fannies of the big money people," said Jim. "I fought my butt off to get where I am in racing—then it all became politics and big money."

A prime target for Jim's lambastic attacks, especially after Firestone dropped from the sport in 1974 when the expense began to outweigh the publicity dividends, was the Goodyear tire company.

Jim insisted they controlled the outcome of races by giving special tires to whomever they wanted to win. Jim was never able to substantiate such charges, though he often would walk the pit lane at Indianapolis with a durometer, an instrument used to gauge the hardness of rubber, checking tire compounds on various cars.

"It's kind of hard on me," once said Leo Mehl, head of Goodyear's racing division. "Herk is my boyhood hero, and every time I pick up the paper he's after me!"

Jim wasn't so much upset with Leo, Goodyear, or any particular company, as he was dismayed by the damage the dumping of huge sums of money into expensive technology had done to the sport. The cost didn't decrease when Firestone dropped from racing. It was too late. The mechanism was already in place. Builders of cars and engines, and countless suppliers of assorted hardware and pieces couldn't decrease their costs. If car owners stayed in racing, they had to pay the price. When the tire money dried up, they turned to other sources of revenue, such as lucrative sponsorships and drivers willing to buy their way into an Indianapolis car, a situation that thoroughly disgusted Jim.

"What built Indianapolis is people rooting for champions from around the country," said Jim. "There are a thousand local racetracks, and every one of them has a track champion. And they're not happy just to be track champions. They've got an urge for better things. But they can't even think about getting to Indianapolis because they don't have the money. We don't get champions at Indianapolis anymore. We get whoever the tire companies want to bring in, or whoever has the money to buy their way in."

During preparations for the 1977 500, a verbal sparring match occurred between Jim, and one of those he considered a ride buyer, Salt Walther. When the qualifying gun sounded at the conclusion of qualifying that year, Walther was left sitting in line. Afterwards, he criticized Jim to the press for taking up track time that should have gone to a "legitimate qualifier."

When told of Walther's remarks, Jim responded, "He's just a little rich kid who has never won a race in his life. His daddy bought his way here. He's had eight attempts to get a car in the race and couldn't do it. And I should give him my place in line?"

The following year Jim's friends had T-shirts made up with the inscription: "Salt Walther Fan Club...Jim Hurtubise President."

Jim's criticism of the state of racing wasn't, in his mind, without a solution. He wanted to see the wings that create aerodynamic down force removed. He wanted to see the tires narrowed to twelve inches, and horsepower decreased. Doing this would reduce the cost of racing, make the driver's skill more important, and provide a better show for the fans.

"In 1973, I went to the Speedway and tried to get these things done," explained Jim. "I told them that one of the tire companies was going to pull out and the other was going to run things. When they went to the pop off valve (a device used to arbitrarily control engine power) I told them that it would up the cost of racing twenty percent."

"It's raised it even more."

"When I set records here I spent less than $3,000 to improve the car. It was up to driver skill and mechanical skill. Not how much money you had to spend. I haven't changed, I still want to race to win. But, I just can't take this stuff seriously anymore, because there's hardly any skill involved."

Even Leo Mehl conceded that Jim's argument about the driver's skill in Indy car racing was accurate. "Herk has a point," admitted Mehl, "when he says a driver's importance has been reduced. It used to be forty or fifty percent driver, now it's getting down to twenty percent."

Jim went on to say, "Racing needs to be brought back to where it relies on a driver's skill. The way it is now a mechanic can get into a car and run it 180 miles per hour. If things don't change, in five years all you'll have left at the Speedway is two buildings, the museum and the motel."

Things didn't deteriorate to that point, but the words of Jim Hurtubise are being echoed today by all who love the sport of Indy car racing, and are concerned about its future. It's leaders, including Indianapolis Motor Speedway president, Tony George, are seeking solutions to the very problems that Jim warned about twenty years ago.

On February 23, 1995 ABC's news magazine program, "*Day One*" called racing, "...a sport that exists to sell."

This is not what auto racing should be about, and it most certainly was not what Jim Hurtubise believed racing should be. To Jim, racing was supposed to be fun; a contest to match man against man in driving skill and mechanical ingenuity.

Seeing it become anything else angered him, and so, for the remainder of his life, Jim became the Don Quixote of racing. A defiant iconoclast tipping away at the windmills of big money interests, but even that he accomplished with his own unique, vigorous sense of humor that often brought smiles to those to whom his satirical barbs were directed.

When Pepsi was his sponsor in 1972, Jim hoisted a twenty-two foot-long "Pepsi Blimp" above his garage as his way of poking fun at the Goodyear blimp. It floated there for several days, until a announcement came over the PA system from Speedway officials: "Jim Hurtubise, you have one hour to remove that thing, or we're going to shoot it down!" Point made, Jim laughingly removed his blimp.

When the Goodyear baseball cap, or one emblazoned with another racing related name, became the headgear of choice at the Speedway, Jim sported a "John Deere Tractors" cap.

Another time, in the midst of the tire war between Goodyear and Firestone, Jim rolled into the pits with a set of Goodyear tires mounted on one side of his car, and a set of Firestones on the other. "You should have seen the look on the face of the tire engineers when they walked up to check the air pressure in the tires," laughed Al Krueger.

In 1975, Jim arrived at the Speedway to file his entries for the upcoming 500. He plopped down the$1,000 entry fee for each of his three cars, along with the appropriate paperwork.

Everything appeared to be in order, but Speedway officials had learned to expect the unexpected from Jim, and so carefully examined his entry blanks. One was for the front engine Mallard, another for a McLaren that Jim had entered the previous two years.

Those were in order. It was the third entry that raised official eyebrows. On the part of the entry form that asked for a description of the car, it was described as a 1975 supercharged Volkswagen powered machine. Darroll and Ed French of the Mechanics Laundry, an Indianapolis industrial laundry, were listed as co-chief mechanics. Ed Zebrowski, a local demolition expert and a friend of Jim's, was listed as the driver.

Jim was on his way out the office door when Al Bloemker caught him. Well aware of Jim's penchant for making bogus entries to reserve extra garage space for entertaining his friends, Al hailed him and said, "Wait a minute, Herk. You can't enter a car or a driver like this."

Blue eyes twinkling with mischief, Jim replied, "Al, I figured that as long as I paid my entry fee, I could enter any kind of car and driver I wanted."

"Of course," Jim continued, quite innocently, "if the car doesn't pass the tech inspection, or Zebrowski doesn't pass his rookie test, then that's up to USAC and you guys here at the Speedway to take care of."

Shaking his head in disbelief while trying to suppress a smile, Al convinced Jim he would have to provide additional technical information on the car and remove Zebrowski from the driver's list, before his entry could be accepted.

"You don't think they have anything against Polish drivers, do you?" Jim asked a group of friends as he told the story that evening.

Undoubtedly, Jim's month of May piece de resistance occurred in 1972. Jim had already qualified his rear engine Coyote for the race, when on the final Sunday of qualifying he put the Mallard in the qualifying line with driver Bud Tinglestad aboard. It appeared Jim was going to attempt a banzai run to get his roadster in the field.

As the crew made its way up the line, however, they would inexplicably wave other cars around them, just as their turn for the track was eminent. When the six PM closing gun sounded, the team's puzzling actions were clarified. Jim reached down, popped open the hood and revealed not an engine, but five cases of Miller beer, his sponsor's product, iced down in the engine compartment. "I tried to get Harlan Fengler [the Chief Steward] to come over and measure my engine," laughed Jim, " but he just turned and walked the other way."

And so Jim rolled through the latter part of his racing career entering the front engine car at Indianapolis year after year and basking in the glow of the fan's loyal adoration, all the while mocking the politics and big money interests that permeated the sport.

The question Jim's fans ask most is, did Jim ever once regret not giving in and playing the game long enough to get that 500 win? He certainly had the talent to win the 500, given the proper equipment, and he had the name recognition to attract a sponsor that could provide that equipment.

Jim's reception at the Speedway was always amazing. A.J. Foyt, Mario Andretti, Johnny Rutherford, or any other number of latter day heroes might have been standing on pit row, but when Jim made his annual appearance with the Mallard, those other champions would be forgotten as the stands erupted in a frenzy of cheers. A sponsor would have leapt at the opportunity to associate themselves with such a popular driver.

Hank Higuchi, who befriended Jim during his racing days in California and later worked with him at the Speedway, is convinced that Jim would have been a racing superstar had he gone with one of the top teams.

"He was one of the very best," says Hank, "a natural driver. I'd try to convince him to go with someone else. To go with one of the big teams. Jim really didn't have the money to do it on his own. But, he would always tell me, 'Aw, Hank, I'd rather do it my own way."

According to a *Sports Illustrated* article, a friend of Jim's once asked, "Herk, what if the Devil himself came to you next May and told you that if you played the game, wore the Goodyear hat straight on your head, and all the rest, that you would go to bed the night of May 28 the winner of the Indianapolis 500. Would you do it?"

After several minutes of contemplation, Jim answered, "No. I'd tell him to get lost. Because I'm doing what I want to do, and I'm having fun doing it. I've built winning cars. I've qualified fastest. I've led the race. I've had fame, I've done all that and I don't have to prove nothing at Indianapolis. I tried like hell to win that race, but I don't care now whether I do or not."

Al Knieech Photo - HFC

Robert Berman Photo - HF

HURTUBISE

23

Hurtubise Family Collection

Viewed strictly from the hard, cold perspective of the win column, it is difficult to rate Jim Hurtubise as successful after 1966. His last career victory came on September 11, 1966, in a Norm Nelson Plymouth at a 150 mile stock car race on his favorite track, Langhorne.

The full measure of a man's success, however, can never be calculated by simply tallying the wins and subtracting the losses. Rather it has to be measured in the light of the satisfaction, peace of mind and happiness he derives in the pursuit of his goals. Using those parameters as a gauge, Jim certainly can be judged a successful man.

Jim's friend, John Laux, recalls an incident that, he believes, emphasizes this very well. "Jim and I were at a USAC awards banquet," says John, "and I was looking around, observing the powerhouse names, the big money sponsors, and I said to Jim, 'Herk, it just ain't fair. Here we are with all the desire, all the know how, and they're the ones with all the money."

"John," replied Jim, a grin crossing his face, "you've got a drink in your hand, I've got a beer, and we got a little money in our pocket. What more could you want?"

"You've got to be happy about what you're doing," Jim said another time. "If your not it's just not worth it. I don't take the 500 seriously anymore, but I still enjoy it. I go there to have a good time, run the old roadster and try to remind people of who I am. On the other hand look at Foyt, he's went along with all the politics and the big companies. When was the last time you saw him smile?"

Good friends and a strong, intimate family gave Jim much to smile about. While not a person to openly express emotions of affection, Jim more than once publicly said of Jane, "She's always there, right by my side."

Jane was indeed always there. Racing is notoriously disastrous to marriages and family life, but Jim had the luxury of being able to concentrate on his racing, with the knowledge that his home and his children were in Jane's good hands.

Jim depended on Jane for the day by day operation of the household, and only on the rare occasion would he attempt to assert his will in those decisions. Such a time occurred at Christmas one year.

"Jim had been complaining," chuckles Jane, "about how much money I'd been spending for Christmas. So, I decided to just buy the kids one gift each. On Christmas Eve, Jim asked me what I'd got the kids. When I showed him, he yelled, 'You've got to be kidding! Is that it?'

"Well, we had to go shopping right then, and he bought everything. Skates, balls, games and hockey sticks. When he finished, he'd spent three times as much as I had ever thought about spending."

Despite his often hectic racing schedule, Jim always made time for his children. "Some of my fondest memories of Dad," says oldest daughter, Karen, "are of the times when he worked in the barn we had back in New York. That's where he built and worked on his race cars. But, I could go out there—just a kid thinking I could really build something —and say, 'Dad, here's what I want to make, how do I do it?' And he'd take the time to tell me. He'd show me what tools to use. Even took time to teach me their proper name.

"This was his career, his livelihood, and I was just playing, yet he took the time for me. All of us kids were always welcome in Dad's barn. When we were finished, he might not be able to find half his tools, but that was okay. He didn't mind."

"Our house was always the place to be for all the neighborhood kids," continues Karen. "We had a pool, and it was always full in the summertime. When Dad dug a pond, he left all the dirt piled up so we would have a hill to sled on in the winter. He even put a light up out there, and then went to the Goodwill store and bought a big box of skates for all the neighborhood kids. Everybody came to the Hurtubise's pond and skated and had hockey games and built bonfires into the night. My poor mother, I don't know how she did it!"

All three of the Hurtubise children recall with fondness the fun that their father constantly provided for them. Of course, Jim loved the toys, the boats, planes, and motorcycles as much as they did. The snowmobile was an especially favorite plaything. Jim had one of the first in the North Tonawanda area, and, fearing Jane's reaction to its purchase, kept it a secret from her for awhile until Andy and Karen gave it away.

"We were out in the barn one evening," laughs Jane, "and Andy said, 'Where's the 'bile Dad? Where's the 'bile?' I said, 'Jim, what in the world is he talking about?' Then, before she caught herself, Karen spoke up and said, 'You know, Mom, the snow....' I turned to Jim, standing there with his head down, and asked him, 'You didn't?'"

He had. It was a big, two cylinder Johnson, and, as with most of Jim's toys, it was as much for the family as it was for himself. He built a sled from plywood and used bumpers from a 1955 Chevy for runners. It was large enough to hold ten people, and Jim would often bundle the children up in blankets, load them in the sled with Jane, and go for long rides on cold, wintry New York days. The children remember those family excursions as especially pleasant. Pat recalls such treks into the woods that were followed by bonfires and wiener roasts, with many of their friends and neighbors on snowmobiles of their own. Sometimes, though, the destinations were a little more out of the ordinary.

"Kids could go into bars in New York," explains Karen, "so Dad would load us in the sled, and we'd take off through the snow covered woods and fields to some of the little taverns around home."

"We were bar hopping!" chimes in Andy. "Sometimes, when a group of friends went with us, there would be a long train of snowmobiles cruising through the woods. I can still remember looking behind us and seeing a long string of headlights that stretched into the night. Everybody would eat chili, and then all of us kids would spend the night playing those bowling machines that all the bars had. It was great."

More important, however, than simply creating fond, childhood memories, Jim and Jane's exercise in child rearing inspired in the children the belief that they could do anything they put their minds to.

"The biggest influence Dad had on me," relates Pat "was that he always insisted that we should do the things that we wanted to do, no matter if it was the popular or the accepted path to follow. I studied mechanical engineering at Purdue University, which wasn't exactly a female kind of thing to do, but Dad supported me in that.

"Then when I was working a co-op job at Allison, where I went to school a semester and worked a semester, Dad always made sure I was up in time for work. He was always up early, no matter how late he might have been out, or how late he might have worked, and I remember Dad sticking his head in my door, usually even before my alarm went off and saying, 'Aren't you up yet?'"

Karen, too, was inspired by her father's example. "We were taught that anything was possible if we were willing to try hard enough. Mom was always preaching that to us, and, of course, we had Dad's example. The one thing Dad couldn't tolerate in us kids was sitting around in front of the TV. He couldn't stand that. You needed to be outside, or doing something. Not just sitting around on your tush."

In whatever they tried to do, Jim insisted his children give it their absolute best. Karen ran track when she was in high school and remembers one track meet in particular where Jim got upset when he perceived her effort wasn't a hundred percent.

"This happened after we had moved back to Indianapolis," says Karen. "Dad and Hank Higuchi had come from practice at the Speedway to watch me. The school we were competing against really wasn't very good, so in my event, the 880 yard dash, I was taking it easy, just running hard enough to stay in front. When I went by the stands on the first lap, I heard Dad yell over the crowd, 'My Gosh Karen, get moving!' And I kicked it in gear! Afterwards he really gave me heck for that. He told me, 'I don't care if they are slow, you should be out there trying to beat your best time."

"It was things like that that really stuck with me. When I got into horses and got interested in competitive riding, Dad encouraged me. But, he wanted me to just compete in events that were timed events. He didn't want me to compete in events where the winner was picked by judges. He believed that someone's opinion was just someone's opinion. But, the clock didn't lie. If you didn't go fast enough, you weren't fooling anybody but yourself."

As might be expected, Jim's son Andy attempted to follow his father's racing footsteps, and in some early racing ventures, did exhibit a bit of promise. While stationed at Grissom Air Force base in southern Indiana, Andy and a friend built and raced a modified stock car, not unlike the cars his father began his racing career in.

After his discharge, Andy continued to pursue his own racing dream, moving from the stock cars, to a midget owned by Charlie Patterson. Charlie is perhaps best known for developing Gasoline Alley, the street on Indianapolis's west side that is home to many racing related businesses, including the shops for several Indy car teams.

Surprisingly, Jim was not supportive of Andy's racing activities. In fact, he seemed to be dead set against it. Once at Terre Haute he even displayed this sentiment publicly. The track announcer was interviewing Jim, and when he finished, he asked Andy to come to the mike. He spoke to Andy for several minutes about his midget race the night before, where he had finished second in the feature at Paragon Speedway. The interviewer then turned to Jim and asked, "Herk, what do you think about your son's racing?"

Andy still remembers his father's blunt reply, "He doesn't belong in a race car."

Jim's discouraging words aside, he was actually very proud of Andy's racing endeavors. "Jim told Andy," states Jane, that if he wanted to race, he would have to do it on his own. But, he was really pleased with his performance. I remember once while we were in Texas Andy was in a midget race back in Indianapolis that was being televised live. Andy was doing real well, and Jim was cheering him on. He had some type of mechanical problem and dropped out, but Jim bragged about him all night long. I really didn't want Andy to know about this because I didn't like the idea of him racing."

Jim wasn't actually opposed to Andy's racing, but he didn't believe, given the vast amounts of money involved, that Andy stood a chance of bettering himself in the sport. At one time midgets and sprint cars were the rungs up the racing ladder to Indianapolis, but by the time Andy became involved, they were a dead-end street.

"The thing that irritated Jim the most about what had happened at Indianapolis," says Jane, "was that he saw all these kids go there whose fathers had money and they bought their way into cars. Rich kids buying rides, Jim just couldn't stand it, and didn't want Andy involved in it."

Despite their differences about his racing career, Andy, like his sisters, was inspired by his father's example. "Dad was awesome," contends Andy. "He could do anything. He could design, build, paint and letter. And anything he did, he made sure he did it right. I think the way I do things myself today, as far as taking time to make sure everything I do is correct, almost to the point of being a perfectionist, I get from Dad."

Jim had always been especially close to his father, and was affected deeply when his father died unexpectedly on February 21, 1971.

An elderly, regular customer of Ernie's had stopped in his service station, for Ernie to look at his car. Examining it with the engine idling, the car somehow jumped in gear, ran over Ernie and dragged him across the parking lot. Jim's mother, Ruth, who was working in the office at the time, called for help, while Pete ran to his father, and lifted the car off of him. Though severely injured, both pelvis bones were broken, and he had many scrapes and cuts, Ernie was alive.

After two weeks in the hospital, he seemed to be well on the way to recovery and had been allowed to set up in a chair for the first time on a Saturday morning. Ruth, following her usual routine, visited with him after she closed the garage that afternoon.

"We had supper together and watched TV until about nine o'clock that night," recalls Ruth. "The next morning the hospital called and said we better come over, but when we got there he was already gone. A blood clot had broken loose and went to his heart."

As was the case with the many times Jim saw his friends die on the race track, he did not openly display his emotions at his father's death. Rather, he withdrew within himself. "The only way you knew Jim was upset," says Jane, "was that he would get very quiet. You could tell then that something was wrong. "Pop's" death really bothered Jim."

"Jim missed his father terribly," says Ruth. "Both the boys were very close to their father. He did a lot with them when they were children. Ernie was quite a sportsman, and he spent a lot of time with them outdoors, hunting and fishing, and of course, the boys loved that."

The first May after his father's death was especially difficult for Jim, because Ernie had always been at the Speedway with his son. He had an Airstream recreational trailer that he towed to the track each year from New York and parked beside the race car haulers behind Gasoline Alley. He would spend the weekends at the track, keeping tabs on what Jim was doing.

"Ernie followed Jim's career diligently," states Ruth. "He was very proud of him and enjoyed watching him. He got a thrill out of it and really enjoyed it when Jim went out on the track because he always got such an ovation. He was a very popular driver."

It has been said that a man's worth can be measured in the number of friends he has. Jim had many friends. Friends that he stayed loyal to, and they to him for years. Although the "California Gang" went their separate ways, pursuing their own busy lives, and couldn't enjoy the fellowship they had experienced traipsing across the Midwest in Jim's old station wagon, they still stayed in touch and visited whenever possible.

Don Shepherd, after helping Jim build the Mallard, tutored both Johnny Rutherford and Bobby Unser into the racing big time. He and Jim were unable to see much of each other after that, but still today this tough, steely-eyed racing man says of his friendship with Jim, "I loved the guy. I really did. Herk was just a lovable, good hearted man."

In the late sixties, Jim and his racing buddy Parnelli Jones drifted apart in the natural evolution of two lives headed in two distinctly different directions. Though never made official, Parnelli retired from Indianapolis racing in 1967, and his energy was absorbed by various businesses, including the part ownership of a top flight Indianapolis team.

Even though it was difficult for them to socialize—Jim lived on the East Coast, Parnelli on the West—there was still a mutual respect between the two great racers, cemented with the hardships they had shared in their early racing days. In 1969, when Parnelli's driver, Al

Unser, broke his leg in a motorcycle accident and was unable to compete in the 500, Parnelli invited Jim to take his place. Jim turned down what was one of the best cars at the track that year, but it was no slight towards Parnelli—he simply wanted to stick with his beloved Mallard.

Al Krueger became a good friend of Jim's when he journeyed to the Speedway with Pete in 1968. After that, Jim wanted Al at the Speedway with him every year, even naming him as the chief mechanic of the Mallard on one occasion.

"I wasn't anything near being a crew chief," laughs Al. "I'd just do what Jim directed me to do. But, he insisted that on all the entry forms I be listed as his crew chief, and he even had my name painted on the sign that hung over the garage door at the Speedway."

Al still has that sign today, displayed proudly for all to see, a unique reminder of his lasting friendship with a special man.

"I was Jim's hands," says Al. "There were many things Jim couldn't do because of his hands, and I would be there to do those things for him. I'd fasten his helmet, tighten his safety belts, all those type things that maybe don't seem important, but that he depended on me to do."

It was Jim's friends who enabled him to continue to race at Indianapolis, for although he was vocally adamant about the system that he saw running and ruining racing there, Jim still could not let go of it.

"They tell me I might as well stay home," he once said "But, I ain't going to stay home. Nobody tells me I have to do anything. They're going to have to put up with me, and I'm going to raise hell while I'm at it!"

By the mid 1970s, the cost of running a car at Indianapolis had risen to a half million dollars and was still escalating. Although Jim's budget to "go raise hell there" was but a fraction of that figure, it still took a person of his creative imagination to devise a way to finance it. He did it by selling memberships in what he called his "Gasoline Alley Club" to many of his friends.

"I can still make a living at Indianapolis," insisted Jim. "In fact I'm probably the only car owner who makes any money. I have a club that I sell memberships to. I enter the Mallard for myself, and with the other two cars, the McLaren and the Eagle, I name one guy the driver, one the crew chief, one as a sponsor, one as a owner. They're all business men from around the country, friends of mine, and they chip in. It's just a fun thing and it helps pay the expenses."

For their "chipping in," the members of Jim's club received credentials that allowed them to come and go as they pleased in the garage area and the pits, where they could rub elbows with the stars of racing and be an intimate part of the excitement, color and pageantry that makes the Indianapolis 500 such a great sporting event.

They also gained access to Jim's garages, numbers 42, 43 and 44. With separate exterior entrances, the garages were connected internally by doors that Jim had installed between each unit. The race cars, of course, were housed there, but occupying a large part of one garage was a highly polished wooden bar, complete with bar stools and all the other amenities that might be found in a local pub.

Adding to the bar room ambience was a set of Victorian-era, swinging saloon doors that connected two of the three garages. Al Krueger says that Jim spotted the doors on the back of a truck as they were being hauled to a salvage yard, chased the truck down, and talked the driver out of them.

Jim's garage area watering hole, that preceeded today's trackside hospitality areas by twenty years, soon became the talk of the Speedway. Garages 42-44 became a gathering place for most of the racing fraternity. Even track owner, Tony Hulman, stopped by on occasion, for a few minutes of solitude from the hustle and bustle of the month of May activities.

In 1978, when Tom Sneva became the first driver to break the 200 mile per hour barrier, he ducked the writers and photographers and disappeared from view. When he reappeared several hours later, he divulged to the press where he had been. "I was over at Hurtubise's garage," admitted Tom, "conferring with Herk's *'consumption engineer,'* Al Krueger."

After the 1974 race, the Speedway made Jim remove his bar from the garage, but he mischievously devised a substitute, an oversize, wooden cover that he perched atop the rear wing of the Eagle. Although his club's patrons found it a convenient place to elbow up to as they sipped beer, Jim insisted it was only a protector for the car's aerodynamic wing. "I don't want anybody running into the wings of these race cars," he said, blue eyes twinkling gleefully. "It makes them handle bad!"

Hurtubise Family Collection

The Jim Hurtubise Family Christmas of 1980.

HURTUBISE

24

mary ann carter photos - HFC

Jim's buoyant, optimistic demeanor aside, there is evidence that the role of the lone, crusading David fighting the Goliath of big money and racing politics was beginning to wear thin on him. He felt alienated, unappreciated, even rejected by the sport he had sacrificed so much for.

His daughter, Karen, remembers a particular incident that drove this truth home to her. "Dad and I were watching the movie, "*The Death of a Salesman,*" one afternoon on TV. I'll never forget it. Dad was sitting there very quiet while we watched it. Neither one of us said a thing until the very end. Then Dad turned to me and said, 'I can understand that. I can understand how that guy [Willie Loman] felt.'

"I was almost in tears," continues Karen. "I had to get up and get out of the room. I was just a teenager, but from that time on, I understood what Dad was feeling. It was a side of Dad that he didn't show to very many people. Most people saw the happy go lucky, nothing bothers him side of Dad. But, he thrived on racing. It was his world, his identity. And I could see that he felt like he had lost the thing that made him a whole person. A complete man."

In 1972, Jim had moved his family from New York to Indianapolis in order to be closer to the Speedway and the sponsors, businesses, and racing industries it attracted. Jim had hoped the closer proximity would further his racing related opportunities, but by the mid-seventies, he came to the realization that he was hanging onto racing by only a tenuous thread. At the Speedway in 1978, the frustration of that realization boiled over into anger, when he believed racing officials were trying to wrest even that remnant of his racing career from his control.

As had been his routine for the previous half dozen years, Jim made his annual trek to Indianapolis with the Mallard in 1978. He had not qualified for the 500 since 1974, and did not seriously believe he would be a threat to do so in 1978. Rather, he was there to revel in the racing community's annual rite of spring, celebrated every May at Indianapolis. He entertained guests and club members in his garage, tossed back some beers with his friends and occasionally pulled the Mallard onto the track amidst the wild cheering of his fans.

Then things turned ugly. Ninety two cars had been entered that year, and sixty four actually showed up at the track, putting garage space at a premium. There were outcries of criticism against Jim, and a few others like him, from those who contended they took garage space and track time away from "serious competitors." Those doing the criticizing preferred to ignore the fact that most of these so called "serious competitors" were the same people entering nonexistent or, at the very least, disassembled backup cars for the express purpose of gaining extra garage space.

Though he tried to dismiss it, Jim was particularly upset by a story circulating the garage area that the first female 500 qualifier, Janet Guthrie, had leveled those type charges against him in the *Buffalo Times*.

Said Jim of those rumors, "There were a lot of articles in the newspaper that said me and Janet Guthrie were going at each other. Hell, none of that is true. She used to come over to my club and drink beer with us. We get along just fine."

Jim and Janet did get along. He had helped her set up her car at Daytona one year and was pleased to see her finish a creditable ninth in the 1978 500 having driven the race with a cracked wrist suffered during a charity tennis match.

For the first time in over a decade the entire first weekend of qualifying was rained out which added to the already building tension. With so much at stake at Indianapolis, the four qualifying days, spread over two consecutive weekends, are under the best of conditions pressure packed. To take what normally transpires in four frantic days and compress it into two places a tremendous strain on officials and competitors alike.

Sunday, May 21, the final day of qualifying dawned with thirteen spots still open and a bevy of talented drivers rushing to fill them. The previous year's winner, A.J. Foyt, was among those who were forced to find a way into the field in those final turbulent hours, as was George Snider, Gary Bettenhausen, Mike Mosley and Pancho Carter.

At 3:45 in the afternoon, with just over two hours left, one spot still remained. Drivers and crews desperately sought a few tenths of a second of speed that could spell the difference between being a part of one of the greatest spectacles in sport, or having to wait another year for the chance to try again. In the short time remaining they knew, at best, they would have but one shot at the track. John Martin tried, but he was too slow and was called in by his crew after just one lap at 181 miles per hour.

Rookie, Rodger Rager was the next to try, but he crashed in turn three, ending his chance at Indianapolis for another year. Another frenzied practice session followed the cleanup of Rager's wreck, but that too was curtailed when Dick Simon hit the wall going through turn four. By the time the safety crews had cleared the wreckage of Simon's car from the track, only one hour of qualifying remained for the 1978 500.

An aura of expectation hung over the Speedway as the 75,000 gathered there, joined by a national TV audience, looked forward to what could prove to be the most dramatic sixty minutes of the entire month. Then, a ruckus broke out at the head of the qualifying line, and it involved Jim. He was in a heated discussion with Chief Steward Tom Binford about his right to qualify.

Jim's crew had pushed his car into the qualifying line and as they sat and waited with everyone else for Simon's car to be removed from the track, race officials approached and informed them that they would not be allowed a qualifying attempt because the Mallard did not have a final inspection sticker.

When crew chief, Hank Higuchi, protested, he was told that in his position of chief mechanic he could be held responsible for not cooperating, and be disciplined accordingly. Hank found Jim, who was on up the line, explained what had happened and asked what he wanted done. Jim's reaction to the situation was to fire Hank on the spot. He sensed a showdown with USAC officials, and it would be he, not his friends, who would take the responsibility.

Jim then went to Chief Steward Tom Binford and demanded to know what was going on. The entry blank, Jim insisted, gave him the right to at least make a qualifying attempt. Binford, on the other hand, argued that USAC had issued a bulletin stating that, for safety considerations, a car that had not practiced at over 180 miles per hour would not be issued a final technical inspection sticker.

Jim contended that neither he nor his team had ever received such a bulletin, and finding no resolution with Binford, became incensed. He believed that he was being singled out by USAC officials as an example for others who were taking time away from the "serious competitors."

Jim could have lodged an official protest at this point, but the time trials would be over long before that could have been processed, so he responded in the only avenue he saw open to him. He would delay the proceedings until something was resolved.

The crowd, restless for any type of action after a day of long delays, began to lend their vocal support to Jim and his protest. Jim's daughter Karen was there that day, and recalls the crowd's reaction, and how it turned from good to bad.

"I was dating my husband John at that time," recalls Karen, "and we decided, of all days, to go to the track. I'm the type of person that enjoys being in a big crowd, and it was always exciting for me to be at the track and hear the fans cheer Dad."

"Anytime he walked in front of the stands they just went berserk. And that's the way it was that day. I'll never forget him walking out there and the crowd yelling, 'Yeah, Go Herk,' and all the other usual stuff. Dad walked by where John and I were standing, and we talked for a minute and he walked on. He wasn't mad, wasn't even upset."

"It was so crowded where John and I were at that I couldn't really see what happened next. I heard the crowd cheering for Dad as he went on down the line, but then, all of a sudden, the crowd got real weird. I didn't know what was going on, but it just got real frantic. They were waving their fists in the air and yelling, 'Get 'em, Herk! Get 'em!' It really frightened me, and I said to John, 'Let's get out of here,' and we went back to Dad's garage."

What had happened was that Jim was now on the track, running a zig-zag pattern across the front straight while Bob Harkey was slowly warming up his car on the backstretch. Jim was chased by a gaggle of pursuers that he eluded for several seconds before being tackled to the track by John Martin. Surrounded and escorted to the pit wall, he was then met by two Indiana State policemen who unceremoniously led him to his garage.

How Jim's protest had escalated to this point is uncertain. According to Al Krueger, although Jim was angry, he was under control. In fact, just before he ran onto the track, he had the presence of mind to ask Al to go back to the garage and take care of things there.

Jim was expecting a throng of reporters and TV crews to follow him back to the garage because of the events that had already taken place. "We're all through out here," he told Al. "There's nothing left to do."

Whether it was because Speedway safety patrolmen grabbed him and attempted to forcibly move him out of the way of Harkey's car, or he just decided he had to make one more protest will never be known. Jim never talked in detail about his reasoning at that time, but he wasn't some out of control zany, as he has often been portrayed in descriptions of that day's events.

Jim Hurtubise was never out of control. Anything he did was done with a purpose, and his actions on this day were no different. While those who were with him that Sunday cannot say with certainty that he planned to run onto the track, most admit that Jim expected a showdown with USAC officials. Perhaps Jim's conversation with his future son-in-law, John Sampson, portrays that understanding best.

"A lot of the family was gathered in Jim's garage just before qualifying began," says John. "I was sitting there drinking a beer, and then everyone left but me and Jim. Jim said to me, 'John, aren't you going out to the track?'

"I said, 'Naw, I think I'll just stay and finish my beer.' Then he said to me, 'John, you better come on out to the track, you don't want to miss this. It's going to make national news!"

Writer Skip Hess, of the *Indianapolis News* talked to Jim several days later, and asked him specifically about his state of mind on May 21.

"There are some people saying you have gone nuts, lost your marbles, because of what you did at the Speedway last Sunday," Hess told Jim. "They're saying you've gone crazy."

Jim responded, "When I went out there Sunday, I was right. USAC officials told me I could not make a qualifying attempt because there was a bulletin they had released which said you had to run 180 miles an hour to be able to try and qualify, but no one could produce that bulletin for me. I knew I was right, and they were going to have to drag me out of there. But, I wasn't mad. I was loud because I wanted to make sure everybody heard me. Half the time I was laughing."

On Monday, Jim returned to Gasoline Alley to pick up some personal belongings. While there he was interviewed by track announcer and local TV sportscaster, Tom Carnegie. "I asked Tom Binford a question and told him I wanted an honest answer," Jim told Carnegie. "I asked him, 'Was there a bulletin that said you had to be practicing over 180 to make a qualifying attempt?' After some hesitation, Tom said, 'No."

Tom Binford served as the Chief Steward at the Indianapolis Motor Speedway until he retired after the 1995 race. He helped guide the 500 to its prominent position as a world class sporting event through his love of the sport and his compassion for its competitors. To this day Binford maintains that there was a written bulletin. Even though this is diametrically opposed to Jim's view and led to the 1978 confrontation, Tom holds no hard feelings towards Jim. In fact Tom has among his cherished auto racing memorabilia, a souvenir from Jim. During a meeting over an incident at Milwaukee, which Tom describes in his book "*A Checkered Past*" Jim left his Champion Spark Plug tie clasp on Tom's desk.

Sadly, the entire situation could have been prevented and resolved with less time lost had USAC officials simply allowed Jim to take his attempt. "Jim wasn't stupid," says Al Krueger. "We had already agreed that if Jim's first lap was too slow, we would yellow flag him, and he would've pulled in. He just wanted to make a qualifying attempt for the sake of his sponsors."

That would have been standard fare at the Speedway. More than one driver has done that very thing to keep his sponsor happy. Many times a driver, even when he realizes he has no chance of making the race, will run the four laps of his trial to completion so he can have an official qualifying photo to satisfy his sponsor.

Even though the Mallard had not run laps at over 180 that year at Indianapolis, it certainly wasn't unsafe. Jim had driven it over 190 miles per hour at Daytona and it had easily passed tech inspection every year at the Speedway from the time he first entered it in 1967. Should it have been considered unsafe because the latest racing technology had outdated it?

If so, USAC reversed that reasoning three years later. In the midst of their battle with rival sanctioning body, CART, they filled the field at Pocono, a paved, high speed, 2 1/2 mile oval, with front engine, upright champ cars, designed specifically to run on one mile dirt tracks.

Would it have been too much on the part of race officials to extend Jim the courtesy of allowing him a qualifying attempt? After all, this was not some rank rookie. This was Hercules. Jim had set records here, led the race, and brought more acclaim to the Speedway than any other driver that appeared on the track that Sunday afternoon, with the possible exception of A.J. Foyt.

Jane wasn't at the track when Jim made his dramatic protest, but she did see it on TV. "I couldn't believe that Jim was out there on the track," recalls Jane. "I almost went into shock. I called my cousin Bob to come quick and take me to the track. I was so upset that we had to stop at the track hospital for a tranquilizer. Jim was the one in trouble, and I was under sedation!"

"For days afterward, Jim was pretty quiet about it, and I think what had happened really bothered him. But, Jim had come up through the ranks when a driver was recognized for his talent. He had lived his own life, and when they started pushing him so hard in those last few years, he felt they were trying to take his racing away from him."

As a result of his actions, Jim was banished from the track until after the race, and although he joked about it with comments like, "I guess I can stand in front of the garage area with the spectators," it was the one part of the whole experience that hurt him the most.

Even today, Jane says, "That's the one thing I'll never forgive them for. They humiliated him. What did they think he was going to do? I remember Patty crying and saying, 'Mom, I was in the garage area, and Dad had to call to me from the other side of the fence.'"

Jane was just as vocal in 1978, when she addressed the situation to *Indianapolis Star* sports editor, Bob Collins. "For a guy who has given twenty-six years of his life to the sport of auto racing and has never tried to take anything from anyone, I'm sick at heart," Jane told Collins. "The people in USAC and the Speedway have driven Jim to the wall and have even taken away his right to enter the garages. Racing is his life, not to mention his livelihood. Drivers who can't afford to run their cars at Indy anymore because they lack a sponsor, or don't have a big company behind them, have had to resort to gimmicks. But there was one who was not even allowed that. Think about it."

"I've said my piece and pray they may all sleep well."

The protest begins. mary ann carter photos - HFC

mary ann carter photos - HFC

The photos are self explanatory. Notice that everyone seems to be laughing.

mary ann carter photos - HFC

The protest ends.

Hurtubise Family Collection

Jim and Hank Higuchi in happier times.

HURTUBISE

25

Hurtubise Family Collection

After the theatrics of 1978, Jim returned as usual to the Speedway in 1979. He held no grudges or hard feelings towards any of the officials, nor they towards him. His reception by the fans when he made his first trackside appearance with the Mallard, if anything, was more exuberant than ever, and, with coverage that far exceeded any ever given to a race car driver in any publication, both *Esquire magazine* and *Sports Illustrated* verified what the fans already knew; Jim Hurtubise was a true auto racing legend.

The problem with being a living legend is that there comes a time when it is no longer possible to provide a suitable encore. Jim realized that his days of being competitive at Indianapolis in the manner he wished, with a car he had designed and built himself, had passed. Although he entered the Mallard, he didn't even make a qualifying attempt in 1979, and 1980 marked the very last time Jim made an appearance at the Speedway with the car that was as legendary as himself.

That didn't mark the end of Jim's relationship with the Speedway, however. The Hulman family doesn't forget the heroes that have made their track the most famous in the world, and they did not forget Jim Hurtubise. They provided him a spot behind Gasoline Alley so he could continue to run his club from his motor home. Jim claimed he liked it even better than when he operated out of his garage.

"The motor home has worked out real good," said Jim. "It gives the members a place to come in and sit down and have a beer. They can have more fun that way because they can walk around outside with their beer. When I was in the garage, I had to keep the doors shut all the time. It was like being in jail."

Jim never liked being penned up, shut in or held down. He was always restless, always on the go, always off to some new adventure. When his racing began to slow in the seventies, he became involved in a number of other activities, including a muffler shop he advertised with the catchy promise: "No Muff Too Tuff." During the month of May, Jim would hang a sign on the door of the closed business that read, "Gone Fishing!"

When even his Speedway racing activities were curtailed after 1980, Jim's restless nature eventually carried him to Port Arthur, Texas.

Al Krueger explains how Jim became interested in Texas. "Jim and I made a trip down there," recalls Al, "just travelling around and visiting some friends of Jim's. We came across this lake that we fished at, and Jim just loved it there. He thought it would be a great place to build a fishing camp, and a great place to live."

Jane picks up the story, "While Jim and Al were in Texas, someone mentioned to them about a new hotel and resort area that was under development on an island near Port Arthur. Jim and Al went over to have a look, and, of course, Jim loved to meet anybody that had anything to do with building or with anything new that was happening. He introduced himself to the developer of the project, and the man, Michael Ryan, said to Jim, 'You can't be the race driver!"

"As it turned out, Michael Ryan and his wife, Lila, were from Minneapolis. When Jim raced there with the IMCA, Lila's father and brother would often be at the track with their tow truck helping push start the sprint cars. They were Hurtubise fans from way back, although Jim didn't know them. They struck up a friendship, and when we moved to Port Arthur, I became the manager of their hotel on Pleasure Island."

Jim made several more exploratory trips to Port Arthur before he sold his Indianapolis home in the summer of 1981, and he and Jane pulled up stakes and moved to Texas. Since the children were all grown, and Jim and Jane were alone, they rented a small condo on Pleasure Island that they shared with their little dog, Klink.

Pleasure Island was located in Sabine Lake, an inlet to the Gulf of Mexico, and with its good fishing and plenty of room for boating and water skiing, it was the perfect setting for Jim. He spent many hours on the lake in "Miss Jenny," a twin Evinrude 185 horsepower, all-wood racing boat that he had hauled to Texas with him.

Jim was happy with his idyllic life in Texas. "I've had everything in life I could possibly want," he told one Texas journalist. "Fame, money, horses, boats, planes and cars. But, down here I'm my own boss. I can do what I want, when I want, and I can go fishing anytime I want to."

When he became bored with fishing and doing odd jobs around the Pleasure Island Hotel, Jim would go to Port Arthur to explore any entrepreneurial opportunities he might find there.

Port Arthur, located near the Louisiana/Texas border, was an economically depressed town, hit hard when the bottom dropped out of the Texas oil market in the seventies. During it's boom years the city had been a rough and rowdy town filled with taverns, gambling dens and houses of ill repute that catered to oil field workers and the merchant marines from the ships that plied their trade on the Gulf of Mexico.

It was one of these former brothels that caught Jim's eye, and he bought it for what he perceived as a great development opportunity. Jim said of his purchase, located on Proctor street just a few blocks from the waterfront, "I can't say it's the 'Best Little Whorehouse in Texas,' but it was one of the best!"

"It used to be the old Melba Hotel, and the top floor was a gambling hall, a bar and a brothel. I bought it to put my shop in the ground floor. I intend to fix up the top two floors as Melba's Hunting Lodge, and sell it like a time sharing condominium to hunters."

"Melba's is fifteen minutes from the duck and geese flight paths and thirty minutes from a horse racing track in Louisiana, and I think there are nine bars located within a block of here. It should go over great."

"Up until '61," Jim continued, revealing how he had already explored the history of his newly adopted home, "Port Arthur was a wide open town for gambling and prostitution because it was a shipping port. Melba is still around. She used to run three houses in town—Melba's, Marcella's and Antoine's. But she was gone when I bought the building, so I didn't have to evict her."

Jim tackled his remodeling project with all the excitement and enthusiasm that he had his racing career. He even tried to interest the Mayor of Port Arthur in his project, hoping the city would finance his effort by declaring the structure a historical monument.

"I had dinner with the mayor and told him what I wanted to do," cracked Jim. "But he told me that he didn't think he could get community support to make an old whorehouse a state monument."

To Jane's way of thinking, Jim, on occasion, got a little too carried away with his enthusiasm for Melba's. "Jim wanted to make us an apartment in that old building," laughs Jane incredulously. "He said, 'Jane I can make that place look like the Taj Mahal.' Well, the building was in a very bad part of town, I think there was even a topless bar across the street. So I said, 'I know you can Jim, but when I walk out the door, I'll still be in the same bad neighborhood."

Jim loved the bawdy, boisterous atmosphere of the Port Arthur waterfront and was soon making friends with businessmen and other residents of his newly adopted community. Most of them were unaware of Jim's racing past and would have cared less had they known. They knew him only as a fun loving, full of life guy who, if he wasn't at his favorite hangout, The Keyhole Club, was fishing in one of his four boats, riding his motorcycle, or cruising around town in his powder blue, 1966 Cadillac Coup de Ville.

Jim showed no more interest in racing during this time than did his new found friends. He had brought the Mallard to Texas with him and installed it in a place of honor in his first floor shop at Melba's. On occasion, he would travel to Golden Triangle Speedway in nearby Beaumont, where old racing friend, Bill Hill, promoted some races, but that was the extent of his racing interest. "Racing was something I did years ago, and now it's finished," is how he explained it to the *Beaumont Enterprise.*

"Besides," he continued, "there's a thousand races a week, and each one is different. I don't like to read about them. It's more important to be there racing."

Without racing to distract him, Jim's life settled into a comfortable routine of fishing, hanging out at the Key Hole Club, and scheming with his Texas friends over new business ventures. Come February, he would make his annual trek to Daytona, followed in May by a journey to Indianapolis for the 500.

In the summer of 1988, Jim began working for millionaire sportsman, John Mecom, restoring vintage sports cars that John raced in historic car events across the country. Jim worked in Mecom's shop with Steve Forrestal, and the job fit his semi retired life style perfectly. The pace of the work was laid back, and Jim was able to come and go as he pleased.

In November of 1988, Jim and Jane met Al Krueger and his wife Jennette at Padre Island, a vacation spot in southern Texas near the Mexican border, for a peaceful retreat with old friends.

"It was really nice," recalls Jane. "We got to spend a lot of time together, and Jim got to do a lot of fishing. He really enjoyed himself."

Near Christmas, a couple of weeks after Jim's fifty sixth birthday, he and Jane traveled to Indianapolis to celebrate the holiday with their children. Karen, Pat and Andy were all married. Andy and Pat had children of their own.

"We had a wonderful Christmas," recalls Jane fondly. "We visited Karen, Pat, Andy and the grandkids. Andy's daughter still talks about how grandpa kept going to sleep on the couch. I told her, 'Honey, grandpa's gone to sleep on every couch he's ever been on!"

Karen recalls a special memory of her own on what turned out to be her father's last Christmas. "Dad wasn't ever a touching person," says Karen. "He would come over and give you a big bear hug, but he wasn't one to be physically tender. I remember we were all sitting around the table at Pat's house, and I'll never forget this, Dad reached over, laid his hand on my hand and just looked at me. Later we all talked about how different Dad was that Christmas. It was like he was reaching out for his family, and I guess he was."

The memory of the last time she saw her father is as vivid to Karen as that poignant Christmas experience.

"Dad and Mom came to our house, just before they went back to Texas," says Karen. "We all went to a little place in Brazil called, 'The Alabama Bar,' because Dad loved the fish and chips they served there. When the evening was over, I walked to their car with them, and while I was standing there watching them drive off, the strangest feeling came over me. It wasn't that I felt like Dad was going to die. I can't say it was a premonition or anything like that. It was just a very sad feeling."

Upon their return to Port Arthur, Jim drove to Mecom's shop in Houston to continue work on the car he was rebuilding. But, parts that he had been waiting on since before Christmas still had not arrived, so he told Steve Forrestall that he was going fishing until they came in.

"We'd had dinner together on Tuesday before Jim left for Houston on Wednesday," Jane recalls. "When he got there, he called and told me that some parts he'd ordered still hadn't came in, so he was going to Toledo Bend. He and several of his buddies had a fishing camp there, and he just loved it."

Jim arrived at the fishing camp on Friday morning, January 6. At two-thirty that afternoon the phone rang in the lobby of The Pleasure Island Motel. Jane, who was on duty, answered it. "I was the manager of the hotel," says Jane, "I was working by myself when the coroner called. I could tell he wasn't expecting me to answer and didn't want to tell me the bad news."

What he told Jane was that the powerful heart that had driven Jim with the intense energy to overcome every obstacle in his path as he climbed to the top of the racing world, had given out. Jim died instantly, without suffering, in the one place, other than a racetrack, he would have most wanted to be.

"The coroner told me," says Jane, "that it was so obvious that Jim had suffered a massive heart attack that there was no need for an autopsy. There was no sign that he had even struggled."

When Jane got off the phone with the coroner, she called the family. "I called Karen and Pat and broke the news to them. But, Andy wasn't home. His wife Carla answered the phone, and I told her what had happened. She drove to where Andy was working and told him about his father."

"And then I had to call Pete..."

On January 12, 1989, Jim returned to Indianapolis for the final time. There, within sight of the track he loved so much, visitation services were held at Conkle Funeral Home. Hundreds of fans, fellow drivers and racing officials paid their respects to the great man they knew as "Herk."

Joe Foster, one of Jim's Texas friends, made the long trip to Indianapolis to pay his respects and arrived at Conkle's late in the evening. Al Krueger, standing off to the side, watched as Joe approached the casket, paused for several minutes, then slipped something into Jim's jacket pocket. When he had gone Al walked up, lifted the lapel of Jim's coat and inside the breast coat pocket he found a fishing lure with a hand written note that simply said: "***Gone Fishing***!"

Postscript

The days after Jim's death were reduced to a blur for Jane. For the first time in thirty one years, she was alone. Al Krueger followed her back to Texas to help her sort and organize the bits, pieces and mementos that remained of Jim's driving career.

Jane struggled to get her life back in order. She wanted to move back to Indianapolis to be near her children and grandchildren, but she had nothing. Jim had not carried Life Insurance for many years.

"When Jim was driving champ cars for Art Lathrop," explains Jane. "Art carried a $50,000 dollar life insurance policy on him. When Jim stopped driving for Art, he asked us if we wanted to pick up the premiums and continue the coverage, but Jim said, 'No way! That's just asking for trouble.' Jim never had life insurance after that. I'd ask him about it from time to time, but he'd always tell me not to worry about it."

"About two weeks after he died," continues Jane, "Jim appeared to me in a dream. He was sitting on the bed in our home on Crawfordsville Road in Indianapolis. In my dream I asked him, 'Jim what am I going to do?' And in this dream, Jim said to me, 'Don't worry, I'll take care of everything.'

"Well, it wasn't long after that, that I was made an offer to sell the Mallard. It was an historic, collectible car because it was the fastest roadster ever at Indianapolis, and the last roadster to make the 500. It just about killed me to have to sell it, because that car had meant so very much to Jim, but I didn't have a choice."

"With the money I was able to buy my house in Indianapolis, and buy a car. I believe to this day that Jim knew I would be able to do that. He knew the car would be worth even more after his death. Even now Jim is taking care of me."

Jim Hurtubise Robert C. Rowe

SPECIAL AWARDS

1965 HARF Banquet "Rollie Jons Sportsmanship Award"

1965 Indy 500 Awards Banquet
"Angelo Angelopolous Sportsmanship Award"
presented by
the American Auto Racing Writers and Broadcasters

"1965 Tony Bettenhausen Memorial Award"
as the outstanding driver at Milwaukee

"1965 Ford Award"

1966 "Hoosier Auto Racing Fans Hall of Fame"

1966 Philadelphia Sports Writers "Most Courageous Athlete"

1966 "R.A. Stranahan Memorial Award"
for outstanding contributions and loyalty to auto racing

1993 National Sprint Car Hall of Fame

USAC Champ Car History

Date	Yr	Place	Car	Finish
9/19	59	Indianapolis, IN	Racing Assoc #3	16th
9/27	59	Trenton, NJ	Racing Assoc #3	7th
10/18	59	Phoenix, AZ	Racing Assoc #3	20th quick
10/25	59	Scramento, CA	Racing Assoc #3	1st
4/10	60	Trenton, NJ	Koopmans #24	17th
5/22	60	Indianapolis 500	Travelon Tr 56	qual Record
5/29	60	Indianapolis 500	Travelon Tr 56	18th
6/5	60	Milwaukee, WI	Travelon Tr #56	11th
6/19	60	Langhorne, PA	Schmidt #44	1st
8/20	60	Springfield, IL		10th
8/28	60	Milwaukee 200	Racing Assoc	26th
9/3	60	DuQuoin, IL		13th
9/10	60	Syracuse, NY	Racing Assoc	15th
9/18	60	Indianapolis, IN	Racing Assoc	12th
9/25	60	Trenton, NJ	Adams Quar Horse	13th
10/30	60	Scramento, CA	Racing Assoc	14th
11/20	60	Phoenix, AZ	Bernco	2nd
4/9	61	Trenton, NJ	Sterling #56	2nd
5/30	61	Indianapolis 500	Delmer #99	22nd
6/10	61	Milwaukee, WI	Hopkins #15	5th
6/18	61	Langhorne, PA	Barnett #56	8th
8/20	61	Milwaukee, WI	Hopkins #15	7th
8/21	61	Springfield, IL	Serling #56	1st
9/3	61	DuQuoin, IL	Sterling #56	18th
9/9	61	Syracuse, NY	Sterling #56	3rd
9/16	61	Indianapolis, IN	Sterling #56	18th
9/24	61	Trenton, NJ	Sterling #56	2nd
10/29	61	Scramento, CA	Barnett #56	14th
11/19	61	Phoenix, AZ		11th
3/8	62	Trenton, NJ	Sterling 56	6th
5/30	62	Indy 500	Jim Robbins #91	13th
6/10	62	Milwaukee, WI	Jim Robbins #72	3rd
6/24	62	Langhorne, PA	Barnett #56	Rain FT
7/1	62	Langhorne, PA	Barnett #56	3rd
7/22	62	Trenton, NJ	Barnett #56	5th
8/18	62	Springfield, IL	Barnett #56	1st
8/19	62	Milwaukee, WI	John Zink #72	21st
8/26	62	Langhorne, PA	Barnett #56	2nd
9/8	62	Syracuse, NY	Barnett #56	4th
9/15	62	Hoosier 100	Barnett #56	8th
9/23	62	Trenton, NJ 200	Barnett #56	9th
10/28	62	Sacramento, CA	Barnett #56	4th
11/18	62	Phoenix, AZ	Barnett #56	5th
4/21	63	Trenton, NJ	Barnett #56	3rd
5/30	63	Indianapolis 500	Novi	22nd
6/9	63	Milwaukee, WI	Konstant Hot #38	19th
6/23	63	Langhorne, PA	Comp- Eng #9	3rd
7/21	63	Trenton, NJ	Konstant Hot #38	22nd qual/rain
7/28	63	Trenton, PA 150	Konstant Hot #38	4th

USAC Champ Car History cont

8/17	63	Springfield, IL	Stearly Motor	17th
8/18	63	Milwaukee, WI	Konstant Hot #38	7th
9/5	63	DuQuoin, IL	Barnett #56	8th
9/14	63	Hoosier 100	Barnett #56	10th
10/27	63	Sacramento, CA	Barnett #56	11th
11/17	63	Phoenix, AZ	Gabriel Shock#81	DNQ
3/22	64	Phoenix Int	Joe Hunt	spun lap 91
4/19	64	Trenton, NJ	Wynn's Oil #5	2nd
5/30	64	Indianapolis 500	DVS #56	14th
6/7	64	Milwaukee, WI	DVS #56	14th
3/28	65	Phoenix 150	DVS	4th
4/25	65	Trenton 100	DVS	18th
5/31	65	Indianapolis 500	Novi	33rd
6/	65	Milwaukee, WI	Orange Juice #7	crash-consi
6/20	65	Langhorne paved	Vita Fresh 88 road	20th
7/18	65	Trenton 150	Vita Fresh #7	2nd
7/25	65	IRP road	Dupont Golden #7	18th
8/1	65	Atlanta 250	Novi	4th
8/8	65	Langhorne 125	Dupont Golden #7	21st
8/15	65	Milwaukee, WI	Dupont Golden #7	16th
8/22	65	Milwaukee, WI	Dupont Golden #7	21st
9/4	65	DuQuoin 100		7th
9/18	65	Hoosier 100	Sterling #56	16th
9/26	65	Trenton 200	Ent Mach #22	25th
11/21	65	Phoenix 200	Gerhardt RE Offy	14th quick
3/20	66	Phoenix AZ	Gerhardt Offy	13th
5/30	66	Indy 500	Gerhardt Offy	17th
6/5	66	Milwaukee WI	Gerhardt Offy	22nd
6/12	66	Langhorne PA	Barnett Bros Road	spun run 4th
6/26	66	Atlanta 300	Gerhardt Offy	26th
8/20	66	Springfield IL	Hyneman	clutch-practice
8/21	66	Milwaukee 200		rain
8/27	66	Milwaukee 200	Gerhardt Offy	26th
9/25	66	Trenton NJ	Gerhardt Offy 56	17th
10/9	66	Mt Fuji Japan	Gerhardt Offy	15th
11/16	66	Phoenix AZ	Gerhardt Offy	qual 29th
5/21	67	Indy 500	Mallard	Bumped
5/21	67	Indy 500	AutoteriaCarWash	6 tenths slow
6/5	67	Milwaukee 150	Leader Card #90	16th
6/11	67	Mosport Canada	Leader Card	rain
6/18	67	Langhorne, PA	Leader Card	15th
7/2	67	Mosport Canada	Leader Card	8th
7/2	67	Mosport Canada	Leader Card	9th
7/23	67	IRP 150	Leader Card	11th
7/30	67	Langhorne PA	Leader Card	12th
8/6	67	Mt Tremblant Can	Leader Card	17th
8/6	67	Mt Tremblant Can	Leader Card	7th
8/19	67	Springfield, IL	Watson Dirt	5th
8/20	67	Milwaukee 200	Leader Card	19th
11/26	67	Riverside CA	A.J. Foyt	17th
5/30	68	Indy500	Pepsi-Frito-Lay	30th

USAC Sprint Car History

Date	Yr	Place	Car	Finish
9/20	59	Reading, Pa	Hyneman #41	4th
10/11	59	Houston, TX	Barnett #56	8th quick
6/12	60	Terre Haute, IN	Barnett #56	2nd
7/3	60	Salem, IN	Barnett #56	4th
10/9	60	Williams Grove, PA	Barnett #56	2nd
3/22	62	Rossberg, OH	Barnett #56	2nd
3/25	62	Reading, PA	Barnett #56	1st
5/6	62	New Bremen, OH	Barnett #56	1st
5/27	62	IRP	Barnett #56	4th
3/20	60	Houston, TX	Barnett #56	2nd
4/17	60	Reading, PA	Barnett #56	2nd
4/24	60	Langhorne, PA	Barnett #56	16th
4/24	60	Langhorne, PA	Barnett #56	1st
6/26	60	Milwaukee, WI	Fray Offy	13th
6/26	60	Milwaukee, WI	Fray Offy	6th
6/26	60	Milwaukee, WI	Barnett #56	21st
7/17	60	Dayton, OH	Barnett #56	DNQ
7/24	60	Hidleburg, PA	Barnett #56	3rd
8/7	60	New Bremen, OH	Barnett #56	3rd
8/14	60	Dayton, OH	Barnett #56	9th
8/21	60	Terre Haute, IN	Barnett #56	1st
9/4	60	Salem, IN	Barnett #56	5th
9/9	60	Lancaster, NY	Barnett #56	Ft, 1st H eng
9/11	60	New Bremen, OH	Barnett #56	2nd
9/24	60	Allentown, PA	Barnett #56	2nd
10/16	60	Reading, PA	Barnett #56	1st
10/23	60	Houston, TX	Barnett #56	5th
11/	60	Clovis, CA	Barnett #56	2nd
12/3	60	Los Angeles Ascot	Barnett #56	1st
3/26	61	Reading, PA	Barnett %^	2nd
4/23	61	Williams Grove, PA	Barnett #56	18th
4/30	61	Salem, IN	Barnett #56	10th consi
6/11	61	Terre Haute, IN	Barnett #56	1st
6/25	61	New Bremen, OH	Barnett #56	8th
7/2	61	IRP	Barnett #56	3rd
7/30	61	IRP	Barnett #56	2nd
8/13	61	Terre Haute, IN	Barnett #56	1st
8/27	61	Langhorne, PA	Barnett #56	1st
8/27	61	Langhorne, PA	Barnett #56	1st
9/2	61	DuQuoin, IL	Barnett #56	3rd
9/4	61	Salem, IN	Barnett #56	4th
9/8	61	Lancaster, NY	Barnett #56	2nd
9/17	61	Reading, PA	Barnett #56	2nd
9/23	61	Allentown, PA	Barnett #56	1st
10/8	61	Williams Grove, PA	Barnett #56	2nd
11/11	61	Los Angeles Ascot	Barnett #56	1st
6/3	62	New Bremen, OH	Barnett #56	1st
6/17	62	Terre Haute, IN	Barnett #56	1st
6/30	62	Williams Grove, PA	Barnett #56	14th
7/8	62	IRP	Barnett #56	2nd
7/29	62	Rossberg, OH	Barnett #56	6th
8/5	62	New Bremen, OH	Steve Stapp	10th

USAC Sprint Car History cont

Date	Yr	Place	Car	Finish
8/12	62	Terre Haute, IN	Barnett #56	1st
9/7	62	Lancaster, PA	Barnett #56	1st
9/16	62	Reading, PA	Barnett #56	12th
9/22	62	Allentown	Barnett #56	8th
10/14	62	Williams Grove, PA	Competition Eng	12th
11/3	62	Los Angeles Ascot	Barnett #56	4th
11/10	62	Los Angeles Ascot	Barnett #56	5th
9/4	63	DuQuoin, IL	Barnett #56	9th
3/24	63	Reading, PA	Barnett #56	9th
3/31	63	Wiliams Grove, PA	Barnett #56	3rd
4/7	63	Langhorne, PA	Barnett #56	7th
4/7	63	Langhorne, PA	Barnett #56	2nd
4/28	63	New Bremen, OH	Barnett #56	1st
6/7	63	Buffalo, NY	Barnett #56	1st
6/16	63	Terre Haute, IN	Barnett #56	17th
7/26	63	Hatfield, PA	Barnett #56	7th
9/1	63	Kansas City, KA	Barnett #56	13th
9/15	63	Reading, PA	Barnett #56	2nd
10/5	63	Williams Grove, PA	Barnett #56	11th
11/3	63	Los Angeles Ascot	Barnett #56	8th
3/29	64	Reading, PA	Holynaki #96	Hit by rock
6/1	64	New Bremen, OH	Key Ent Chevy	Engine run2nd
7/16	67	Oswego, NY	Barnett Bros #3	5th
7/16	67	Oswego, NY	Barnett Bros #3	18th

USAC Midget Record

Date	Yr	Place	Car	Finish
10/3	59	Gardena, CA stadium		engine run 2nd
8/27	60	Milwaukee, WI	Stapp Offy	21st
10/30	59	San Jose, CA		8th
11/26	59	Gardena, CA stadium		
2/7	60	Los Angeles Ascot		
5/1	60	New Bremen, OH		2nd
6/9	60	Grand Rapids, MI		14th
6/10	60	Anderson, IN		hit frombehind
6/25	60	Kokomo, IN		Spun
11/25	60	Los Angeles Ascot	Denee	2nd
8/18	61	Milwaukee, WI	Leader Card	3rd
10/1	61	Terre Haute, IN		23rd
10/21	61	Los Angeles Ascot	Glen Dennee Offy	flipped
11/25	61	Los Angeles Ascot	Weaver Offy	3rd
12/31	61	Saugus, CA		14th
10/7	62	Terre Haute, IN	Nowicke	3rd
10/20	62	Los Angeles Ascot	Guttry #27	2nd semi
11/25	62	Ascot Turkey Nite	Guttry #27	missed show
10/6	63	Hut 100	Turner Offy	2nd
12/26	59	Saugus, CA	Linhares Offy	10th

USAC Stock Car Record

Date	Yr	Place	Car	Finish
11/15	59	Los Angeles Ascot		radiator
11/22	59	Clovis, CA		flipped lap 10
1/20	63	Riverside, CA	60 Pontiac	27th
7/7	63	IRP	63 Ford	20th
7/14	63	Milwaukee, WI	Ford #38	29th
8/11	63	Milwaukee, WI 150	Ford #56	3rd
8/20	63	Milwaukee, WI 200	Ford #56	29th
8/25	63	Springfield, IL 100	Ford #56	3rd
4/26	64	Langhorne 150	Norm Nelson Ply	1st
5/3	64	IRP Yankee 300	Norm Nelson Ply	6th
	65	Hanford CA 200	Norm Nelson Ply	engine
5/2	65	IRP Road	Norm Nelson Ply	3rd
6/13	65	Indianola, IA	Norm Nelson Ply	crashed
7/4	65	Illiana 100 lap	Norm Nelson Ply	3rd
7/11	65	Milwaukee 200	Norm Nelson Ply	2nd
8/14	65	Milwaukee 150	Norm Nelson Ply	26th
8/19	65	Milwaukee, WI	Norm Nelson Ply	crash in qual
9/19	65	Milwaukee 250	Norm Nelson Ply	1st
10/10	65	Wentzville MO	Norm Nelson Ply	2nd
10/24	65	Langhorne 250	Norm Nelson Play	2nd
9/11	66	Langhorne PA	Norm Nelson Ply	1st

NASCAR Record

Date	Yr	Place	Car	Finish
2/22	63	Daytona	Petty #42	17th
2/22	63	Daytona	Petty 41	7th
2/24	63	Daytona	Petty #41	28th
3/17	63	Atlanta, GA	63 Plymouth	22nd
4/5	64	Atlanta 500	Junior Johnson	4th
1/23	66	Riverside CA	N Nelson 65 Ply	6th
2/29	66	Daytona 500	N Nelson 65 Ply	6th
3/27	66	Atlanta 500	N Nelson 66 Ply	1st
7/4	66	Daytona Firecrack	Norm Nelson Ply	5th
2/26	67	Daytona 500	Norm Nelson Ply	9th
2/25	68	Daytona 500	68 Mercury	27th
3/30	68	Atlanta 500	68 Murcery	11th
4/21	68	North Wilkesboro	68 Murcery	24th
7/4	68	Daytona Firecrack	68 Murcery	10th
8/4	68	Atlanta Dixie 500	68 Murcery	38th
9/2	68	Darlington 500	68 Murcery	30th

World Close Course Record

Date	Yr	Place	Car	Finish
7/5	68	Daytona Int	Mallard	191.938

Hurtubise Family Album

Hurtubise Family Album

Hurtubise Family Album

56

Hurtubise Family Album

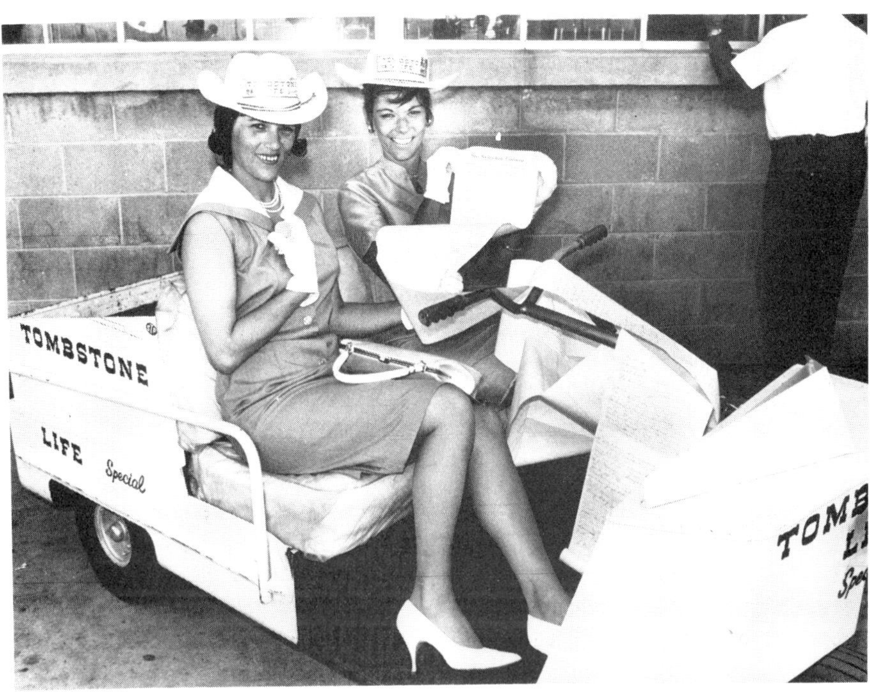

Hurtubise Family Album

Credits

"Go Hercules! Go Go Go" by Charles N. Barnard, True Magazine, June 1967 Issue.
"The Ghost of Indy Past." Sports Illustrated, May 15 1978 Issue
"Gadfly of the Indy 500," by Roy Blount, Jr., Esquire, June 6, 1978.
Andy Granatelli, "They Call Me Mister 500"Bantam Books.
"Fastest Ever" by Greg Sharp, Circle Track April 1984.
"Jim Hurtubise" by Dick Gerald, Stock Car Racing, July 1966 issue.
"Jim Hurtubise" by Joe Scalzo, Auto Sports, February 1963.
1960 St. Petersberg newspaper story by Jack Ellison.
"A Checkered Past" by Tom Binford.
Beaumont Sunday Enterprise & Journal
"Parnelli" by Bill Libby
"Dusty Heroes" by John Sawyer
Open Wheel Magazine.
Hot Rod Magazine.
Sage Magazine.
National Speed Sport News
Indianapolis Star
Indianapolis News
Indianapolis Times.
Los Angeles Times
Los Angeles Herald Examiner
Buffalo Courier Express
Buffalo Evening News
News American
Daytona Beach Evening News
Tonawanda News
Niagara Falls Gazette
Virginia Gazette

The Herk Edwards Story
as told to
Earl C. Fabritz

The BOBBY: Charlie Bobby's eight valve Fronty Ford which won the 1928 Pacific Coast Dirt Track Championship.

The BABE: Elbert "Babe" Stapp, a veteran of twelve Indianapolis 500 Mile Races and one of California's most popular drivers.

and Me: Herk Edwards, the third part of the team that dominated California race tracks in the late 1920s and early '30s.

Hard Cover, 128 pages, 40 photos
$16.00 postage paid

317-597-2487
Witness Productions
Dept P, Box 34
Marshall, IN 47859

Joie Chitwood ain't in the Sprint Car Hall of Fame because he ran a thrill show.

I started reading the book with the full intention to close the covers when the thrill show portion of his life started, but Chitwood raced and ran the thrill show at the same time in the early days, and did both with such zest that even when the racing ended, well, by then I'd gotten to like the guy so much I didn't want to leave before his performance ended. You won't either. This one gets four stars.

Dick Berggren

$25.00 postage paid

317-597-2487
Witness Productions
Dept P, Box 34, Marshall, IN 47859

TATTERSALL
The Legend

The inside story of USAC Midget Champion and Australian Legend, Bob Tattersall, as told by Ed Watson and Dennis Newlyn

*256 pages
*Complete USAC Record
*New Zealand Records
*54 pages of photos
*Australian Records
*Non-USAC Records

$14.95 Indiana residents add $.75 Tax

WITNESS PRODUCTIONS BOX 34 Marshall, IN 47859

PHONE ORDERS
317-597-2487

The AAA/USAC National Midget Auto Racing Hall of Fame Now Has A Home. YOURS!

Now you can have the first presentation of the National Midget Hall of Fame in your own home with this leather covered special edition book which honors the fifty members of the Midget Auto Racing Hall of Fame.

Larry Wright and Ed Watson have teamed to create special tribute pages to the greatest men in Midget Auto Racing History.

AAA/USAC National Midget Auto Racing Hall Of Fame

LARRY RICE

Rice was the 1973 USAC National Midget Champion and he quietly amassed a number of major victories during an impressive 24-year USAC career which ended in retirement in 1991.

Turning to broadcasting, he became a familiar face as part of ESPN's "Larry and Gary Show" on the popular "Saturday Night Thunder" telecasts.

In 1972 he gave the Shannon Brothers from Dayton, Ohio their long-sought-after Midget Owners Championship, while placing third in the point battle as a driver.

He won the prestigious "Hut Hundred" in 1970 driving for Gene Willman and used his midget racing knowledge to become the USAC Silver Crown Champion in both 1977 and 1981.

In 1985 he won two legs of the 4-Crown Nationals at the Eldora Speedway when he captured both the sprint and Silver Crown events. He won the Silver Crown leg at Eldora again in 1987.

He drove in two Indianapolis 500 Mile Races and was voted the "Co-Rookie of the Year" with Rick Mears in 1978.

The AAA/USAC National Midget Auto Racing Hall Of Fame

Fred Agabashian
J.C. Agajanian
Henry Banks
Gary Bettenhausen
Tony Bettenhausen, Sr.
Duane Carter
Pancho Carter
Art Cross
Doug Caruthers
Jimmy Caruthers
Jimmy Davies
Len Duncan
Teddy Duncan
Rex Easton
Don Edmunds
A.J. Foyt
Joe Garson
Earl Gilmore
Perry Grimm
Sam Hanks
Mel Hansen
Gene Hartley
Allen Heath
Ronney Householder
Parnelli Jones
Mel Kenyon
Frank Kurtis
Mike McGreevy
Harry McQuinn
Duke Nalon
Johnnie Parsons
Johnny Parsons
Larry Rice
Chuck Rodee
Paul Russo
Bill Schindler
Bob & Gene Shannon
Bob Stroud
Bob Swanson
Bob Tattersall
Shorty Templeman
Johnnie Tolan
Sleepy Tripp
Jack Turner
Bill Vandewater
Rich Vogler
Bill Vukovich
Leroy Warriner
Bob Wente
Wally Zale

160 pages featuring
The Hall of Fame Members Photo Gallery
The History of Midget Racing
by Ed Watson
The National Champion Owners and Drivers
and a
A Full Record Section

$20.00 postage paid

Witness Productions
Box 34
Marshall, IN 47859
317-597-2487

MC Visa

56
TRAVELON TRAILER
56
NOVI
STP
56
LARRY WRIGHT ©
56